PROGRAMED COLLEGE VOCABULARY 3600

Programed College Vocabulary 3600

SECOND EDITION

George W. Feinstein
Pasadena City College

Prentice-Hall, Inc., Englewood Cliffs, New Jersey 07632

Library of Congress Cataloging in Publication Data

FEINSTEIN, GEORGE W., (date).
 Programed college vocabulary 3600.

 1. Vocabulary—Programed instruction. I. Title.
PE1449.F38 1978   428'.1'077   78-15524
ISBN 0-13-729806-4

© 1969, 1979 by Prentice-Hall, Inc., Englewood Cliffs, N.J. 07632

All rights reserved. No part of this book
may be reproduced in any form or
by any means without permission in writing
from the publisher.

Printed in the United States of America

10 9 8 7 6 5 4 3 2

PRENTICE-HALL INTERNATIONAL, INC., *London*
PRENTICE-HALL OF AUSTRALIA PTY. LIMITED, *Sydney*
PRENTICE-HALL OF CANADA, LTD., *Toronto*
PRENTICE-HALL OF INDIA PRIVATE LIMITED, *New Delhi*
PRENTICE-HALL OF JAPAN, INC., *Tokyo*
PRENTICE-HALL OF SOUTHEAST ASIA PTE. LTD., *Singapore*
WHITEHALL BOOKS LIMITED, *Wellington, New Zealand*

To the Instructor

Answer *True* or *False:* A mastery of vocabulary contributes to a student's success in college courses. _____

If you answered *True* (as powerfully supported by research studies), you will appreciate this second edition of *Programed College Vocabulary 3600*.

The average freshman English course is not without its gaps. Students grind out themes and scramble through novels, plays, and poems; and in the frenzy a small continent of literary terminology is often overlooked. Thus, freshmen manage somehow to misinterpret test questions about "irony" or "imagery" or "social criticism": "There isn't any social criticism in *Uncle Tom's Cabin*, it's just a novel against slavery." In themes, too, an occasional pen-wizard will "take things for granite." But the English instructor should not leave vocabulary training to chance or take it for granted.

Psychologists insist that a student can learn practically anything, including the theory of relativity, if only it is broken down into easy steps. But how does an English instructor find enough class time or conference time to help each student individually with the thousand details of composition and literature? Programed learning offers a possible solution, not of course where value judgments are concerned but where factual data such as vocabulary must be mastered. In recent seasons industrial firms and educators have adopted programed techniques with startling success.

Programed College Vocabulary 3600 has been designed to supplement freshman English. This book differs from most vocabulary textbooks in that (1) it focuses on literary and academic terms, and (2) it is autoinstructional. In short, the approach is pragmatic. *Programed College Vocabulary 3600* stresses those words that are particularly useful to English students, and it elicits from each student a stream of active responses with immediate verification, a process that psychologists call *reinforcement*. Furthermore, hundreds of additional responses are called for in the teacher-administered tests which accompany this book, so that even the reinforcement gets reinforcement. In any case, the system works. The book has now been adopted in more than two hundred colleges and universities—the reports as to the program's effectiveness are extremely encouraging.

This second edition incorporates several vital improvements. For example, it substitutes eighteen short programed chapters—each suitable as a day's assignment—for the eleven lengthy ones of the original edition; adds useful new programed chapters, including "Words Often Misused," "Figures of Speech," "Psychology," and "Business and Law"; indicates the pronunciation of more words than previously; revises many exercises and tests; and is accompanied by a new Instructor's Manual that provides the teacher with chapter tests and review materials.

Class procedures are flexible. The teacher can leave vocabulary instruction entirely to the programed text itself and simply give chapter tests to his class, as a checkup, at convenient intervals. But the Instructor's Manual includes additional study suggestions as well as tests, and the teacher may wish to devote further class time to enrichment of each chapter. Thus, the freshman English course may take on brave new dimensions.

I sincerely thank the reviewers of this second edition—particularly Margo Connolly of Chabot College, California; Lisa Feinstein of Santa Monica City College, California; Professor Evelyn Fracasso of Quinnipiac College, Connecticut; Susan Gurman of Newbridge School, California; Professor Kathy E. Justice of Southeastern Community College, North Carolina; and Professor Robert Serum of Northwood Institute, Michigan. . . . And to this book of words, let me add a beautiful word—*Edith*.

GEORGE W. FEINSTEIN
Pasadena City College

Contents

v		To the Instructor
1		How to Use This Manual

PART ONE

5	1	Latin Derivatives
6		*Roots*
22		*Review test*
24	2	Latin Derivatives
25		*Roots*
31		*Prefixes*
36		*Review test*
38		*Supplementary Lists: Exercises 2-A, 2-B, 2-C*
42	3	Greek Derivatives
43		*Roots*
59		*Review Test*
61	4	Greek Derivatives
62		*Roots*
68		*Prefixes*
73		*Review Test*
75		*Supplementary List: Exercise 4*
77	5	Descriptive Words
93		*Review Test*
95		*Supplementary List: Exercise 5*
97	6	Descriptive Words
112		*Review Test*
114		*Supplementary List: Exercise 6*
116	7	Action Words
131		*Review Test*
133		*Supplementary List: Exercise 7*

135	8	Words Often Misused
147		*Review Test*
149	9	Words Often Misused
162		*Review Test*
164		*Supplementary List: Exercise 9*
166	10	Name Derivatives
178		*Review Test*
180		*Supplementary Lists: Exercises 10-A, 10-B, 10-C, 10-D*

PART TWO

184	11	Figures of Speech
192		*Review Test*
194	12	Rhetoric
209		*Review Test*
211	13	Psychology
224		*Review Test*
226		*Supplementary List*
228	14	Business and Law
238		*Review Test*
240		*Supplementary List*
242	15	Fiction
256		*Review Test*
258		*Supplementary List*
260	16	Drama
273		*Review Test*
275		*Supplementary List*
277	17	Poetry
289		*Review Test*
291		*Supplementary List*
293	18	General Literature
307		*Review Test*
309	19	Academic Terms
309		*Fine Arts*
312		*Natural Science*
316		*Philosophy*
318		*Social Science*
321		*Miscellany*

How to Use This Manual

1. Cover the answers at the left side of each page with a strip of paper or with your hand.
2. Study carefully the definitions and examples at the beginning of each "frame," or word group.
3. Complete each statement—and immediately verify your answer—throughout the rest of the frame. Fill blanks with word choices, letter choices, or completions as indicated, without looking back to the definitions.
4. After completing each statement, uncover enough of the key at the left to check your answer.
5. If your answer is correct, go on to the next statement.
6. If you have made an error, study the explanations again at the top of the frame, or consult a dictionary, before you go on.
7. Take the quizzes and the review tests when you reach them, but wait until you have completed each quiz or review test before checking or grading your answers to it.
8. Throughout this manual, fill in the blanks completely and with correct spelling. The act of writing, as well as the repetition, will help the learning process.

PRONUNCIATION KEY

a	cat	ê	hero	ô	corn	ū	amuse
ā	hate	ẽ	lover	o͞o	fool	û	burn
â	rare	i	hit	oo	took	ũ	fur
ä	far	ī	kite	oi	coil	zh	*for* si *in* vision
e	men	o	hot	ou	out	ə	*for* a *in* alone
ē	evil	ō	note	u	up	n̲	*as in French* bon

PART ONE

1

Latin Derivatives

ROOTS

1. *am, amat*
2. *ann, enn*
3. *aqu*
4. *aud, audit*
5. *capit*
6. *cent*
7. *cred, credit*
8. *dic, dict*
9. *duc, duct*
10. *fid*
11. *frater*
12. *greg*
13. *litera*
14. *loc*
15. *loqu, locut*
16. *mal*
17. *man*
18. *mater, matr, metr*
19. *mit, miss*
20. *mor, mort*
21. *mov, mot, mob*
22. *nov*
23. *omni*
24. *ped*
25. *pon, posit*

Latin derivatives make up at least half of our language. A student without this half of English vocabulary would be like a sprinter with one leg. Luckily you are already familiar with hordes of useful Latin derivatives and by one technique or another you can learn hundreds more. Taking six years of classical Latin is an excellent method, but if that route is inconvenient, you can study common Latin roots and prefixes that have enriched our English language.

Chapters 1 and 2 focus on fifty important Latin terms and their clusters of derivatives. An additional seventy-five Latin roots are presented in three supplementary exercises at the end of Chapter 2.

First, memorize the Latin term and its definition, given at the beginning of each frame. Next, note carefully the example derivatives that follow in parentheses. Try to understand the connection between each of these derivatives and its Latin root. Then fill in the blanks.

Exercises

Roots

1. **am, amat:** love.
   Derivatives: *amateur, amative, amatory, amiable, amity, amorist, amours*.

   ▶ Since *amat* means *love,* an *amative* young man is _loving_ [hostile / loving].

   ▶ An *amateur* golfer plays for _love_ [love / the fat fees] of the game.

   ▶ The two letters in the words *amorist* and *amatory* that suggest *love* are _am_.

   ▶ The Casanova devoted to *love*-making is an _amorist_ [atheist / amorist], and he has _amatory_ [amatory / mandatory] adventures.

   ▶ Cleopatra's *love* affairs are her _amou_rs.

   ▶ Warm friendship between nations is international _amity_ [animosity / amity].

   ▶ Friendly people are _amiable_ [amiable / alienated].

2. **ann, enn:** year.
   Derivatives: *annals, anniversary, annual, annuity, biennial, centennial, millennium, perennial, superannuated*.

   ▶ The three letters in the words *annals* and *annual* that suggest *year* are _ann_.

   ▶ *Per annum* means *per* _year_ [month / year].

   ▶ *Yearly* income from a fund is called an _annuity_ [excise / annuity].

COVER THIS STRIP

loving

love

am

amorist
amatory

amours

amity

amiable

ann

year

annuity

superannuated

▶ A man who has lived many *years* is said to be ___superannuated___ [superannuated / supercilious].

enn

▶ In some words, like *biennial, centennial,* and *perennial,* the Latin root for *year* is ___enn___ [ial / enn].

---

3. **aqu**: water.
   Derivatives: *aquacade, aqualung, aquamarine, aquaplane, aqua regia, aquarium, aquatint, aqua vitae, aqueduct, aqueous humor, aqiculture, subaqueous.*

water

▶ To make an *aqueous* solution you dissolve something in ___water___ [alcohol / water].

aqu

▶ The three letters in *aqualung* and *aqiculture* that suggest *water* are ___aqu___.

water

▶ An *aquaplane* is towed on ___water___ [snow / water / rocks].

aquacade

▶ A *water* festival which involves swimming and diving is sometimes called an ___aqua___cade.

aquarium

▶ Small fish may be kept in an ___aquar___ium.

Aquarius

▶ The sign of the zodiac that represents a *water* bearer is ___Aquarius___ [Aquarius / Taurus].

aqueous

▶ The *watery* fluid between the cornea and the lens of the eye is known as ___aqueous___ [aqueous / amorous] humor.

---

4. **aud, audit**: hear.
   Derivatives: *audible, audience, audile, audio-frequency, audiophile, audio-visual, audiphone, audit, audition, auditor, auditorium, auditory.*

hear
audit

▶ You can assume that *auditory* nerves help you to ___hear___ [hear / see], since the five-letter Latin root for *hear* is ___audit___ [ditor / audit].

audition
audience
auditorium

▶ After a successful critical *hearing*, or *audit*ion, a singer might entertain an *audience* in an *audit*ium.

hearing

▶ An *audiometer* is an instrument which measures sensitivity of *hearing* [hearing / sight].

hi-fi

▶ An *audiophile* is enthusiastic about *hi-fi* [stamps / hi-fi].

adenoids

▶ Find the word that has no business being in the following list: *audible, audiphone, audio-frequency, adenoids, auditor* *adenoids*

---

5. **capit**: head.
Derivatives: *cap, capital, capitalism, capitate, capitol, caption, decapitate, per capita, recapitulate.*

head
caption

▶ *Capit* is a root that means *head*; so the *heading* of a chapter or an article is called a *caption* [decoction / caption].

head

▶ *Capitation* is a tax or fee on each *head* [head / foot].

head

▶ A per *capita* tax is assessed as so much per *head*.

capit

▶ The Latin root for *head* is *capit*.

capital
decapitated

▶ In Paris, the *capit*al of France, King Louis XVI got a sovereign cure for headaches—he was de*capitated*.

recapitulate
(b)

▶ Newscasters sometimes re*capitulate* the day's news; such a *recapitulation* literally restates the news (a) in full, (b) by headings. (b)

Quiz

Write the meaning of each boldface Latin root.

1. **aud**ience   *hear*
2. **capit**ol   *head*

8

1. hear
2. head
3. water
4. love
5. year

3. sub**aqu**eous   _water_

4. **am**atory   _love_

5. **anni**versary   _year_

---

6. **cent:** hundred.
Derivatives: *cent, centavo, centenarian, centenary, centennial, centigrade, centigram, centiliter, centime, centimeter, centipede, centuple, centurion, century, tercentennial.*

▶ The Latin root for *hundred* is _cent_; thus, a *centenarian* has lived a _100_ years, in other words, an entire _cent_ury.

cent
hundred
century

▶ There are one *hundred* degrees between the freezing and boiling points of water on the _centigrade_ [Fahrenheit / centigrade] thermometer.

centigrade

▶ One-*hundredth* of a meter is a _centimeter_ [centimeter / kilometer].

centimeter

▶ One-*hundredth* of a gram is a _centigram_.

centigram

▶ One-*hundredth* of a liter is a _centiliter_.

centiliter

▶ A *centenary*, or _centenn_ial, is celebrated after one _100_ years.

centennial
hundred

▶ Since *ter* means *three*, the *tercentennial* of the Declaration of Independence should occur in the year _2076_ [1976 / 2076]. You are all invited.

2076

---

7. **cred, credit:** believe; trust.
Derivatives: *accredit, credence, credentials, credible, credit, creditable, creditor, credo, credulity, credulous, creed, discredit.*

▶ Since the Latin root for *believe* is _cred_ [cred / crud], a *credible* story is _believable_ [believable / absurd].

cred
believable

▶ Your *creed*, or *credo*, is what you (a) fight, (b) believe in. (_b_)

(b)

9

believe
▶ To give *credence* to a rumor is to __believe__ [deny / believe] it.

accredited
credentials
▶ An ac__credited__ college hires only those teachers who have proper __credent__ials.

believe
▶ Your *credulity* is your readiness to __believe__ [love / believe].

incredulous
▶ Sometimes news is so amazing that you are __incredulous__ [cretinous / incredulous].

---

8. **dic, dict:** say.
   Derivatives: *addict, benediction, contradict, dictaphone, dictate, diction, dictograph, dictum, edict, indicative, indict, interdict, jurisdiction, malediction, predicate, predict, valedictorian, verdict.*

dict
say
▶ The four-letter Latin root of *dictate* and *dictum* is __dict__ and it means __say__.

predict
▶ To *say* what will happen, or foretell, is to pre__dict__.

edict
▶ An order issued by an absolute ruler is an __edict__ [edict / audit].

verdict
▶ The judgment of a jury is a __verdict__.

predicate
▶ The part of a sentence which *says* something about the subject is the pre__dicate__.

indicative
▶ The mood of a verb that merely states a fact is __indicative__ [subjunctive / indicative].

duck
▶ *Dictaphone, contradict, indicate, duck, addict*—which word floated in by mistake? __duck__

---

9. **duc, duct:** lead.
   Derivatives: *abduct, aqueduct, conducive, conduct, deduce, duchess, duct, ductility, duke, educate, educe, Il Duce, induce, introduce, produce, reduce, reproduce, seduction, traduce.*

duc lead	▶ To *educate* is literally to "lead out." The three-letter root of *education* is __duc__ and it means __lead__.
Leader	▶ Mussolini was called *Il Duce*, which means "The __lead__er."
dukes conducive duchesses	▶ Europe has had many princely *leaders* known as __dukes__ [schlemiels / dukes], but America's democratic climate is hardly con__ducive__ to the growth of a crop of *dukes* and their wives, __duchess__es.
aqueduct	▶ Water is sometimes *led* into a city through an __aqueduct__.
seducer	▶ An innocent girl may be *led* astray by a __seducer__ [seducer / centuple].
ductility	▶ The ability of a metal to be *led* into various shapes is called __ductility__ [motility / ductility].

10. **fid**: faith; trust.
    Derivatives: *affidavit, confidant, confide, confidence, confidential, diffident, fidelity, fiduciary, infidel, perfidious, perfidy.*

faith	▶ To *confide* in a stranger is an act of __faith__ [leading / faith].
fid	▶ The Latin root for *faith* is __fid__.
unfaithfulness	▶ *Infidelity* means __unfaithfulness__ [unfaithfulness / inability to provide].
perfidious	▶ In betraying his *trust*, Benedict Arnold did a __perfidious__ [perfervid / perfidious] thing.
perfidy	▶ In fact, Benedict Arnold committed an act of __perfidy__ [perfidy / persiflage].
confident	▶ A prizefighter who has *faith* in himself is said to be con__fident__.

diffident

▶ A lad who is shy and lacks *faith* in himself is said to be *diffident* [amative / diffident].

Quiz

Write the meaning of each boldface Latin root.

1. lead
2. hundred
3. believe
4. faith
5. say

1. de**duct**ion   l_ead_____
2. **cent**ury   h_undred____
3. **cred**ential b_elieve____
4. af**fid**avit   f_aith_____
5. bene**dict**ion s_ay_____

11. **frater**: brother.
    Derivatives: *confraternity, frater, fraternal, fraternity, fraternize, fratricide.*

brother

▶ *Frater* means __brother__.

brotherly

▶ *Fraternal* obligations are __brotherly__ [fatherly / brotherly].

fraternize

▶ To mingle with conquered people in a social or *brotherly* way is to __frater__nize with them.

fratricide

▶ Killing one's own *brother* is called __fratri__cide.

brother

▶ A girls' club should not be called a *fraternity* because *frater* means __brother__.

confraternity

▶ A *brotherly* group devoted to charitable work is sometimes called a __confraternity__ [fiduciary / confraternity].

12. **greg**: flock.
    Derivatives: *aggregation, congregate, egregious, gregarious, segregate.*

greg

▶ The Latin root for *flock* is __greg__.

congregation ▸ A minister's *flock* is called a con*gregation*.

segregation ▸ Separation from the main group or *flock* is se*gregation*.

flock
society ▸ Since *greg* means *flock*, we may assume that *gregarious* people like *society* [solitude / society].

▸ Insulting your teacher during examination week might stand out from your *flock* of lesser mistakes as an *egregious* [egregious / diffident] blunder.

egregious

▸ Bismuth is ineligible to play with the football *aggregation* [aggravation / aggregation].

aggregation

---

13. **litera:** letter.
    Derivatives: *alliteration, literacy, literal, literalism, literally, literary, literate, literati, literature, litterateur, transliteration.*

litera
letter ▸ The Latin root of the word *literary* is *litera*, and it means *letter*.

▸ Translating *letter* for *letter* results in a *liter*al translation.

literal

▸ A person who can't read or write is *unlettered*, or *illiterate* [illegitimate / illiterate].

illiterate

literate
literature ▸ The person who reads and writes is *literate* [literate / libelous] and possibly enjoys *literat*ure.

▸ *Literalism* in art means drawing things to the *letter,* that is, *realistically* [realistically / imaginatively].

realistically

▸ A *litterateur* is (a) a man who keeps rabbits, (b) a man of letters. (b)

(b)

---

14. **loc:** place.
    Derivatives: *allocate, dislocate, locale, localism, locality, localize, location, locative,* loco citato, *locus, relocate.*

loc	▶ A three-letter Latin root that means *place* is __loc__.
place	▶ The *locale* of a train wreck refers to the __place__ [place / cause].
locality localism	▶ An expression that is used only in a certain *place*, or __locali__ty, is called a __localism__ [barbarism / localism].
locus *loci*	▶ In mathematics the set of points or *places* which satisfy a given condition is called the __loc__us. The plural of *locus* is __loci__ [locusts / loci].
place	▶ In footnotes *loco citato* is abbreviated as *loc. cit.* and means "in the __place__ cited."
place	▶ In Latin and Greek grammar the *locative* case denotes __place__ [time / place].

---

15. **loqu, locut:** talk.
    Derivatives: *allocution, circumlocution, colloquial, colloquium, colloquy, elocution, eloquent, grandiloquent, interlocutor, loquacious, prolocutor, soliloquy.*

talkative	▶ A *loquacious* child is __talkative__ [sulky / talkative].
colloquial	▶ Most people talk informally, that is, in __colloquial__ [literary / colloquial] English.
locut	▶ In *interlocutor* and *locution* the five-letter root that suggests *talk* is __locut__.
eloquent	▶ Webster was an inspired *talker;* in fact, he was often el__oquent__.
grandiloquent	▶ A windy orator who uses grand, phony expressions is __grandiloquent__ [magnanimous / grandiloquent].
circumlocution	▶ Saying a thing in a roundabout way is known as __circumlocution__ [circumspection / circumlocution].

soliloquy

▶ Hamlet's "To be or not to be," spoken alone on stage, is a _soliloquy_ [solecism / soliloquy].

Quiz

Write the meaning of each boldface Latin root.

1. al**liter**ation _letter_
2. col**loqu**ium _talk_
3. **frater**nal _brother_
4. dis**loc**ate _place_
5. ag**greg**ate _flock_

1. letter
2. talk
3. brother
4. place
5. flock

16. **mal:** bad.
    Derivatives: *maladjusted, maladminister, maladroit, malaise, malapropos, malaria, malcontent,* mal de mer, *malediction, malefactor, malevolent, malfeasance, malformed, malice, malign, malignant, malinger, malnutrition, malocclusion, malodorous, malpractice.*

bad

▶ *Malfeasance* in office refers to _bad_ [bad / admirable] conduct.

bad

▶ *Mal* means _bad_.

malignant

▶ The truly *bad* tumors are the _malignant_ [benign / malignant] ones.

(b)

▶ To hurl *maledictions* is to fling (a) small rocks, (b) evil words or curses. (b)

malevolent

▶ Evil wishers are _malevolent_ [benevolent / malevolent].

bad

▶ *Malaise* is physical discomfort that hints of _bad_ [good / bad] health.

maladroit

▶ A clumsy child is said to be _maladroit_ [maladroit / adroit].

malnutrition ▸ If the child has *bad* nutrition he suffers from *malnutri*tion.

malodorous ▸ If the child smells like no geranium he is *mal*odorous.

---

17. **man:** hand.
Derivatives: *amanuensis, manacle, manage, mandate, mandatory, maneuver, manicure, manifest, manifesto, manipulate, manual, manufacture, manumit, manuscript.*

hands ▸ *Manacles* are worn on the *hands* [eyes / hands].

man ▸ The Latin root for *hand* is *man*.

manicure ▸ *Hands* with ugly nails should be given a *manicure* [manicure / pedicure].

hand ▸ Both *emancipate* and *manumit* mean to set free, that is, to let go from the *hand*.

hand ▸ An *amanuensis* is a copyist—he works with his *hand* [jaw / hand].

man
manuscript ▸ Another word derived from the root *man*, meaning *hand*, is *manuscript* [amnesia / amenity / enema / manuscript].

---

18. **mater, matr, metr:** mother.
Derivatives: *alma mater, maternal, maternity, matriarch, matricide, matrilineal, matrimony, matrix, matron, metronymic, metropolis.*

matriarch ▸ A *mother* who rules a family or tribe is a *matriarch* [matriarch / patriarch].

matr
mother ▸ In the words *matrix* and *matrimony* the four-letter Latin root is *matr*, and it means *mother*.

matricide ▸ Slaying one's own *mother*, an ungrateful business, is known as *matricide* [uxoricide / matricide].

matron
maternity

▸ A hospital ___*matr*on___ supervises the care of expectant *mothers* in the ___*matern*___*ity* ward.

mother

▸ *Matrilineal* descent refers to kinship through the ___*mother*___ [father / mother].

metronymic

▸ Henry Cabot Lodge derived his middle name from the maiden name of his mother; therefore for him the name *Cabot* is a ___*metronymic*___ [metronymic / patronymic].

---

19. **mit, miss:** send.
    Derivatives: *admissible, admit, commissary, commit, emissary, emit, intermittent, mission, missionary, missive, omission, permit, premise, promise, remit, submit, transmit.*

miss
send

▸ The Latin root in *mission* is ___*miss*___ and it means ___*send*___.

missionary

▸ The man we *send* to convert the heathens is called a ___*missionary*___.

emissary

▸ The diplomat we *send* out is an ___*emissary*___ [emissary / auditor].

missive

▸ A tourist usually *sends* his home-town friends a ___*missive*___ [missive / missile].

mit

▸ Which three letters in *remit* mean *send*? ___*mit*___

intermittent

▸ Shots *sent* out at intervals are said to be ___*intermittent*___ [interdicted / intermittent].

---

20. **mor, mort:** death.
    Derivatives: *immortal, moribund, mortal, mortality, mortgage, mortician, mortify, mortuary, post-mortem,* rigor mortis.

death

▸ The root *mort* suggests that a *mortician* is concerned with ___*death*___ [birth / death].

mortuary
mortis

▸ The *mortician* operates a funeral home known as a ___*mortuary*___ and he is, no doubt, acquainted with the *stiffness of death* known as *rigor* ___*mortis*___.

dying
immortal

(a)

▶ A sweet old lady complains that the custom of sending valentines is, alas, *moribund*—that is, *dying* [too lively / dying]. She wishes that the valentine custom would never die, that it would be *immortal* [immortal / immoral].

▶ If you develop gangrene, your flesh *mortifies;* this means that it (a) decays and dies, (b) glows with health. (*a*)

Quiz

Write the meaning of each boldface Latin root.

1. **man**ual   *hand*
2. **mat**ernal   *mother*

1. hand
2. mother
3. death
4. send
5. bad

3. **mort**gage   *death*
4. **e**mis**s**ion   *send*
5. **mal**efactor *bad*

---

21. **mov, mot, mob:** move.
    Derivatives: *automobile, commotion, demote, emotion, immobile, immovable, locomotive, mobile, mobility, motile, motion, motivation, motor, promote, remote, remove.*

mov
mot
mob
move

▶ Give the root of *movable*: *mov*; of *motor*: *mot*; of *mobile*: *mob*. These variant Latin roots mean *move*.

move

▶ From the letters *mot* it's a safe guess that *motile* cells are able to *move* [talk / move].

mobility

▶ An army's ability to *move* is referred to as its *mobility* [stability / mobility].

motivation

▶ Whatever *moves* a man to study or marry or assassinate is his *motivation* [innovation / motivation].

emotions

▶ You are often *moved*, or stirred, by *emotions* [emotions / omissions].

promotion	▶ Another word derived from the root meaning *move* is *promotion* [mother / matador / promotion / smote].

22. **nov**: new.
   Derivatives: *innovation, nova, Nova Scotia, novel, novelette, novella, novelty, novice, novitiate, novocain, renovate.*

new	▶ The letters *nov* in *novelty* mean *new*.
new	▶ An *innovation* is a *new* [crazy / new] idea or custom.
novice novitiate	▶ In a religious order a *new* member is called a *nov*ice and he serves a probationary period, or a *novitiate*.
(b)	▶ A *nova* star is (a) a faithful old planet, (b) a brilliant new exploding star. (b)
novel	▶ A hint of something *new* also occurs in the word *novel* [naval / novel / venerable / Navaho].
renovate new	▶ When our landlord promises to *renov*ate our apartment, we hope he knows that the word-root *nov* means *new* [air / new].

23. **omni**: all.
   Derivatives: *omniactive, omnibenevolent, omnibus, omniferous, omnipotent, omnipresent, omniprevalent, omniscient, omnium-gatherum, omnivorous.*

omni	▶ In the words *omniscient* (all-knowing) and *omnipotent* (all-powerful) the four-letter root that means *all* is *omni*.
many	▶ An *omnium-gatherum* is a collection of *many* [many / one or two] different things.
omniferous	▶ A tree that produces *all* varieties is *omniferous* [mellifluous / omniferous].

19

all (b)	▸ Because *omni* means ___all___ [*all* / *small*], we can assume that an *omnivorous* reader reads (a) only the funnies, (b) practically everything. (b)
omnibuses	▸ To transport loads of students, a school usually buys *omnibuses* [compacts / omnibuses].

24. **ped:** foot.
    Derivatives: *biped, centipede, expedient, expedite, expedition, impediment, pedal, pedestal, pedestrian, pedometer, quadruped, sesquipedalian.*

foot	▸ A *pedestrian* travels by ___foot___ [foot / jet plane].
ped	▸ The three-letter word-root meaning *foot* is ___ped___.
walked	▸ A *pedometer* measures the distance ___walked___ [driven / walked].
biped	▸ A man has two *feet* and so according to Aristotle is a featherless ___biped___ [biped / slob].
feet	▸ An *impediment* is literally something that obstructs or holds up the ___feet___ [feet / meals].
(a)	▸ To *expedite* means, in a sense, to free the *feet*, hence, (a) to speed up the action, (b) to snarl things up. (a)
feet	▸ Since *sesqui* means "one and a half," a *sesquipedalian* is a word that is supposedly about one and a half ___feet___ [feet / years] long.

25. **pon, posit:** place.
    Derivatives: *apposite, appositive, component, composition, depose, deposit, dispose, exponent, expose, impose, interpose, juxtapose, opponent, position, positive, postpone, proponent, propose, repository.*

posit *place*	▸ The words *position, deposit,* and *appositive* all contain the five-letter root ___posit___, which means ___place___.

pon
▸ Another root that means *place* is ___pon___ [pan / pon].

components
▸ Stereo set parts that must be *placed* together are called ___components___ [compartments / components].

juxtaposed
▸ Objects *placed* alongside each other are ___juxtaposed___ [juxtaposed / coincident].

repository
dispose
▸ You can *place* old books in a ___repository___ [repertory / repository] or otherwise dis___pose___ of them.

exponent
▸ One who sets forth, or advocates, a doctrine is its ___exponent___ [expatriate / exponent].

apposite
▸ Appropriate or *well-placed* remarks are said to be ___apposite___ [apposite / appellate].

Quiz

Write the meaning of each boldface Latin root.

1. foot
2. new
3. place
4. all
5. move

1. **ped**al ___foot___
2. **nov**elette ___new___
3. com**posit**ion ___place___
4. **omni**present ___all___
5. de**mote** ___move___

21

Review Test

Write *True* or *False*.

True 1. A *pedestrian* is one who walks.
True 2. An *innovation* is something newly introduced.
false 3. A *localism* is a universally popular pet phrase.
false 4. A *missive* is a small female ballet dancer.
True 5. A *literal* translation follows the original very closely.
True 6. In a *matriarchy* the mother rules the family or tribe.
false 7. A *dictum* is someone injured in an accident.
True 8. *Loquacity* refers to talkativeness.
false 9. To *mobilize* means to hypnotize and to stop action.
false 10. The name *Il Duce* means the "deuce" or "two-spot."

Write the meaning of each boldface Latin root. The first letter of each answer is given.

11. a **frater**nity of poets — b_rother_
12. guilty of **mal**practice — b_ad_
13. **aqu**atic sports — w_ater_
14. an in**cred**ible plot — b_elieve_
15. a Robert Frost **cent**ennial — h_undred_
16. an **am**orous sonnet — l_ove_
17. the im**mort**al Chaucer — d_eath_
18. an e**greg**ious idiot — f_lock_
19. an illuminated **man**uscript — h_and_
20. dis**posit**ion of funds — p_lace_

Write the letter that indicates the best completion.

(d) 21. An *infidel* is one who has no (a) married parents, (b) schooling, (c) musical ability, (d) religious faith.
(c) 22. An *audible* kiss is one that (a) lasts a long time, (b) can be seen, (c) can be heard, (d) gives off steam.
(b) 23. That which is *omnipresent* is (a) nowhere, (b) everywhere, (c) a welcome gift, (d) invisible.
(b) 24. The Latin root for *head* is used in which word?—(a) aquatint, (b) caption, (c) deception, (d) amour.
(a) 25. The Latin root for *year* is used in which word?—(a) perennial, (b) banana, (c) birthday, (d) decade.

Key to Review Test

Check your test answers by the following key. Deduct 4% per error from a possible 100%.

1. True	6. True	11. brother	16. love	21. (d)
2. True	7. False	12. bad	17. death	22. (c)
3. False	8. True	13. water	18. flock	23. (b)
4. False	9. False	14. believe	19. hand	24. (b)
5. True	10. False	15. hundred	20. place	25. (a)

Score: 100 %

2
Latin Derivatives

ROOTS	PREFIXES	
1. *port, portat*	11. *ante*	18. *post*
2. *scrib, script*	12. *bi*	19. *pre*
3. *sign*	13. *circum*	20. *retro*
4. *spec, spect*	14. *contra*	21. *semi*
5. *spir, spirat*	15. *inter*	22. *sub*
6. *tempor*	16. *intra, intro*	23. *super*
7. *terra*	17. *multi*	24. *trans*
8. *urb*		25. *uni*
9. *vid, vis*		
10. *voc, vocat*		

Chapter 2 continues our study of Latin derivatives. Follow the same procedure as in Chapter 1.

Exercises

Roots

COVER THIS STRIP

1. **port, portat:** carry.
   Derivatives: *comport, deport, disport, export, import, portable, portage, portfolio, porter, portmanteau, purport, rapport, report, support, transport.*

   | port
   | carry

   ▸ The words *porter, export,* and *purport* all have the root __*port*__, which means __*carry*__.

   | transport
   | portable
   | portfolio
   | portmanteau

   ▸ One can easily *trans*__*port*__ a __*port*__able typewriter, a __*portfol*__io (brief case), or a __*portman*__teau (leather suitcase that opens into two compartments like a book).

   | (a)

   ▸ To make a *portage* between lakes means (a) to carry gear, (b) to stop for lunch. (*a*)

   | deportment

   ▸ Your __*deport*__*ment* is your behavior or way of *carrying* yourself.

2. **scrib, script:** write.
   Derivatives: *ascribe, circumscribe, conscription, describe, inscribe, manuscript, nondescript, postscript, prescribe, proscribe, scribble, scribe, scripture, subscribe, transcribe, typescript.*

   | scrib
   | write

   ▸ The five-letter root of *subscribe, proscribe,* and *inscribe* is __*scrib*__, and it means __*write*__.

   | postscript

   ▸ An afterthought *written* at the end of a letter is a __*postscript*__.

   | conscription

   ▸ The army draft, or enrollment, is known as *con*__*scription*__.

   | written
   | transcribed
   | manuscripts
   | scribes

   ▸ The Scriptures were so named because they were __*written*__ [sung / written], possibly __*transcribed*__ [transfused / transcribed] into beautiful *manu*__*script*__ by industrious __*scribes*__ [porters / scribes].

25

prescription	▶ My doctor peered at my tongue, then hastily wrote a *pre*scription.
(b)	▶ A *nondescript* dog is (a) a very individual type, (b) hardly individual enough to be written about. (b)

3. **sign:** sign.
   Derivatives: *assign, consign, countersign, design, designate, ensign, insignia, resign, signal, signalize, signatory, signature, signet, significant, signify.*

sign sign	▶ In the words *signalize, countersign,* and *designate* the root is _sign_, and—who'd guess it?—it means _sign_.
signature	▶ A man *signs* his checks with, we trust, his own _sign_ture.
significant signifies	▶ A man's *signature* on a document is very _significant_ [sagacious / significant] since it _signifies_ [beclouds / signifies] his intentions.
signet	▶ An initial or other special *sign* is carried on a _signet_ [signet / garnet] ring.
an ensign	▶ A military banner or other *sign* of authority is known as _an ensign_ [lasagne / an ensign].
signatory	▶ Countries that have *signed* a treaty are _signatory_ [secessionist / signatory] nations.
sign assignment	▶ Remember that the Latin root *sign* means _sign_. If necessary, repeat it ten times—what an _assign_ment!

4. **spec, spect:** look.
   Derivatives: *aspect, circumspect, inspect, introspection, perspective, prospect, respect, retrospect, spectacle, specter, spectroscope, spectrum.*

spect look	▶ The root in *inspect, aspect,* and *prospect* is _spect_, and it means _look_.

26

circumspect	▶ To be cautious and *look* around before acting is to be *circumspect* [circumspect / circumscript].
introspection	▶ Marcel Proust had a habit of *looking* into his mind and memories—he was given to *introspection* [introspection / interdiction].
retrospect	▶ *Looking* back he saw things in ret*rospect*.
perspective	▶ Another viewpoint would have given him a different per*spective*.
(d)	▶ One word that did *not* develop from the root for *look* is (a) specter, (b) spectrum, (c) spectacles, (d) spaghetti. (d)

5. **spir, spirat:** breathe.
   Derivatives: *aspirate, aspire, conspire, expire, inspire, perspire, respiration, spiracle, spirit, spirometer.*

breathe	▶ *Spirat* means *breathe* [spin / breathe].
respiration perspiration	▶ To *breathe* through the lungs is called resp*iration*; to *breathe* through the skin—that is, to sweat—is per*spiration*.
spiracle	▶ The whale Moby Dick had an air hole called a *spiracle* [spiracle / oracle].
spirit expired	▶ In the sea battle Captain Ahab yielded up his *spir*it and ex*pired*.
spirometer	▶ A machine which measures one's lung capacity, or *breath*, is called a *spirometer* [spectroscope / spirometer].
(a)	▶ Poetic *inspiration* was originally thought to be (a) a breathing in of a divine influence, (b) the product of indigestion. (a)

Quiz

Write the meaning of each boldface Latin root.

1. in**spect**ion _look_
2. con**spire** _breathe_
3. im**port** _carry_
4. de**script**ion _write_
5. con**sign** _sign_

1. look
2. breathe
3. carry
4. write
5. sign

---

6. **tempor:** time.
   Derivatives: *contemporary, contretemps, extemporaneous, extempore, extemporize, pro tem, tempo, temporal, temporary, temporize.*

▶ Emerson and Thoreau lived at the same *time*—they were _contemporary_ [congruent / contemporary] writers.

contemporary

▶ The root _tempor_ means *time*.

tempor

▶ To be chairman *pro tem* means "for the _time_ being," or _temporar_ily.

time
temporarily

▶ Talks or remarks made at the *time* without preparation are said to be _extemporaneous_ [extenuating / extemporaneous].

extemporaneous

▶ To delay, or consume *time*, by needless discussions is to _temporize_ [temporize / expedite].

temporize

▶ An inopportune or embarrassing occurrence is known as a _contretemps_ [nondescript / contretemps].

contretemps

▶ Parade music has a brisk _tempo_.

tempo

---

7. **terra:** earth.
   Derivatives: *disinter, inter, terrace, terra cotta, terra firma, terramycin, terraqueous, terrazzo, terrestrial, terrier, territory.*

28

terramycin	▶ One antibiotic derived from an *earth* is called _terra_mycin.
terra	▶ The Latin root for *earth* is _terra_.
earth	▶ *Terra firma* refers to firm _earth_ [water / earth].
terra	▶ Unglazed, brown-red earthenware is known as _terra_ cotta.
(a)	▶ *Terrain* has to do with (a) land surfaces, (b) ammunition. (a)
terrestrial	▶ The earth's land as distinct from water is _terrestrial_ [global / terrestrial].
terrier	▶ A small hunting dog which burrowed into the *earth* for small game was called a _terr_ier.
(b)	▶ A body that is *interred* has been (a) cremated, (b) buried. (b)

8. **urb**: city.
   Derivatives: *interurban, suburban, suburbanite, suburbs, urban, urbane, urbanism, urbanite, urbanity, urbanize.*

city	▶ To *urbanize* a district is to make it become like a _city_ [city / farm].
urb	▶ The three-letter Latin root that means *city* is _urb_.
interurban	▶ Buses that travel between *cities* are inter_urban_.
suburbs	▶ On the outskirts of the *cities* lie the _suburbs_ [subways / suburbs].
(a) urbanities	▶ An *urbane* fellow is (a) polished and suave, (b) countrified and crude. (a) He is accustomed to those *citified* refinements of manners known as the _urbanities_ [gaucheries / urbanities].

9. **vid, vis:** see.
   Derivatives: *advise, envision, evidence, improvisator, invidious, providence, revise, supervise, visible, visionary, visit, vista, visualize.*

▸ The words *visible, visit,* and *supervise* have the same three-letter root ___vis___, which means ___see___.

▸ A *vista* is a ___view___ [view / southern mansion].

▸ The words *evidence* and *providence* have the same three-letter root ___vid___, which also means ___see___.

▸ To the Puritans *divine providence* meant that God would ___foresee___ [ignore them / foresee].

▸ Comparisons which are unfair and offensive are said to be ___invidious___ [invaluable / invidious].

---

10. **voc, vocat:** call.
    Derivatives: *advocate, avocation, convocation, equivocal, evoke, invoke, irrevocable, provoke, revoke, vocable, vocabulary, vocal, vocation, vociferous.*

▸ A *calling* together of students to assembly is a ___convocation___ [convocation / convection].

▸ *Vocal* promises are ___spoken___ [written / spoken]; after all, the root *voc* means ___call___.

▸ Your career job, or *calling,* is your ___vocat___ion.

▸ Your hobby is your av___ocation___.

▸ I ad___vocate___ (recommend) that you choose your field of specialization wisely because by commencement day that decision will be practically ___irrevocable___ [irrepressible / irrevocable].

▸ At the beginning of an epic, the poet Homer ___invokes___ [invokes / inspires] the gods.

invocation

▶ Today a minister usually gives the *in*__invocation__.

equivocal

▶ A sentence which seems to say two opposite things is said to be __equivocal__ [omniscient / equivocal].

Quiz

Write the meaning of each boldface Latin root.

1. **urb**anite   __city__
2. en**vis**ion   __see__
3. **voc**iferous   __call__
4. **terr**itory   __earth__
5. **tempor**ary   __time__

1. city
2. see
3. call
4. earth
5. time

Prefixes

11. ante: before.

before

▶ *Antebellum* days came __before__ [before / after] the Civil War.

antedated

▶ The Civil War __antedated__ [antedated / succeeded] the first World War.

anterior

▶ That which is toward the front or which comes *before* is __anterior__ [anterior / posterior].

12. bi: two.

two

▶ A *bicameral* legislature has __two__ [one / two] chambers.

bifocals

▶ Glasses with *two* different focal lengths are called __bifocals__ [monocles / bifocals].

31

bipartisan

▸ A committee which represents *two* parties is _bipartisan_ [bipartisan / partisan].

13. **circum:** around.

circumference

▸ The line *around* a circle is the _circumference_ [circumference / diameter].

(a)

▸ To *circumvent* the villain is (a) to get around him and outwit him, (b) to fall into his trap. (a)

about

▸ Dante's *Divine Comedy* was written *circa* 1320, that is, _about_ [after / about] 1320.

14. **contra, contro, counter:** against.

(b)

▸ A *countercharge* is (a) an admission of guilt, (b) a charge by the accused against his accuser. (b)

controvert

▸ To argue *against* a certain idea is to _controvert_ [corroborate / controvert] it.

illegal

▸ *Contraband* is _illegal_ [legal / illegal] merchandise.

15. **inter:** between.

between

▸ An *interlinear* translation has the meaning inserted _between_ [opposite / between] the lines.

between

▸ The *interregnum* is the period _between_ [during / between] the rule of kings.

intercultural

▸ Relations *between* cultural groups are said to be _intercultural_ [intercultural / subcultural].

16. **intra, intro:** within.

within

▸ *Intramuscular* pains are _within_ [between / within] the muscles.

intravenous

▸ That which is *within* the veins is _intravenous_ [invidious / intravenous].

Albany

▸ *Intrastate* commerce goes on between New York City and _Albany_ [Chicago / Albany].

---

17. multi: many.

many

▸ A *multiped* insect has _many_ [many / two] feet.

multivalent

▸ An atom having a valence of three or higher is _multivalent_ [bivalent / multivalent].

multiparous

▸ An animal having two or more offspring at a birth is _multiparous_ [uniparous / multiparous].

---

18. post: after.

after

▸ Mark Twain's *The Mysterious Stranger* was published *posthumously,* that is, _after_ [before / after] his death.

posterity

▸ Those generations which come *after* us are our _posterity_ [ancestors / posterity].

posterior

▸ That part of us which comes *after* us is our _poster_ior.

---

19. pre: before.

before

▸ That which has *precedence* comes _before_ [before / after] the rest.

before

▸ The word *prejudice* implies that a judgment is made _before_ [before / after] the facts are studied.

preamble

▸ The beginning of a constitution is a good place for the _preamble_ [amendments / preamble].

33

20. retro: back.

▶ If civilization is *retrogressing,* it is (a) improving, (b) going back to a worse condition. (b)

▶ A *retrorocket* tends to ___retard___ [speed up / retard] a space ship.

▶ A law or ruling which affects an earlier period is ___retroactive___ [retroactive / radioactive].

---

21. semi: half.

▶ A *semilunar* shape is like that of the ___half___ [full / half] moon.

▶ *Semicentennials* celebrate a period of ___fifty___ years.

▶ The *semidiameter* of a circle is equal to its ___radius___ [radius / circumference].

---

22. sub: under.

▶ The *subconscious* operates ___under___ [within / under] the conscious mind.

▶ A *subcutaneous* infection is ___under___ [on / under] the skin.

▶ In subtraction the number written *under* the other number is called the ___subtrahend___ [subtrahend / minuend].

---

23. super: above; beyond.

▶ *Supersensory* impressions are ___beyond___ [within / beyond] the normal limits of the senses.

▶ The *superstructure* of a warship is ___above___ [above / below] the main deck.

supersonic

▶ Speeds *beyond* the speed of sound are __super__sonic.

24. trans: across.

▶ A *transpolar* flight goes __across__ [around / across] the pole.

across

▶ In geometry a line that cuts *across* two other lines is called a __transversal__ [tangent / transversal].

transversal

▶ To *transgress* is (a) to respect the rules, (b) to step across the rules or violate them. (b)

(b)

25. uni: one.

▶ A legislature with *one* chamber is __unicameral__ [unicameral / bicameral].

unicameral

▶ The horns on a *unicorn* reach the grand total of __one__.

one

▶ Since the word *unique* means "the only *one* of its kind," such phrases as "more unique" and "most unique" are __illogical__ [logical / illogical].

illogical

35

Review Test

Write *True* or *False*.

False 1. A *spectroscope* is a listening device.

False 2. To *countermand* an order is to repeat it.

False 3. *Intrastate* traffic goes between states.

True 4. An ostrich is a *biped*.

True 5. World War I *antedates* the invention of the atom bomb.

True 6. A *unicycle* has one wheel.

False 7. *Semiannual* conventions meet once in two years.

False 8. To *retrogress* is to advance rapidly.

True 9. William Shakespeare and his friend Ben Jonson were *contemporaries*.

True 10. A *subterranean* road runs under the earth.

Write the meaning of each boldface Latin root or prefix. The first letter of each answer is given.

11. **circum**navigate the globe — a_round_

12. an im**port**ed tobacco — c_arry_

13. a sentimental in**scrip**tion — w_ritten_

14. a **mult**itude of unpaid bills — m_any_

15. an **inter**change of ideas — b_etween_

16. the irre**voc**able finger of fate — c_all_

17. in**spir**ation for Homer's epic — b_reathe_

18. inspection of the **terr**ain — e_arth_

19. Lord Chesterfield's **urb**anity — c_ity_

20. Chapman's **trans**lation — a_cross_

Write the letter that indicates the best completion.

(a) 21. The *preamble* to a document comes (a) at the beginning, (b) in the middle, (c) at the end, (d) in the amendments.

(c) 22. A *signet* ring has on it (a) a diamond, (b) an emerald, (c) a sign, (d) a curse.

(b) 23. A *post-mortem* is held on a person who is (a) old, (b) dead, (c) diseased, (d) dying.

(a) 24. The Latin prefix for *above* is used in which word?—(a) supernatural, (b) anteroom, (c) submerge, (d) retrorocket.

(c) 25. The Latin root common to both *supervise* and *television* means (a) hear, (b) send, (c) see, (d) above.

Key to Review Test

Check your test answers by the following key. Deduct 4% per error from a possible 100%.

1. False	6. True	11. around	16. call	21. (a)
2. False	7. False	12. carry	17. breathe	22. (c)
3. False	8. False	13. write	18. earth	23. (b)
4. True	9. True	14. many	19. city	24. (a)
5. True	10. True	15. between	20. across	25. (c)

Score: 100 %
mostly

Supplementary Lists

Exercise 2-A

One derivative of each Latin root is given. Fill the blanks at the right with three more derivatives. If in doubt about a word, check its etymology in a dictionary.

ROOT	MEANING	DERIVATIVES
1. *ac, acr*	sharp	acrimony, _____, _____, _____
2. *aer*	air	aerial, _____, _____, _____
3. *agr*	field	agrarian, _____, _____, _____
4. *ali*	another	alias, _____, _____, _____
5. *alter, altr*	change	alternate, _____, _____, _____
6. *anim*	spirit; life	animosity, _____, _____, _____
7. *apt, ept*	adjust	aptitude, _____, _____, _____
8. *arm*	arm; weapon	armistice, _____, _____, _____
9. *art*	art; craft	artificial, _____, _____, _____
10. *avi*	bird	aviary, _____, _____, _____
11. *bel, bell*	war	rebel, _____, _____, _____
12. *ben, bene*	well	benefit, _____, _____, _____
13. *brev*	short	abbreviate, _____, _____, _____
14. *carn*	flesh	incarnate, _____, _____, _____
15. *cid, cis*	kill; cut	precise, _____, _____, _____
16. *civ*	citizen	civil, _____, _____, _____
17. *clam*	shout	exclaim, _____, _____, _____
18. *claud, claus*	close	closet, _____, _____, _____
19. *cogn*	know	incognito, _____, _____, _____
20. *cord*	heart	cordial, _____, _____, _____

ROOT	MEANING	DERIVATIVES
21. *corp*	body	corpse, _____, _____, _____
22. *cruc*	cross	crux, _____, _____, _____
23. *dent*	tooth	indent, _____, _____, _____
24. *dign*	worthy	dignity, _____, _____, _____
25. *doc, doct*	teach; prove	doctor, _____, _____, _____

Exercise 2-B

One derivative of each Latin root is given. Fill the blanks at the right with three more derivatives. If in doubt about a word, check its etymology in a dictionary.

ROOT	MEANING	DERIVATIVES
1. *dom*	master	domineer, _____, _____, _____
2. *don*	bestow	donate, _____, _____, _____
3. *du*	two	duet, _____, _____, _____
4. *ego*	I	egotist, _____, _____, _____
5. *err*	wander	error, _____, _____, _____
6. *fin*	end; limit	define, _____, _____, _____
7. *fort*	strong	fortify, _____, _____, _____
8. *fus*	pour	effusive, _____, _____, _____
9. *gen*	birth; race	progeny, _____, _____, _____
10. *grat*	please; favor	gratify, _____, _____, _____
11. *grav*	heavy	gravity, _____, _____, _____
12. *jac, jact, jec*	throw	eject, _____, _____, _____
13. *junct*	join	adjunct, _____, _____, _____
14. *labor*	work	elaborate, _____, _____, _____
15. *leg*	law	legal, _____, _____, _____

ROOT	MEANING	DERIVATIVES
16. *lev*	light; rise	levity, _____, _____, _____
17. *lib*	book	libel, _____, _____, _____
18. *luc*	light	elucidate, _____, _____, _____
19. *magn*	large	magnify, _____, _____, _____
20. *mar*	sea	mariner, _____, _____, _____
21. *medi*	middle	medium, _____, _____, _____
22. *min*	little; less	minimum, _____, _____, _____
23. *mon, monit*	warn	premonition, _____, _____, _____
24. *mor*	custom	moral, _____, _____, _____
25. *mut*	change	mutation, _____, _____, _____

Exercise 2-C

One derivative of each Latin root is given. Fill the blanks at the right with three more derivatives. If in doubt about a word, check its etymology in a dictionary.

ROOT	MEANING	DERIVATIVES
1. *nav*	ship	navigator, _____, _____, _____
2. *nomen, nomin*	name	nominee, _____, _____, _____
3. *ocul*	eye	monocle, _____, _____, _____
4. *par*	equal	parity, _____, _____, _____
5. *pater, patr*	father	patron, _____, _____, _____
6. *prim*	first	prime, _____, _____, _____
7. *rat, ration*	reason	rational, _____, _____, _____
8. *rect*	right	direct, _____, _____, _____
9. *rupt*	break	erupt, _____, _____, _____
10. *sanct*	holy	sanction, _____, _____, _____

ROOT	MEANING	DERIVATIVES
11. *seg, sect*	cut	bisect, _____, _____, _____
12. *sequ, secut*	follow	sequel, _____, _____, _____
13. *simil*	like	simile, _____, _____, _____
14. *sol*	alone	soliloquy, _____, _____, _____
15. *son*	sound	assonance, _____, _____, _____
16. *struct*	build	construct, _____, _____, _____
17. *ten*	hold	tenacious, _____, _____, _____
18. *tract*	draw; pull	extract, _____, _____, _____
19. *turb*	agitate	turbine, _____, _____, _____
20. *umbr*	shade	umbrage, _____, _____, _____
21. *vac*	empty	vacant, _____, _____, _____
22. *vert, vers*	turn	revert, _____, _____, _____
23. *vinc, vict*	conquer	victory, _____, _____, _____
24. *vit*	life	vital, _____, _____, _____
25. *vulg*	common	divulge, _____, _____, _____

3

Greek Derivatives

ROOTS

1. *anthrop*
2. *astr*
3. *auto*
4. *bibli*
5. *bio*
6. *chrom*
7. *chron*
8. *crypt*
9. *cycl*
10. *dec*
11. *dem*
12. *derm*
13. *dyn*
14. *gram, graph*
15. *hetero*
16. *homo*
17. *hydr*
18. *log*
19. *metr, meter*
20. *morph*
21. *neur*
22. *orth*
23. *paleo*
24. *pan*
25. *path*

Socrates never heard of a *telephone* or an *astronaut* or *psychiatry*—and yet these words are derived from Greek roots. As more scientific discoveries are made next year and the year after that, the chances are good that new names will also be built on the old Greek stems and prefixes. Knowing the meaning of these Greek forms can throw a high-wattage light on many English words.

Historically, Greek and Latin came flooding into our language in three waves: (1) religious terms at about the beginning of the Christian era; (2) literary and cultural terms during the Renaissance, the revival of learning of the fifteenth and sixteenth centuries; and (3) scientific terms in recent centuries.

Chapters 3 and 4 focus on fifty important Greek terms and their clusters of derivatives. An additional twenty-five Greek roots are presented at the end of Chapter 4 in a supplementary exercise.

First, memorize the Greek term and its definition, given at the beginning of each frame. Next, note carefully the example derivatives that follow in parentheses. Try to understand the connection between each of these derivatives and its Greek root. Then fill in the blanks.

Exercises

Roots

COVER THIS STRIP

1. **anthrop:** man.
   Derivatives: *anthropocentric, anthropogenesis, anthropogeography, anthropoid, anthropology, anthropometry, anthropomorphism, anthropophagy, misanthropy, philanthropy.*

anthropoids
▶ The *man*-like apes are called _____poids.

anthrop
▶ The Greek root for *man* is _____.

▶ The study of *man* is _____ [philology / anthropology].
anthropology

▶ Cannibalism, or the eating of man's flesh, is known as _____ [anthropophagy / herbivorousness].
anthropophagy

man
▶ *Anthrop* means _____.

anthropocentric
▶ A *man*-centered universe is obviously _____ic.

▶ One who hates *mankind* is a _____ [misanthrope / metronymic].
misanthrope

philanthropist
anthrop
man
▶ A charitable fellow is a _____ist (from *phil,* meaning *loving,* and _____, meaning _____).

2. **astr:** star.
   Derivatives: *aster, asterisk, asteroid, astral, astrobiology, astrodome, astrogate, astrolabe, astrology, astrometry, astronaut, astronomy, astrophysics, disaster.*

stars
▶ *Asteroids* are tiny planets that look like _____ [apes / stars].

astr
▶ The Greek root for *star* is _____.

43

astronomy astrology	▸ The scientific study of the *stars* is _____my, and fortune-telling by the *stars* is _____gy.
astrogate astronauts	▸ Those who fly toward the *stars* are said not to navigate but to _____gate, and the fliers themselves are called _____ [dreadnaughts / astronauts].
asterisks	▸ Printer's *stars* (as in H*Y*M*A*N K*A*P*L*A*N) are called _____.
disaster	▸ The word *dis*_____ hints that the *stars* were contrary.

3. **auto:** self.
   Derivatives: *autobiography, autocrat, autogenesis, autograph, autohypnosis, autoinfection, automat, automation, automaton, automobile, autopsy, autosuggestion.*

self	▸ An *autobiography* is written by one's _____ [critic / self].
self	▸ *Autosuggestion* is given by one's _____ [doctor / self].
auto	▸ The Greek root for *self* is _____.
automation	▸ A system of *self*-operating machinery is called _____ion.
automat	▸ A *self*-operating restaurant service is an _____at.
autocrat automobile autograph	▸ I can't admire any _____crat (dictator, having *self*-power) riding in his bullet-proof _____, but I might ask him for his _____ (*self*-written name).

4. **bibli:** book.
   Derivatives: *Bible, Biblicist, bibliofilm, bibliography, bibliolatry, bibliomania, bibliophile, bibliopole, bibliotheca.*

bibli	▸ The Greek root for *book* is _____.
bibliography	▸ A list of *book* sources is called a _____phy.

a bibliotheca	▶ A library or *book* collection is sometimes called _____ [volumetrics / a bibliotheca].
bibliomania	▶ A craze for collecting *books* is _____ [numismatics / bibliomania].
bibliophile bibliopole	▶ The _____*phile* (book-lover) gets his *books* from a _____*pole* (book-dealer).
bibliofilm	▶ Scholars record rare *books* on special microfilm known as _____ [movifilm / bibliofilm].
book	▶ The root *bibli* means _____.

5. **bio:** life.
   Derivatives: *biochemist, biodynamics, biogen, biogenesis, biography, biology, biolysis, biometrics, biophysics, biopsy, biotics.*

life	▶ *Biology* deals with plant and animal _____ [life / fiction].
bio	▶ The three-letter Greek root for *life* is _____.
biography	▶ The written account of a *life* is a _____.
biopsy	▶ The diagnostic examination by microscope of a piece of *living* tissue is a _____*psy*.
biometrics	▶ The calculation of the probable span of human *life* is called _____ [kinematics / biometrics].
biophysics	▶ The branch of physics that deals with *living* matter is _____.
biochemistry	▶ The branch of chemistry that deals with *life* processes is _____.
(a)	▶ *Biogenesis* is the theory that living things can come from (a) living things only, (b) lifeless matter. ( )

Quiz

Write the meaning of each boldface Greek root.

1. **bibli**omania   _____

2. **auto**infection   _____

3. **anthrop**ocentric _____

4. **astr**al   _____

5. anti**bio**tics   _____

1. book
2. self
3. man
4. star
5. life

---

6. **chrom:** color.
    Derivatives: *chromatic, chromatism, chromatology, chrome, chromium, chromoplasm, chromosome, chromosphere, panchromatic, polychrome.*

▶ A many-colored print is _____ [polyglot / polychromatic].

polychromatic

▶ A lens with *chromatic* aberration distorts _____ [sound / color].

color

▶ The Greek root for *color* is _____.

chrom

▶ The *colorful* gases seen around the sun during a total eclipse are called the _____ [biolysis / chromosphere].

chromosphere

▶ *Chrom* means _____.

color

▶ Our hereditary markings depend on tiny _____ somes.

chromosomes

---

7. **chron:** time.
    Derivatives: *chronic, chronicle, chronograph, chronological, chronology, chronometer, chronometry, chronoscope, synchronize.*

▶ *Chronological* order is _____ [time / place] order.

time

▶ *Chron* means _____.

time

46

synchronized	▶ A motion picture film and its sound effects should be *timed* together, or *syn*_____.
chronometer chronometry	▶ A watch or clock is sometimes called a _____*meter*, and the scientific measurement of *time* is _____*try*.
chron	▶ The Greek root for *time* is _____.
chronic	▶ If your back aches for a long *time* you have a _____ backache.

8. **crypt:** secret.
   Derivatives: *crypt, cryptic, cryptogram, cryptographer, cryptography, cryptology, cryptonym.*

secret	▶ A *cryptic* remark has a _____ [clear / secret] meaning.
crypt	▶ The Greek root for *secret* is _____.
cryptogram cryptographer	▶ A *secret,* coded message is a _____*gram,* and the fellow who decodes it is a _____*er.*
cryptonym	▶ A *secret* name is a _____ [cognomen / cryptonym].
crypt	▶ Bodies were often hidden away in a _____ [chromosphere / crypt].

9. **cycl:** circle; wheel.
   Derivatives: *cycle, cyclograph, cycloid, cyclometer, cyclone, cyclorama, cyclotron, encyclical, encyclopedia.*

(b)	▶ An *encyclopedia* gives instruction in (a) science only, (b) the *circle* of arts and sciences. ( )
cycl	▶ The Greek root for *circle* or *wheel* is _____.
cyclone	▶ A storm that has *circling* winds is called a _____.

cyclorama ▸ A *circular* room with large pictures is a _____ama.

cyclotron ▸ An apparatus that accelerates atomic patricles in *circles* is a _____on.

wheel
motorcycle
▸ A *cyclometer* measures _____ [wheel / Russian] revolutions and might be useful on a _____ [foot / motorcycle].

---

10. **dec:** ten.
   Derivatives: *decade, decagon, decaliter, Decalogue,* Decameron, *decameter, decasyllable, decathlon, decennial, decimal, decimate.*

decade
decaliter
decameter
▸ *Ten* years equal a _____; *ten* liters equal a _____; *ten* meters equal a _____.

dec ▸ The Greek root for *ten* is _____.

ten ▸ A *decathlon* consists of _____ [five / ten] athletic events.

ten ▸ A *decennial* celebrates _____ years.

Decalogue ▸ The *Ten* Commandments are called the _____ [Heptateuch / Decalogue].

Decameron ▸ Boccaccio's tales were supposedly told during a plague by *ten* people on *ten* days—hence, they are entitled the _____ [Pentateuch / *Decameron*].

Quiz

Write the meaning of each boldface Greek root.

1. **crypt**ogram   _____

2. bi**cycle**   _____

3. **dec**imal   _____

48

1. secret
2. wheel
3. ten
4. color
5. time

4. **chrom**atism   _____

5. **chron**ology   _____

---

11. **dem:** people.
    Derivatives: *demagogue, demiurge, democracy, democrat, demography, endemic, epidemic, pandemic.*

democracy
▶ Government by the *people* is called _____cy.

demagogue
▶ One who uses false claims and emotional appeals to stir up the common *people* is a _____gue.

people
▶ The Greek root *dem* means _____.

endemic
▶ A disease restricted to *people* in one locality is _____ [endemic / cycloid].

epidemic
pandemic
▶ A disease that spreads among *people* is epi_____, and if it hits *people* over a very wide area it is _____ [panoramic / pandemic].

people
▶ *Demography* is a study of how _____ [people / cattle] are distributed.

dem
▶ The Greek root for *people* is _____.

---

12. **derm:** skin.
    Derivatives: *dermatitis, dermatoid, dermatologist, dermatophyte, endoderm, epidermis, hypodermic, pachyderm.*

skin
▶ *Dermatitis* is an inflammation of the _____ [joints / skin].

dermatologist
▶ A *skin* infection should be treated by a _____ist.

derm
▶ The Greek root for *skin* is _____.

pachyderms	▶ Thick-*skinned* animals, like elephants and rhinoceroses, are _____ [anthropoids / pachyderms].
epidermis	▶ Our outermost layer of *skin* is *epi*_____.
hypodermic	▶ An under-the-*skin* injection is *hypo*_____.

13. **dyn:** power.
    Derivatives: *dynamic, dynamism, dynamite, dynamo, dynamometer, dynasty, dynatron, dyne, electrodynamics, hydrodynamics, thermodynamics.*

(b)	▶ A *dyne* is a unit of (a) time, (b) force or power. ( )
dynamometer	▶ Mechanical *power* can be measured by a _____*meter*.
dyn	▶ The Greek root for *power* is _____.
dynamic	▶ An energetic person is said to be _____*ic*.
dynasty	▶ A *powerful* family which has ruled for some generations is a _____*sty*.
power	▶ *Dyn* means _____.
power	▶ The *dynamos* at Niagara produce electrical _____.
dynamite	▶ One *powerful* explosive is _____.

14. **gram, graph:** write.
    Derivatives: *autograph, biography, calligraphy, cryptogram, diagram, epigram, geography, graffiti, gramophone, grammar, graphic, graphite, graphology, holograph, lithograph, mimeograph, photograph, seismograph, telegram, typography.*

writing	▶ A *mimeograph* makes duplicates of _____ [secrets / writing].

writing	▶ *Graphite* is used in pencils for _____ [*erasing / writing*].
write	▶ The Greek roots *gram* and *graph* mean _____ [*heavy / write*].
calligraphy	▶ One's penmanship, or *handwriting,* is called _____ [*calliope / calligraphy*].
seismograph	▶ Seismic disturbances, or earthquakes, are *recorded* on the *seis_____*.
(b)	▶ *Graphology* tries to analyze character by means of (a) head bumps, (b) handwriting. ( )
(b)	▶ The *graffiti* found on walls are (a) insects, (b) rude sketches and writing. ( )
grandma	▶ Which word wandered into the wrong line-up?—*epigram, telegram, grammar, grandma, lithograph.* _____

15. **hetero:** other.
    Derivatives: *heterodox, heterodyne, heterogeneous, heterograft, heteromorphic, heteronym, heteroplasty, heterosexual.*

other (a)	▶ *Hetero* means _____. Members of a *heterogeneous* group are (a) of various types, (b) all alike. ( )
other	▶ A *heterosexual* person is attracted to the _____ [*same / other*] sex.
heterodox	▶ Religious or political beliefs that are *other* than the usual kind are _____*dox*.
heteroplasty heterograft	▶ Surgery in which the grafted tissue comes from *another* person is called _____*plasty* or _____*graft*.

51

Quiz

Write the meaning of each boldface Greek root.

1. **dem**ocrat _____

2. litho**graph** _____

3. **dyn**amism _____

4. **hetero**geneity _____

5. pachy**derm** _____

1. people
2. write
3. power
4. other
5. skin

---

16. **homo:** same.
    Derivatives: *homeopathy, homochromatic, homogamy, homogeneous, homogenize, homograft, homologous, homonym, homosexual.*

▶ If those in a group are the *same,* that group is _____ [homogeneous / heterogeneous].

homogeneous

▶ Words that have the *same* sound, like "bare" and "bear," are called _____ [antonyms / homonyms].

homonyms

▶ The Greek root for *same* is _____.

homo

▶ *Chrom* means _____, and flowers which are all the *same* color are _____ [homochromatic / heterochromatic].

color
homochromatic

▶ Milk which is uniformly of the *same* texture has been _____ed.

homogenized

▶ One who has sexual desire for those of the *same* sex is _____ [homosexual / heterosexual].

homosexual

---

17. **hydr:** water.
    Derivatives: *hydraulics, hydrocarbon, hydrocephaly, hydrogen, hydrography, hydrokinetics, hydrometer, hydropathy, hydrophobia, hydroponics, hydrotherapy.*

▶ *Hydraulics* deals with the mechanical properties of _____ and other liquids.

water

water	▶ *Hydropathy* and *hydrotherapy* involve treatment of disease by use of _____.
hydr	▶ The Greek root for *water* is _____.
hydrophobia	▶ Because rabies brings on a fear of *water*, the disease is also known as _____bia.
hydrocephaly	▶ Excessive fluid in the skull is called _____ [hydrocephaly / heteroplasty].
fluids	▶ *Hydroponics* is the science of growing plants in _____ [sand / fluids].

18. **log:** word; study.
    Derivatives: *apology, biology, decalogue, dialogue, doxology, embryology, eulogy, geology, hydrology, logic, logorrhea, mineralogy, monologue, philology, prologue, tautology, theology.*

study	▶ *Biology* is the _____ [breeding / study] of plant and animal life.
study	▶ *Mineralogy* is the _____ of minerals.
log	▶ The Greek root for *study* is _____.
hydrology	▶ The *study* of water and its distribution is _____ [hydrolysis / hydrology].
embryology	▶ The *study* of embryo development is _____ [embryology / embryectomy].
word	▶ The root *log*, as in *monologue, dialogue* and *eulogy*, means _____ [word / log].
words	▶ A *tautology*—as in "small little midget"—uses too many _____.
words	▶ A person with *logorrhea* pours out too many _____.

53

19. **metr, meter:** measure.
   Derivatives: *ammeter, barometer, centimeter, chronometer, geometry, hexameter, hydrometer, metrology, metronome, micrometer, pentameter, seismometer, speedometer, thermometer, trigonometry.*

measure
▶ A *barometer* is used to _____ [measure / lower] air pressure.

measure
▶ A *chronometer* is used to _____ time.

micrometer
▶ One instrument which *measures* tiny distances is the _____ [micrometer / microcosm].

geometry
trigonometry
metr
▶ Mathematics courses that deal with *measurement* include geo_____ and trig_____. In these two words the root that means *measure* is _____.

(b)
▶ *Metrology* is the science of (a) metals, (b) weights and measures. ( )

20. **morph:** form.
   Derivatives: *amorphous, anthropomorphic, isomorph, metamorphosis, morpheme, Morpheus, morphine, morphology.*

(b)
▶ Ovid's *Metamorphoses* tells how the gods caused people to change their (a) financial condition, (b) form or shape. ( )

form
▶ *Morph* means _____.

morphology
▶ In linguistics the study of the internal structure and *form* of words is called _____ology.

amorphous
▶ *Formless* sulphur is _____ [amorphous / crystalline].

forms
▶ *Morpheus* was the god of dreams, named after the _____ [colors / forms] seen in dreams.

form
man
▶ An *anthropomorphic* god is in the _____ (*morph*) of a _____ (*anthrop*).

54

Quiz

Write the meaning of each boldface Greek root.

1. hydro**meter** _____
2. **hydr**ophobia _____
3. geo**logy** _____
4. iso**morph** _____
5. **homo**logous _____

1. measure
2. water
3. study
4. form
5. same

---

21. **neur:** nerve.
    Derivatives: *neural, neuralgia, neurasthenia, neurocirculatory, neurogenic, neurologist, neuromotor, neuromuscular, neuron, neurosis, neurotic.*

▶ A *neurotic* suffers from a _____ [speech / nervous] disorder.

nervous

▶ *Neuritis* is a painful inflammation of the _____ [skin / nerves].

nerves

▶ The Greek root for *nerve* is _____.

neur

▶ The *neurotic* has what is called a _____ [neurosis / psychosis].

neurosis

▶ If you develop fatigue, worries, and pains without apparent cause, your condition is called _____ *nia*.

neurasthenia

▶ If you need a *nerve* specialist, go to a _____ *ist*.

neurologist

---

22. **orth:** right; true.
    Derivatives: *orthocephalic, orthochromatic, orthodontics, orthodox, orthoepy, orthogenesis, orthography, orthopedics, orthopsychiatry, orthoscope.*

▶ The *orthodox* religion is (a) the established "true" faith, (b) a modern variation of religious faith. ( )

(a)

55

orth	▸ The Greek root for *right* or *true* is _____.
orthopedist	▸ To *right* or correct skeletal deformities is the job of the _____ [orthopedist / cyclopedist].
orthodontist	▸ The straightening and *trueing* of teeth is done by the _____ [neurologist / orthodontist].
right	▸ *Orthography* deals with _____ [right / foreign] spelling.
right	▸ *Orthoepy* deals with _____ pronunciation.

23. **paleo:** ancient.
    Derivatives: *paleobotany, Paleocene, paleography, paleolithic, paleontology, Paleozoic, paleozoology.*

ancient	▸ The *Paleozoic, Paleocene,* and *paleolithic* periods belong to an _____ [ancient / recent] era.
paleo	▸ The Greek root for *ancient* is _____.
paleontology	▸ The study of *ancient* forms of plant and animal life is called _____ology.
paleolith	▸ An *ancient* stone tool is a _____lith.
ancient writing	▸ The word *paleography* has two Greek roots, meaning _____ and _____.

24. **pan:** all.
    Derivatives: *panacea, Pan-American, Pan-Asiatic, panchromatic, pancreas, pandemic, pandemonium, panegyric, Panhellenic, panorama, pantheism, pantheon, pantomime.*

all	▸ *Panchromatic* film is sensitive to _____ [no / all] colors.
all	▸ A *panacea* is a supposed cure for _____ [one / all] disease or trouble.

pan

▸ The Greek root for *all* is _____.

panorama

▸ A picture with a view in *all* directions is a _____*ama*.

pandemic

▸ A disease that is very widespread is _____*ic*.

Panhellenic

▸ A league of *all* the campus Greek-letter (Hellenic) fraternities and sororities is _____*ic*.

Pantheon

▸ A temple for *all* the gods was the _____ [Colosseum / Pantheon].

all

▸ *Pan* means _____.

---

25. **path:** disease; feeling.
    Derivatives: *antipathy, apathy, empathy, neuropathy, osteopathy, pathetic, pathologist, pathos, psychopath, sympathy, telepathy.*

path

▸ The Greek root _____ means *feeling*.

pathetic

▸ A *feeling* of pity is aroused by *pathos* or that which is _____*ic*.

sympathy
empathy

▸ Your compassion for another person is *sym*_____, and your complete projection of yourself into the *feelings* of another person is *em*_____.

▸ The root *path* means *feeling*, but it can also mean *disease;* thus, a *pathologist* is a specialist in _____ [paths and trails / diseases].

diseases

psychopath

▸ A serious mental disorder would be found in a _____ [psychopath / bibliopole].

Quiz

Write the meaning of each boldface Greek root.

1. **orth**ography   *r*_____

2. **neur**on   _____

57

1. right
2. nerve
3. ancient
4. feeling
5. all

3. **paleo**botany   _____

4. a**path**etic   *f*_____

5. **pan**acea   _____

Review Test

Write *True* or *False*.

_____ 1. *Cryptography* deals with secret writing.

_____ 2. *Bibliomania* refers to excessive use of alcohol.

_____ 3. *Graphite* can be used to write with.

_____ 4. *Paleontologists* are interested in fossils.

_____ 5. *Autosuggestion* requires two or more people.

_____ 6. *Orthodox* beliefs are new and daring.

_____ 7. *Homogenized* milk has its cream floating at the top.

_____ 8. *Dermatology* deals with the skin.

_____ 9. *Neurasthenia* refers to a hardening of the arteries.

_____ 10. A wristwatch is a type of *chronometer*.

Write the meaning of each boldface Greek root. The first letter of each answer is given.

11. an **anthrop**omorphic god   m_____

12. **pan**hellenic organizations   a_____

13. suffering from de**hydr**ation   w_____

14. the Dewey **dec**imal system   t_____

15. the **chrom**osome number   c_____

16. a sudden meta**morph**osis   f_____

17. overuse of anti**bio**tics   l_____

18. faith in **dem**ocracy   p_____

19. the **hetero**doxies of Berkeley   o_____

20. a sensitive volt**meter**   m_____

Write the letter that indicates the best completion.

( ) 21. An *asterisk* is a printing symbol that looks like (a) a number, (b) a star, (c) a slanted line, (d) a question mark.

( ) 22. *Pathogenesis* has to do with the origin of (a) a disease, (b) a path, (c) God, (d) sin.

( ) 23. A *dynamometer* measures (a) speed of rotation, (b) spark, (c) power, (d) sound.

( ) 24. The Greek root for *circle* is used in which word?—(a) cryptic, (b) cardiac, (c) encyclical, (d) eclipse.

( ) 25. The Greek root which is common to both *geology* and *proctology* means (a) *earth,* (b) *study,* (c) *tunnel,* (d) *the end.*

Key to Review Test

Check your test answers by the following key. Deduct 4% per error from a possible 100%.

1. True	6. False	11. man	16. form	21. (b)
2. False	7. False	12. all	17. life	22. (a)
3. True	8. True	13. water	18. people	23. (c)
4. True	9. False	14. ten	19. other	24. (c)
5. False	10. True	15. color	20. measure	25. (b)

Score: _____%

4

Greek Derivatives

ROOTS

1. *phil*
2. *phon*
3. *physi*
4. *pseudo*
5. *psych*
6. *pyr*
7. *soph*
8. *tele*
9. *the*
10. *therm*

PREFIXES

11. *amphi*
12. *anti*
13. *arch*
14. *dia*
15. *epi*
16. *eu*
17. *hyper*
18. *hypo*
19. *kilo*
20. *meta*
21. *mono*
22. *neo*
23. *peri*
24. *poly*
25. *syn, sym*

Chapter 4 continues our study of Greek derivatives. Follow the same procedure as in Chapter 3.

Exercises

Roots

COVER THIS STRIP

1. **phil:** loving.
   Derivatives: *Anglophile, bibliophile, Francophile, philander, philanthropy, philatelist, philharmonic, philodendron, philogynist, philology, philoprogenitive, philosophy, philter.*

phil
▶ The Greek root for *loving* is _____.

bibliophile
▶ One who *loves* books (*bibli*) is a _____.

philanthropist
▶ One with *love*, or charity, for man (*anthrop*) is a _____ist.

philosopher
▶ One who *loves* wisdom (*soph*) is a _____er.

philogynist
philanderer
▶ One who *loves* women (*gyn*) is a _____ist; but if he trifles with their *love* he may be called a _____ [demagogue / philanderer].

philharmonic
▶ If you *love* musical harmony, you might join a _____ic orchestra.

Francophile
▶ If you *love* or admire the French, you are a _____ [Francophobe / Francophile].

philatelist
▶ If you *love* stamps and collect them, you are a _____ [psychopath / philatelist].

2. **phon:** sound.
   Derivatives: *phonautograph, phoneme, phonetic, phonics, phonograph, phonology, phonometer, phonoscope, telephone.*

phon
▶ The word *telephone* deals with *sound*, as is suggested by its Greek root _____.

sound
▶ *Phonetic* spelling is based on the _____ [sound / general appearance] of words.

phoneme	▶ In linguistics, a specific speech *sound* is called a _____eme.
phonometer	▶ An instrument which measures (*meter*) the intensity and the frequency of *sound* vibrations is a _____[chronometer / phonometer].
(b)	▶ *Phonics* deals with (a) picture transmission, (b) speech sound, especially as related to the teaching of reading and pronunciation. ( )
sound	▶ *Phon* means _____.

3. **physi:** nature.
   Derivatives: *physical, physician, physicist, physiocrat, physiognomy, physiography, physiology, physiotherapy.*

nature	▶ A *physicist* studies the laws of _____ [poetry / nature].
physi	▶ The Greek root for *nature* is _____.
physiography	▶ The description of *nature* and natural phenomena is sometimes called _____ [empathy / physiography].
(a)	▶ A *physiocrat* believes that the only true source of wealth is (a) the land and its products, (b) gambling. ( )
nature	▶ *Physi* means _____.
physiology	▶ The branch of biology that deals with the parts and the functions of the body is _____gy.
physiognomy	▶ Your face is your _____nomy.

4. **pseudo:** false.
   Derivaties: *pseudoaquatic, pseudoclassic, pseudomorph, pseudonym, pseudopod, pseudoscience.*

pseudonym
> An author's fictitious or *false* name, such as *Mark Twain* or *George Eliot* or *Lewis Carroll*, is his _____ [surname / pseudonym].

false
> *Pseudo* means _____.

(b)
> When a critic refers to a novel as "a pseudoclassic," he means that it is (a) a genuine classic, (b) not a genuine classic. ( )

pseudosciences
> Unreliable studies such as phrenology and astrology are actually _____ [social sciences / pseudosciences].

is not
> A *pseudoaquatic* plant _____ [is / is not] genuinely aquatic.

false form
> A *pseudomorph* is a mineral which looks like another one, and the word literally means _____ _____.

---

5. **psych:** mind; spirit.
   Derivatives: *psyche, psychedelic, psychic, psychiatrist, psychoanalysis, psychodrama, psychograph, psychology, psychometry, psychoneurosis, psychopath, psychosis, psychosomatic, psychotherapy.*

mind
> *Psychiatry* treats disorders of the _____ [eye / mind].

psychoanalysis
> Freudian analysis, which aims to cure the *mind*, is _____*sis*.

psych
> The Greek root for *mind* is _____.

psychograph
> A chart of one's personality traits is a _____ [psychograph / pseudomorph].

mind
> A *psychic* shock or trauma has a permanent effect on the _____ [heart / mind].

psychedelic
> Drugs like LSD which affect the *mind* are _____*lic*.

Quiz

Write the meaning of each boldface Greek root.

1. **pseudo**pod   _____

2. **physi**cian   _____

3. **phon**ograph   _____

4. **psych**osis   _____

5. **phil**harmonic   _____

---

1. false
2. nature
3. sound
4. mind
5. loving

---

6. **pyr:** fire.
   Derivatives: *pyre, pyretic, Pyrex, pyrexia, pyrites, pyritology, pyrochemical, pyrogenic, pyrolysis, pyromancy, pyromaniac, pyrometry, pyrophobia, pyrosis, pyrostat, pyrotechnics.*

▶ A *pyromaniac* has a compulsion to _____ [steal things / start fires].

start fires

▶ *Pyrotechnics* is the art of making and displaying _____ [advertisements / fireworks].

fireworks

▶ The Greek root for *fire* is _____.

pyr

▶ Hindu widows used to be cremated on their husband's funeral _____*e*.

pyre

▶ American women use heat-resistant glassware called _____.

Pyrex

▶ A child with *pyrexia* is suffering from _____ [chills / fever].

fever

▶ A *pyrostat* is an alarm device protecting against _____ [burglar / fire].

fire

▶ An irrational fear of *fire* is called _____*bia*.

pyrophobia

▶ A *pyromaniac* and a *pyrophobe* would probably be _____ [happy / unhappy] together.

unhappy

65

7. **soph:** wisdom.
   Derivatives: *gymnosophist, philosophy, Sophia, sophism, sophisticated, sophistry, Sophocles, sophomore, sophomoric, theosophy.*

wise sophomoric	▶ The word *sophomore* has two Greek roots: *soph,* which means _____ [wise / strong], and *mor* (as in *moron*), which means *foolish.* Therefore an immature person who acts like a know-it-all is said to be _____ [sophomoric / heterogeneous].
sophistry	▶ Since the *sophists* were notorious for their clever but deceptive logic, a misleading argument is sometimes called a _____ry.
sophisticated	▶ People who are *worldly-wise,* rather than simple, are _____ed.
sophisticated	▶ A rocket or electronic device that is very subtle and complicated in design is also said to be _____ed.
wisdom	▶ According to its Greek roots, the word *philosophy* means *the love of* _____.

8. **tele:** far.
   Derivatives: *telecast, telegenic, telegraph, telekinesis, telemechanics, telemeter, telepathy, telephone, telephoto, telescope, telethermometer, telethon, teletype, television.*

far *writing*	▶ The word *telephone* literally means *far* + *sound.* Similarly, *telegraph* means _____ + _____.
far *seeing*	▶ *Television* means _____ + _____ [advertising/ seeing].
tele	▶ The Greek root for *far* is _____.
telethermometer	▶ A thermometer that measures temperature from *afar* is a _____er.
telephoto	▶ Photos can be taken from *afar* by _____to.
telemechanics	▶ Mechanisms can be radio-operated from *afar* by techniques of _____mechanics.

telepathy
▶ Transmitting thoughts without use of the five senses is called _____pathy.

9. **the:** god.
   Derivatives: *atheism, monotheism, pantheism, Pantheon, polytheism, theanthropic, theism, theocentric, theocracy, theology, theosophy.*

God
▶ *Theism* and *monotheism* generally refer to a belief in _____.

polytheism
▶ Belief in many *gods* is *poly_____*.

atheism
▶ Belief in no *god* is *a_____*.

the
▶ The Greek root for *god* is _____.

theocracy
▶ Puritan New England, ruled by *God* and the church, was a _____ [democracy / theocracy].

theology
▶ The study of *God* and religious doctrines is called _____gy.

god
▶ *The* means _____.

theocentric
▶ A cultural pattern in which *God* is the center of interest is _____ [anthropocentric / theocentric].

10. **therm:** heat.
    Derivatives: *diathermy, hydrothermal, isotherm, thermal, thermesthesia, thermocouple, thermodynamics, thermograph, thermolysis, thermometer, thermonuclear, thermopile, thermos, thermostat.*

heat
▶ In a *thermonuclear* blast the nuclear fission releases _____ [psychic waves / heat].

(a)
▶ A *thermostat* controls (a) heat, (b) water. ( )

(b)
▶ The word *hydrothermal* literally means (a) electric power, (b) hot water. ( )

thermograph

▶ A record of temperature is made by the _____ph.

isotherm

▶ A line on the weather map between points of equal temperature is an _____ [isotherm / isobar].

thermodynamics

▶ The relations between *heat* and other forms of energy are dealt with in _____ics.

thermos

▶ Coffee keeps its *heat* in a _____ jug.

Quiz

Write the meaning of each boldface Greek root.

1. **the**osophy _____

2. **pyr**ometry _____

1. God
2. fire
3. far
4. wisdom
5. heat

3. **tele**scope _____

4. **soph**omore _____

5. dia**therm**y _____

Prefixes

11. amphi: around; on both sides.

▶ Since frogs live *both* on land and in water they are _____ [bisexuals / amphibians].

amphibians

amphitheater

▶ An arena with the spectators seated *around* it is an _____ter.

▶ A statement with two possible meanings—such as "The Duke yet lives that Henry shall depose"—is _____ [amphibolous / anthropomorphic].

amphibolous

12. anti: against.

against

▶ An *antipathy* is a feeling _____ [for / against] something.

68

contrast	▸ In *antithesis* the two parts of a sentence present a _____ [similarity / contrast].
(a)	▸ Sofas which might get soiled by hair oil from Macassar were often protected by a small cover known as (a) an antimacassar, (b) a paleolith. ( )

13. arch: chief.

chief	▸ An *archangel* is a _____ [common / chief] angel.
(b)	▸ In Milton's *Paradise Lost* the *archfiend* is (a) a run-of-the-mill devil, (b) Satan himself. ( )
an archetype	▸ A dominant, often-repeated pattern or theme in literature is said to be _____ [a stenotype / an archetype].

14. dia: through.

through	▸ *Diathermy* sends heat _____ [through / around] one's body.
diameter	▸ The distance *through* a circle is called the _____.
(b)	▸ A *diaphanous* garment (a) has diamonds around it, (b) can be seen through. ( )

15. epi: upon; beside.

upon	▸ The *epidermis* is the outer, nonsensitive layer that lies _____ [upon / below] the true skin.
epicenter	▸ The point above and *upon* the center of an earthquake is the _____ [seismograph / epicenter].
epitaph	▸ The inscription *upon* a tomb is an _____ [anagram / epitaph].

16. eu: good; well.

well being

▶ *Euphoria* is a feeling of _____ [pain / well being].

good

▶ *Eupepsia* means _____ [good / bad] digestion.

praises

▶ A *eulogy* _____ [praises / condemns].

euthanasia

▶ Mercy killing is known as _____ [asphyxia / euthanasia].

17. hyper: excessive.

hypercritical

▶ One who finds fault with an *excessive* number of details is _____ [hypocritical / hypercritical].

hyperopia

▶ A person whose eyes can see an *excessive* distance probably has _____ [myopia / hyperopia].

excessive

▶ *Hyperthyroidism,* marked by rapid pulse and sleeplessness, may be caused by _____ [insufficient / excessive] activity of the thyroid gland.

18. hypo: under.

below

▶ A patient with *hypothermia* has a temperature _____ [above / below] normal.

hypothesis

▶ An assumption which *underlies* an investigation is called a _____ [hypothesis / prosthesis].

hypopituitarism

▶ *Underactivity* of the pituitary gland, characterized by bodily fat and a loss of sexuality, is called _____ [hyperpituitarism / hypopituitarism].

19. kilo: thousand.

thousand

▶ A *kilocycle* equals one _____ [hundred / thousand] cycles per second.

kilometer	▶ One *thousand* meters equal one _____.
one	▶ Problem: One *thousand* watts of electrical energy used for sixty minutes equal _____ [one / 60,000] kilowatt-hour[s].

20. meta: change; after.

metamorphic	▶ Rocks such as marble which have *changed* their form under pressure are _____ [anthropomorphic / metamorphic].
metabolism	▶ The body's chemical and physical *changes,* with release of energy, are aspects of _____ [morphology / metabolism].
(b)	▶ *Metempsychosis* assumes that at one's death his soul (a) also dies, (b) makes a change, passing into another body. ( )

21. mono: one.

one	▶ A *monolith* consists of _____ [one / more than one] stone.
monodrama	▶ A play with *one* performer is a _____ [monodrama / melodrama].
monomania	▶ Captain Ahab's irrational interest in *one* subject, Moby Dick, amounts to _____ [bipolarity / monomania].

22. neo: new.

new	▶ A *neophyte* in a religious order is a _____ [new / elderly] member.
neologism	▶ A *new* word, freshly coined, is a _____ [neologism / hyperbole].
neoclassicism	▶ A period of a *new* version, or revival, of classical literary style is known as _____ [romanticism / neoclassicism].

23. peri: around.

around

▶ The *perimeter* of a ranch is the distance _____ [across / around] it.

(b)

▶ Aristotle and his young Athenian friends have been called *peripatetic* philosophers because (a) they sat in a classroom, (b) they walked around. ( )

(a)

▶ *Periphrasis* is a *roundabout* way of phrasing, as illustrated in (a) "I did dance and Joe did shout," (b) "I danced and Joe hollered." ( )

24. poly: many.

many

▶ A *polytechnic* institution offers courses in _____ [one or two / many] technical fields.

polygon

▶ A plane figure with *many* sides is a _____ [polygon / mastodon].

(b)

▶ A *polysyllable* has *many* (at least four) syllables, like the word (a) "logic," (b) "transcendentalism." ( )

25. syn, sym: together.

(a)

▶ *Synthesis* involves (a) bringing things together, (b) taking things apart. ( )

synchronized

▶ Actions that are timed *together* are _____ [acclimated / synchronized].

syndrome

▶ Symptoms which occur *together* and indicate a specific disease are called a _____ [syndrome / eupepsia].

72

Review Test

Write *True* or *False*.

_____ 1. The *archdeacon* has a higher rank than the deacon.

_____ 2. *Hyperacidity* refers to a lack of enough stomach acid.

_____ 3. *Metamorphic* rocks have undergone a change of form.

_____ 4. A *polytheist* believes in the oneness of God.

_____ 5. The feminine name *Sophia* originally meant "stupid."

_____ 6. An *amphibian* plane can take off from land or sea.

_____ 7. *Antipathy* is warm affection.

_____ 8. A *phonoscope* enables one to see certain characteristics of sounds.

_____ 9. *Synchronized* movements are timed together.

_____ 10. A *kilogram* weighs one thousand pounds.

Write the meaning of each boldface Greek root or prefix. The first letter of each answer is given.

11. a **pseudo**medieval ballad   f_____

12. a jutting **peri**scope   a_____

13. the doctor's **dia**gnosis   t_____

14. cooking with **Py**rex   f_____

15. the actor's **mono**cle   o_____

16. **neo**-impressionism in art   n_____

17. the gentle **phil**osopher   l_____

18. suffering from **hypo**glycemia   u_____

19. a sensitive **therm**ocouple   h_____

20. cutting the **epi**cardium   u_____

Write the letter that indicates the best completion.

( ) 21. *Euphoria* refers to a feeling of (a) well-being, (b) weariness, (c) drowsiness, (d) hunger.
( ) 22. *Physics* is the study of (a) diseases, (b) chemicals, (c) nature, (d) beauty.
( ) 23. *Psychosurgery* involves cutting into (a) the lungs, (b) the face, (c) the muscles, (d) the brain.
( ) 24. *Tele* means (a) *sound,* (b) *star,* (c) *far,* (d) *sight.*
( ) 25. The Greek root which is common to both *pantheism* and *theology* means (a) *all,* (b) *god,* (c) *study,* (d) *nature.*

Key to Review Test

Check your test answers by the following key. Deduct 4% per error from a possible 100%.

1. True	6. True	11. false	16. new	21. (a)
2. False	7. False	12. around	17. loving	22. (c)
3. True	8. True	13. through	18. under	23. (d)
4. False	9. True	14. fire	19. heat	24. (c)
5. False	10. False	15. one	20. upon	25. (b)

Score: _____%

Supplementary List

Exercise 4

One derivative of each Greek root is given. Fill the blanks at the right with three more derivatives. If in doubt about a word, check its etymology in a dictionary.

ROOT	MEANING	DERIVATIVES
1. *agog*	leader	pedagogue, _____, _____, _____
2. *cosm*	world; order	cosmic, _____, _____, _____
3. *crac, crat*	power	plutocrat, _____, _____, _____
4. *erg*	work	energy, _____, _____, _____
5. *gam*	marriage	monogamy, _____, _____, _____
6. *gen*	race; kind	genetics, _____, _____, _____
7. *geo*	earth	geometry, _____, _____, _____
8. *gon*	corner; angle	hexagon, _____, _____, _____
9. *gyn*	woman	gynecology, _____, _____, _____
10. *hem*	blood	hemophilia, _____, _____, _____
11. *iatr*	heal	geriatrics, _____, _____, _____
12. *iso*	same	isobar, _____, _____, _____
13. *lith*	rock	monolith, _____, _____, _____
14. *mega*	great	megaphone, _____, _____, _____
15. *micro*	small	microbe, _____, _____, _____
16. *necr*	dead	necrosis, _____, _____, _____
17. *nom*	law; order	economy, _____, _____, _____
18. *onym*	name	antonym, _____, _____, _____
19. *ped*	child	pedant, _____, _____, _____
20. *phos, phot*	light	photograph, _____, _____, _____

ROOT	MEANING	DERIVATIVES
21. *pod*	foot	podiatrist, _____, _____, _____
22. *poli*	city	police, _____, _____, _____
23. *scop*	see; watch	episcopal, _____, _____, _____
24. *techn*	art; skill	technique, _____, _____, _____
25. *zo*	animal	zoo, _____, _____, _____

5
Descriptive Words

concupiscent — lusty

1. affable
2. altruistic
3. ambidextrous
4. aromatic
5. asinine
6. astute
7. bawdy
8. bellicose
9. berserk
10. bizarre
11. boorish
12. bovine
13. buoyant
14. buxom
15. cadaverous
16. candid
17. carnivorous
18. clandestine
19. craven
20. dastardly
21. deft
22. defunct
23. deleterious
24. derogatory
25. destitute
26. diabolic
27. discreet
28. disenchanted
29. docile
30. doddering
31. dogmatic
32. droll
33. dubious
34. eccentric
35. effeminate
36. emaciated
37. enigmatic ✓
38. erotic
39. exorbitant
40. feasible
41. fetid
42. flamboyant
43. fluent
44. frugal
45. furtive
46. gullible
47. iconoclastic
48. impassive
49. impeccable
50. impromptu

The right descriptive word can be worth diamonds in a composition. Of course, as Mark Twain has said, it must be the right word, not its second cousin. Naturally, if you know thirty ways to describe a man or a voice or a smile instead of only five ways, you have a wider selection and your chances of picking an effective word are much improved.

Chapters 5 and 6 each present fifty descriptive words which should be part of the stock in trade of any writer of themes or reader of literature. Additional adjectives appear in supplementary exercises at the ends of these chapters.

Study carefully the definitions at the beginning of each frame. Then fill in the blanks with words defined in that frame, unless other choices are offered.

Exercises

COVER THIS STRIP

1. **affable** (af'ə-bəl): easy to talk to; amiable.
2. **altruistic** (al'trōō-is'tik): unselfish; concerned for the welfare of others.

(b) ▶ An *affable* professor is (a) hostile, (b) friendly. (b)

(a) ▶ An *altruistic* woman is one who sacrifices to help (a) others, (b) only herself. (a)

affable ▶ We found Elmer in a friendly, talkative mood, in fact, quite af*fable*.

altruistic ▶ Devoted to public charities, Straus was certainly al*truistic*.

affable
altruistic
▶ In *A Tale of Two Cities,* the executioner stands grim and silent, hardly an af*fable* fellow. Then Sydney Carton gives his life—loses his head, in fact—to save a friend. What an al*truistic* deed!

3. **ambidextrous** (am'bə-dek'strəs): able to use both hands with equal ease.
4. **aromatic** (ar'ə-mat'ik): fragrant; spicy; sweet-smelling.

(b) ▶ *Aromatic* plants are (a) odorless, (b) pleasantly scented. (b)

ambidextrous ▶ A basketball player who shoots baskets with either hand is *ambidextrous* [ambidextrous / paraplegic].

ambidextrous ▶ Wilma bats the baseball equally well from either side of the plate because she is *ambidextrous*.

aromatic ▶ Her boudoir was *aromatic* with subtle perfumes and incense.

aromatic ambidextrous	▶ At harvest these orchards are *aromatic*, and the owner hires a few fast, cheap, *ambidextrous* pickers.
	5. **asinine** (as′ə-nīn′): stupid; silly; ass-like. 6. **astute** (ə-stoot′): shrewd; keen in judgment; cunning.
(a)	▶ The baseball fan's *asinine* comments made it clear that he was (a) a knucklehead, (b) a deep thinker. (*a*)
astute	▶ Our nation needs *astute* [astute / asinine] diplomats.
astute	▶ Get rich by making *astute* investments.
asinine	▶ Grandpa Fudd tried to play a pizza on his record player. What an *asinine* thing to do!
astute asinine	▶ Even the most *astute* student can make a mistake, but to keep repeating the same mistakes is *asinine*.
	7. **bawdy** (bô′dē): indecent; obscene. 8. **bellicose** (bel′ə-kōs′): hostile; eager to fight; warlike.
(b)	▶ *Bawdy* shows can be expected at (a) Sunday schools, (b) Las Vegas. (*b*)
bellicose	▶ World tension is increased when national leaders exchange *bellicose* [affable / bellicose] remarks.
bellicose	▶ Bouncing his knuckles off my nose seemed to me a *bellicose* gesture.
bawdy	▶ The minister's daughter blushed at the *bawdy* anecdote.
bawdy bellicose	▶ When I tried to hush the drunken stranger who was singing a vulgar, *bawdy* song in our church, he became quite *bellicose*.

9. **berserk** (bər-sûrk′): crazed; in a destructive frenzy.
10. **bizarre** (bi-zär′): odd in appearance; grotesque; queer.

bizarre

▶ Halloween masks are usually _bizarre_ [bazaar / bizarre].

(a)

▶ People who go *berserk* belong in (a) asylums, (b) crowded buses. (*a*)

berserk

▶ The brand-new straitjacket looks nice on the man who went *ber_serk_*.

bizarre

▶ The green wig gave my aunt a *bi_zarre_* appearance.

bizarre
berserk

▶ The painting was so *bi_zarre_* that Twain thought it depicted a cat going _berserk_ in a platter of tomatoes.

Quiz

Write the letter that indicates the best definition.

1. (d)	(d)	1. affable	a. extremely odd; peculiar in appearance
2. (e)	(e)	2. altruistic	b. obscene; vulgar
3. (j)	(j)	3. ambidextrous	c. shrewd; cunning
4. (h)	(h)	4. aromatic	d. pleasant; easy to talk to
5. (g)	(g)	5. asinine	e. unselfish; concerned for others
6. (c)	(c)	6. astute	f. crazed; in violent rage or frenzy
7. (b)	(b)	7. bawdy	g. stupid; silly
8. (i)	(i)	8. bellicose	h. fragrant
9. (f)	(f)	9. berserk	i. quarrelsome; warlike
10. (a)	(a)	10. bizarre	j. skilled with both hands

11. **boorish**: rude; ill-mannered; awkward.
12. **bovine** (bō′vīn): cow-like; sluggish, patient, and stupid.

(a)

▶ Ballet dancers should be (a) slender and agile, (b) bovine types. (*a*)

(a)

▶ *Boorish* people are (a) crude, (b) sophisticated. (*a*)

80

boorish

bovine

boorish
bovine

▸ Tracking mud over the hostess's white rug is rather _boor_ish.

▸ Half awake, the big boy sat with a dull, stolid, _bov_ine expression on his face.

▸ Taking camera shots of the natives was _boor_ish, Gwen realized, but she simply had to have pictures of the huge, slow-moving, _bov_ine types.

---

13. **buoyant** (boi′ənt): tending to float; light of spirit; cheerful.
14. **buxom** (buk′səm): healthily plump; full-bosomed; attractive.

(a)

▸ When drowning, grab a *buoyant* material, like (a) cork, (b) a lead pipe. (a)

buxom

▸ The Flemish women painted by Rubens tend to be fleshy—that is, _buxom_ [buxom / fashionably anemic].

buxom

▸ After thirty days of butter and cream Amy looked rosy and _buxo_m.

buoyant

▸ The balloonist said that hydrogen was lighter and more _buoyant_ than helium, and that he got a bigger bang out of using it.

buxom
buoyant

▸ The milkmaid, who was pillowy and _buxo_m, embraced Luke; and suddenly his spirits were _buoyant_.

---

15. **cadaverous** (kə-dav′ẽr-əs): gaunt; haggard; corpse-like.
16. **candid**: frank; unprejudiced; outspoken.

(b)

▸ A *cadaverous* person should probably (a) reduce, (b) put on weight. (b)

candid

▸ I want the unvarnished truth, so give me a _candid_ [candid / candied] report.

candid

▸ The editor said that my poems stank—he was quite _candid_.

cadaverous

▸ After forty days of fasting Lou looked pale and _cadaverous_.

81

cadaverous candid	▶ The sick hermit was so wasted and _cadaverous_ that, to be _candid_, the doctor hardly knew whether to feed him or bury him.

17. **carnivorous** (kär-niv′ə-rəs): flesh-eating.
18. **clandestine** (klan-des′tin): secret; furtive; underhanded.

carnivorous	▶ Lions are _carnivorous_ [carnivorous / herbivorous].
(a)	▶ A *clandestine* affair is (a) hush-hush, (b) well publicized. (_a_)
carnivorous	▶ Deer and rabbits are eaten by _carnivorous_ animals.
clandestine	▶ My boss and the blonde secretary must be working on a top-secret report—they have had several _clandestine_ meetings.
carnivorous clandestine	▶ Our neighbor's beagle, which has _carnivorous_ tastes, makes _clandestine_ visits to our chicken coop.

19. **craven**: cowardly; timid; chicken-hearted.
20. **dastardly**: sneaky and mean; brutal.

(b)	▶ It was *dastardly* of Punky Jones to (a) tie up the cattle rustlers, (b) trip and rob the blind man. (_b_)
(a)	▶ It was *craven* of me (a) to flee from the dachshund, (b) to challenge the bully. (_a_)
craven	▶ Amid flying bullets one tends to develop a timid, even a _craven_ spirit.
dastardly	▶ Beating his infants was _dastardly_, even if they did pour syrup on his stamp collection.
dastardly craven	▶ Who painted the captain's horse blue? Private Jubbs did the _dastardly_ deed, but he was too _craven_ to admit it.

Quiz

Write the letter that indicates the best definition.

1. (h)	(h)	1. boorish	a. cowardly
2. (g)	(g)	2. bovine	b. flesh-eating
3. (e)	(e)	3. buoyant	c. like a corpse; thin and pale
4. (j)	(j)	4. buxom	d. frank; honest
5. (c)	(c)	5. cadaverous	e. floating; light-spirited
6. (d)	(d)	6. candid	f. done in secret; hidden
7. (b)	(b)	7. carnivorous	g. like a cow or an ox; sluggish
8. (f)	(f)	8. clandestine	h. rude; lacking manners
9. (a)	(a)	9. craven	i. outrageous; brutal
10. (i)	(i)	10. dastardly	j. pleasingly plump

---

21. **deft**: skilled and neat in action; adroit; dexterous.
22. **defunct** (di-fungkt′): dead; deceased; no longer existing.

(a) ▶ One must be particularly *deft* to (a) do needlework, (b) ride escalators. (a)

(a) ▶ A *defunct* enterprise belongs to (a) the past, (b) the future. (a)

deft ▶ I found that to play Chopin's "Minute Waltz" in less than five minutes requires quick, __deft__ fingers.

defunct ▶ Alas, poor Yorick, whose skull I hold—he is __defunct__.

deft
defunct ▶ To walk across this boulevard of speeding cars, you must be __deft__ or soon you'll be __defunct__.

---

23. **deleterious** (del′ə-tēr′i-əs): harmful; injurious to health.
24. **derogatory** (di-rog′ə-tôr′ē): belittling; disparaging.

deleterious ▶ Nicotine is considered to be __deleterious__ [deleterious / a body builder].

83

(b)

derogatory

deleterious

derogatory
deleterious

▶ *Derogatory* remarks are (a) complimentary, (b) uncomplimentary. (b)

▶ Calling the guest speaker "an egregious halfwit" was a rather __derogat__ory comment.

▶ Upton Sinclair alluded to the del__eterious__ effects of tainted meat.

▶ The factory owner sniffed in der__ogatory__ fashion: "And what makes you think that a few gallons of pesticide can be so __deleterious__ in that big lake?"

---

25. **destitute** (des′ti-toot′): extremely poor; lacking the necessities of life.
26. **diabolic** (dī′ə-bol′ik): devilish, fiendish.

(a)

(b)

destitute

diabolic

destitute
diabolic

▶ His *diabolic* ambition was to destroy (a) mankind, (b) disease. (a)

▶ The *destitute* have more than their share of (a) money, (b) poverty. (b)

▶ Her husband died three days after his insurance lapsed, and she was left __destitute__.

▶ He hated women, so he invented the dress that buttons in the back. How dia__bolic__!

▶ The melodrama dealt with a penniless old couple—absolutely des__titute__—the victims of a __diabolic__ villain who foreclosed on the mortgage.

---

27. **discreet:** prudent; tactful; careful not to talk or act unwisely.
28. **disenchanted:** set free from one's rosy illusions.

disenchanted

▶ Those who expected to find fat gold nuggets lying on the Yukon snowbanks were quickly __disenchanted__ [vindicated / disenchanted].

84

(a)

▶ A *discreet* housewife (a) keeps her secrets, (b) blabs about her former lovers. (a)

discreet

▶ This juicy story should not be publicized, fellows, so please be dis__creet__.

disenchanted

▶ Those who trusted Stalin's promises were soon dis__enchanted__.

discreet
disenchanted

▶ After marriage William was less __discreet__ in his drinking; and his bride, stumbling among his bottles, was __disenchant__ed.

29. **docile** (dos'əl): easy to handle or train; teachable.
30. **doddering:** shaky; senile; tottering, as from age.

docile

▶ A child that sits quietly for an hour at a time is unusually __docile__ [docile / bellicose].

doddering

▶ At age ninety a man is ordinarily __doddering__ [buxom / doddering].

docile

▶ I'm no cowboy, so please give me a well-behaved, __doci__le horse.

doddering

▶ We need young, vigorous leaders, not men who are old and __dodder__ing.

doddering
docile

▶ If your ancient and dod__dering__ grandmother runs your life for you, should you remain __docile__?

Quiz

Write the letter that indicates the best definition.

1. (i)	(i)	1. deft	a. prudent in speech and conduct
2. (d)	(d)	2. defunct	b. needy; penniless
3. (g)	(g)	3. deleterious	c. fiendish; outrageously wicked
4. (e)	(e)	4. derogatory	d. dead
5. (b)	(b)	5. destitute	e. uncomplimentary; belittling
6. (c)	(c)	6. diabolic	f. losing one's romantic beliefs
7. (a)	(a)	7. discreet	g. harmful to health
8. (f)	(f)	8. disenchanted	h. trembling and tottering
9. (j)	(j)	9. docile	i. skillful; nimble
10. (h)	(h)	10. doddering	j. obedient; teachable

---

31. **dogmatic** (dog-mat′ik): asserting opinions in a dictatorial way; positive; strongly opinionated.
32. **droll** (drōl): comical; quaintly amusing.

▶ A *droll* fellow at the circus is (a) the tiger, (b) the clown. (b)

(b)

▶ Highly *dogmatic* conversationalists are usually (a) popular, (b) obnoxious. (b)

(b)

▶ The audience laughed at Will Rogers' dr__oll__ remarks.

droll

▶ Military men often become opinionated and do__gmatic__.

dogmatic

▶ Our landlord kept ordering us in do__gmatic__ fashion to clean our rooms, nor did he smile at Bill's __droll__ remark that the garbage disposal must have backfired.

dogmatic
droll

---

33. **dubious** (doo′bi-əs): doubtful; vague; skeptical; questionable.
34. **eccentric** (ik-sen′trik): odd; peculiar; unconventional; off-center.

▶ The bearded gentleman skating around in the drugstore is thought to be rather __eccentric__ [eccentric / conventional].

eccentric

dubious
▶ Although madman Columbus said the world was round, his listeners could see it was flat, and so they were naturally _dubious_ [dubious / delusive].

eccentric
▶ Mrs. Doodle often takes her Flemish rabbit for a walk on a leash, another one of her e_ccentric_ habits.

dubious
▶ The drug addict claimed he could fly from the hotel roof, but his level-headed friends were d_ubious_.

eccentric
dubious
▶ The farmer decided that the nudists were either crazy or highly e_ccentric_; he was d_ubious_ about them.

---

35. **effeminate** (i-fem′ə-nit): womanish; unmanly; weak or decadent.
36. **emaciated** (i-mā′shi-āt′id): very thin; wasted away, as by disease or starvation.

effeminate
▶ Most people have tended to look upon knitting as an _effeminate_ [effeminate / manly] hobby.

effeminate
▶ Pierre's voice is high-pitched and ef_feminate_.

emaciated
▶ After a wasting disease an invalid looks _emaciated_ [buxom / emaciated].

emaciated
▶ The bodies found in the death camp were thin and _emaciated_.

effeminate
emaciated
▶ Mary accused Joe of being ef_feminate_, so he swung his purse at her; and having gained thirty pounds this summer he is certainly not em_aciated_.

---

37. **enigmatic** (en′ig-mat′ik): puzzling; perplexing; mysterious.
38. **erotic** (i-rot′ik): pertaining to sexual love; amatory.

erotic
▶ "Adult movies" are usually more _erotic_ [prudish / erotic] than "family movies."

(b)

enigmatic

erotic

erotic
enigmatic

▶ We refer to Mona Lisa's smile as *enigmatic* because it is (a) dazzling, (b) puzzling. (b)

▶ I was mystified by the en_igmatic_ warning.

▶ The sexy passages in *Tropic of Cancer* were so _erotic_ that they gave off blue smoke.

▶ If you cut all the er_otic_ passages from Noodle's last novel, the book would disappear. When asked why he wrote it, Noodle winked in en_igmatic_ fashion.

---

39. **exorbitant** (ig-zôr′bə-tənt): extravagant; excessive in price; unreasonable.
40. **feasible** (fē′zə-bəl): capable of being done; practicable; suitable.

exorbitant

not feasible

feasible

exorbitant

exorbitant
feasible

▶ Five dollars an egg, as paid by those early miners, would ordinarily seem _exorbitant_ [cheap / exorbitant].

▶ To build a bridge across the Pacific is at present _not feasible_ [feasible / not feasible].

▶ Your plan to feed the whole world is charitable, but is it f_easible_?

▶ "Twenty dollars to clip my dog is an _exorbitant_ fee— you've clipped me, too!"

▶ Your scheme to charge e_xorbitant_ prices for "Hungarian goulash made from real Hungarians" does not strike me as f_easible_.

88

Quiz

Write the letter that indicates the best definition.

1. (j)	(j) 1. dogmatic	a. having to do with sexual desire
2. (f)	(f) 2. droll	b. mysterious; having a hidden meaning
3. (d)	(d) 3. dubious	c. practicable; reasonable
4. (i)	(i) 4. eccentric	d. doubtful; questionable; skeptical
5. (h)	(h) 5. effeminate	e. thin; wasted away by disease
6. (e)	(e) 6. emaciated	f. whimsically amusing; comical
7. (b)	(b) 7. enigmatic	g. excessive; too high-priced
8. (a)	(a) 8. erotic	h. womanish; unmanly
9. (g)	(g) 9. exorbitant	i. peculiar; having odd traits
10. (c)	(c) 10. feasible	j. opinionated; dictatorial

---

41. **fetid** (fet′id): having a foul odor; stinking.
42. **flamboyant** (flam-boi′ənt): too showy; strikingly colorful; brilliant; gorgeous.

▶ *Fetid* odors often come from (a) rose bushes, (b) gym lockers. (b)

(b)

▶ Dad loves *flamboyant* neckties, so give him one that is very (a) black, (b) colorful. (b)

(b)

▶ Olga fainted when she smelled the ____fetid____ garbage can.

fetid

▶ Jeeter painted his jalopy orange and purple, and now it looks rather ____flamboyant____

flamboyant

▶ The crowd failed to appreciate the ____flamboyant____ oratory, and so they flung ancient eggs with a ____fetid____ odor.

flamboyant
fetid

---

43. **fluent** (floo′ənt): able to speak or write readily; flowing smoothly.
44. **frugal** (froo′gəl): costing little; spending little; meager; scanty.

▶ A tongue-tied immigrant who learned English from a book will probably (a) be fluent, (b) not be fluent. (b)

(b)

89

(a)	▶ A *frugal* meal (a) is cheap and plain, (b) contains fruit. (a)
frugal	▶ On his tiny pension Mr. Snurd eked out a fr_ugal_ existence.
fluent	▶ To make the debate squad you should be a fl_uent_ speaker.
frugal fluent	▶ For thirty years the woman saved, suffered, lived a _frugal_ life, for her dream was to become a lawyer and to deliver _fluent_ speeches in court.

45. **furtive**: stealthy; sly; done in secret; clandestine.
46. **gullible** (gul′ə-bəl): easily cheated or tricked; credulous.

gullible	▶ Brooklyn Bridge has often been sold to the _gullible_ [gullible / sophisticated] visitor.
furtive	▶ A stealthy gesture is said to be _furtive_ [ambidextrous / furtive].
furtive	▶ Mike stole a _furtive_ glance at the blonde.
gullible	▶ The con man got rich selling swampland to g_ullible_ investors.
gullible furtive	▶ Nancy believed the handsome stranger's promises, for she was innocent and _gullible_; and she gave his hand a f_urtive_ squeeze.

47. **iconoclastic** (ī-kon′ə-klas′tik): attacking cherished beliefs.
48. **impassive** (im-pas′iv): not showing emotion; calm; serene.

smash	▶ *Iconoclastic* leaders _smash_ [respect / smash] traditions.
impassive	▶ When a good poker player picks up excellent cards, his face is usually _impassive_ [impassive / jolly].

impassive	▶ Even when his enemies peeled off his scalp, Chief Little Water stood unblinking and im_passive_.
iconoclastic	▶ Those women who first took up the fight against male chauvinism were truly ic_onoclastic_.
iconoclastic impassive	▶ Many listened in 1850 to the Abolitionists and their _iconoclastic_ arguments, and few could remain _impassive_.

49. **impeccable** (im-pek'ə-bəl): faultless; without sin or error.
50. **impromptu** (im-promp'too): done on the spur of the moment; offhand.

impeccable	▶ Banks should hire employees of _impeccable_ [dubious / impeccable] honesty.
(a)	▶ *Impromptu* remarks are (a) spontaneous, (b) planned in advance. (_a_)
impromptu	▶ Called on unexpectedly, Daniel Webster delivered a brilliant _improm_tu talk.
impeccable	▶ Our eminent minister was presumably of _impeccable_ moral character.
impromptu impeccable	▶ College freshmen must often write an _improm_tu theme in class; and naturally the professor feels insulted if the production is not brilliant and _impecc_able.

Quiz

Write the letter that indicates the best definition.

(c)	1. fetid	a. emotionless; calm
(e)	2. flamboyant	b. improvised; done without preparation
(j)	3. fluent	c. smelly
(g)	4. frugal	d. smashing traditional doctrines
(f)	5. furtive	e. colorful and showy
(h)	6. gullible	f. sly; stealthy
(d)	7. iconoclastic	g. meager and costing little
(a)	8. impassive	h. easily swindled
(i)	9. impeccable	i. flawless
(b)	10. impromptu	j. smooth flowing in speech or writing

1. (c)
2. (e)
3. (j)
4. (g)
5. (f)
6. (h)
7. (d)
8. (a)
9. (i)
10. (b)

Review Test

Write *True* or *False*.

False 1. *Bellicose* children are *docile*.

True 2. *Emaciated* prisoners sometimes look *cadaverous*.

True 3. *Eccentric* people are likely to do *bizarre* things.

False 4. *Asinine* observations are *astute*.

False 5. *Aromatic* sprays are *fetid*.

True 6. *Bawdy* stories have an *erotic* quality.

False 7. *Diabolic* plans are *altruistic*.

True 8. Being *ambidextrous* and *deft* should help you play basketball.

False 9. Being *boorish* and *impassive* should help you become a successful salesman.

False 10. *Frugal* and *deleterious* foods are best for your health.

Write the letter that indicates the best definition of the italicized word.

(b) 11. A *craven* soldier: (a) brave, (b) cowardly, (c) hungry, (d) ill.

(d) 12. A *gullible* buyer: (a) wealthy, (b) affable, (c) hard to convince, (d) easy to cheat.

(a) 13. *Impeccable* grammar: (a) flawless, (b) full of errors, (c) enigmatic, (d) discreet.

(c) 14. *Flamboyant* shirts: (a) bovine, (b) large, (c) colorful, (d) made of silk.

(b) 15. *Iconoclastic* policies: (a) dastardly, (b) tradition-smashing, (c) conventional, (d) highly expensive.

(b) 16. A *buxom* maiden: (a) innocent, (b) plump, (c) well-dressed, (d) flirtatious.

(d) 17. *Clandestine* conferences: (a) impromptu, (b) candid, (c) midnight, (d) secret.

(c) 18. A *feasible* project: (a) rather foolish, (b) exorbitant, (c) practicable, (d) utopian.

(b) 19. A *carnivorous* animal: (a) fierce-looking, (b) flesh-eating, (c) powerful and dangerous, (d) thick-skinned.

(a) 20. *Fluent* remarks: (a) smooth-flowing, (b) astute, (c) droll, (d) somewhat misleading.

Matching. Write the letter that indicates the best definition.

(g) 21. candid
(e) 22. destitute
(a) 23. derogatory
(h) 24. furtive
(c) 25. effeminate

a. belittling; uncomplimentary
b. fur-bearing
c. womanish
d. isolated; lonesome
e. very poor; needy
f. well-mannered; polite
g. straightforward and honest
h. sneaky; sly

Write the word studied in this chapter that will complete the sentence.

26. The waiter screamed and threw soup at us— he had gone b*erserk*.
27. My hungry uncle found his false teeth just as the banquet began, and his spirits were bu*oyant*.
28. The widow distrusted Mr. Finn because of his du*bious* reputation.
29. Those who expected modern plumbing in Morocco were soon dis*illusioned*.
30. Our corset factory had expired—it was as def*unct* as Benedict Arnold.
31. The swindler had been talkative and friendly, an af*fable* fellow.
32. Four dollars for a dish of prunes? Isn't that a bit ex*orbitant*?
33. Discuss this untidy affair with no one. Try to be dis*creet*.

Key to Review Test

Check your test answers by the following key. Deduct 3% per error from a possible 100%.

1. False	8. True	15. (b)	22. (e)	29. disenchanted
2. True	9. False	16. (b)	23. (a)	30. defunct
3. True	10. False	17. (d)	24. (h)	31. affable
4. False	11. (b)	18. (c)	25. (c)	32. exorbitant
5. False	12. (d)	19. (b)	26. berserk	33. discreet
6. True	13. (a)	20. (a)	27. buoyant	
7. False	14. (c)	21. (g)	28. dubious	

Score: _____ %

Supplementary List

Exercise 5

Fill in the blanks at the left with the descriptive words that fit the definitions. Although these words were not defined in this chapter, you should recognize most of them. Check your answers with the key at the end of the exercise. Use your dictionary to study any unknown words.

abstemious, articulate, auspicious, avid, bland

1. _____ mild; nonstimulating; insipid
2. _____ very eager; greedy
3. _____ temperate; eating and drinking sparingly
4. _____ favorable; propitious; of good omen
5. _____ able to express oneself well; clearly presented

caustic, compatible, coy, culpable, deferential

6. _____ able to get along well together
7. _____ very respectful; courteous
8. _____ at fault; deserving blame
9. _____ corrosive; stinging; sarcastic
10. _____ shy; bashful; coquettishly modest

delectable, delusive, derisive, disgruntled, disoriented

11. _____ ridiculing; mocking
12. _____ disappointed; displeased; sulky
13. _____ misleading; false; deceptive
14. _____ delightful; enjoyable
15. _____ confused; out of adjustment to one's environment

dissident, dormant, dyspeptic, erudite, exotic

16. _____ strangely beautiful; foreign and fascinating
17. _____ grouchy and gloomy because of indigestion

18. _____ as if asleep; inactive

19. _____ not agreeing; differing; dissenting

20. _____ learned; scholarly

heinous, illicit, immaculate, imperturbable, impotent

21. _____ pure; flawless; completely clean

22. _____ atrocious; extremely wicked

23. _____ powerless; helpless; without virility

24. _____ calm; unruffled

25. _____ unlawful; improper

Key

1. bland	6. compatible	11. derisive	16. exotic	21. immaculate
2. avid	7. deferential	12. disgruntled	17. dyspeptic	22. heinous
3. abstemious	8. culpable	13. delusive	18. dormant	23. impotent
4. auspicious	9. caustic	14. delectable	19. dissident	24. imperturbable
5. articulate	10. coy	15. disoriented	20. erudite	25. illicit

6
Descriptive Words

1. indomitable
2. inept
3. innate
4. inscrutable
5. insidious
6. intrepid
7. itinerant
8. lecherous
9. lethal
10. lethargic
11. lucid
12. lunar
13. mercenary
14. meticulous
15. myopic
16. naive
17. nebulous
18. nostalgic
19. occult
20. ominous
21. opaque
22. ostentatious
23. petulant
24. phlegmatic
25. picayune
26. prolific
27. pusillanimous
28. raucous
29. sacrilegious
30. sagacious
31. sanctimonious
32. sardonic
33. secular
34. sedentary
35. senile
36. sinister
37. sinuous
38. spurious
39. stoical
40. succinct
41. taciturn
42. therapeutic
43. toxic
44. vacuous
45. venerable
46. verbose
47. verdant
48. vicarious
49. vindictive
50. zealous

Chapter 6 continues our study of descriptive words. Follow the same procedure as in Chapter 5.

Exercises

COVER THIS STRIP

1. **indomitable** (in-dom′i-tə-bəl): unconquerable; unyielding.
2. **inept:** clumsy; incompetent; not suitable.

(a) ▸ An *indomitable* fighter (a) fights on and on, (b) quits. (*a*)

inept ▸ A pianist wearing mittens would probably be ___*inept*___ [effective / inept].

indomitable ▸ Every nation speaks of its soldiers' ___*indomitable*___ courage.

inept ▸ The Dodgers made five errors in the field and were just as ___*inept*___ at the plate.

indomitable
inept ▸ Wanda climbed to the mountain peak, for her spirit was ___*indomitable*___; but I slipped off a boulder, for I was ___*inept*___.

3. **innate** (i-nāt′): inborn; natural, not acquired.
4. **inscrutable** (in-skroo′tə-bəl): mysterious; not able to be understood.

not innate ▸ One's political beliefs are ___*not innate*___ [innate / not innate].

cannot ▸ When we speak of "*inscrutable* fate," we mean that we ___*cannot*___ [can / cannot] easily foresee the future.

inscrutable ▸ At one time no mystery melodrama was complete without its slinking and *ins*___*crutable*___ Oriental butler.

innate ▸ Ducklings seem to have an ___*inna*___te attraction to water.

98

innate
inscrutable

▸ At age five Capablanca had already shown an _innate_ talent for chess; and his face over the tournament board was tight-lipped and _inscrutable_.

---

5. **insidious** (in-sid′ē-əs): treacherous; crafty; more dangerous than is apparent.
6. **intrepid** (in-trep′id): very brave; dauntless; bold.

insidious

▸ Traitors who bore from within are _____ [innate / insidious].

intrepid

▸ Courageous aviators are said to be _____ [intrepid / craven].

intrepid

▸ Only hardy and _____ men could reach the North Pole.

insidious

▸ Socrates was accused of corrupting the Athenian youths with *ins*_____ doctrines.

intrepid
insidious

▸ Sam danced into the lion's cage to prove how _____ he was—but some _____ fellow had left a banana peel on the floor.

---

7. **itinerant** (i-tin′ər-ənt): wandering; going from place to place.
8. **lecherous** (lech′ər-əs): lustful; lewd.

lecherous

▸ Lustful people are said to be _____ [lethargic / lecherous].

(b)

▸ *Itinerant* laborers (a) have permanent jobs, (b) keep moving. ( )

lecherous

▸ The chaste heroine was chased, all right, by a *l*_____ villain who wore a handlebar mustache.

itinerant

> Steinbeck implied that the i_____ fruit-pickers were being exploited.

lecherous
itinerant

> Many risque anecdotes allude to the l_____ nature of the i_____ salesman.

9. **lethal** (lē'thəl): causing death; deadly; fatal.
10. **lethargic** (li-thär'jik): sluggish; dull; drowsy.

chlorine

> A *lethal* gas used in the first World War was _____ [oxygen / chlorine].

lethal

> A gun, a knife, an automobile—any of these may be considered a l_____ weapon in a court case.

lethargic

> Basketball coaches don't want _____ [ambidextrous / lethargic] athletes.

lethargic

> Having swallowed the pig, the snake became _____ and sleepy.

lethargic
lethal

> This heavy smog has slowed me up—made me feel _____; I hope the stuff is not _____.

Quiz

Write the letter that indicates the best definition.

1. (g)
2. (f)
3. (b)
4. (a)
5. (i)
6. (h)
7. (j)
8. (e)
9. (d)
10. (c)

( ) 1. indomitable   a. mysterious; beyond understanding
( ) 2. inept   b. inborn; inherent
( ) 3. innate   c. slow-moving; sluggish
( ) 4. inscrutable   d. deadly
( ) 5. insidious   e. lustful
( ) 6. intrepid   f. awkward; lacking dexterity
( ) 7. itinerant   g. unable to be defeated
( ) 8. lecherous   h. courageous; fearless; brave
( ) 9. lethal   i. stealthily treacherous
( ) 10. lethargic   j. traveling on a circuit

11. **lucid** (lōō′sid): clear; easily understood; mentally sound.
12. **lunar:** (lōō′nər): pertaining to the moon.

(b)

▸ A *lunar* eclipse blots out (a) the sun, (b) the moon. ( )

lucid

▸ Technical directions ought to be _____ [enigmatic / lucid].

lunar

▸ On the moon the astronauts conducted certain _____*ar* experiments.

lucid

▸ Velma says her friend is crazy but that he has his _____ moments.

lucid
lunar

▸ The friendly astronomer gave us a _____*d* description of the _____ landscape.

13. **mercenary** (mûr′sə-ner′ē): greedy; serving for pay only: as *mercenary* troops.
14. **meticulous** (mə-tik′yoo-ləs): extremely careful about details; painstaking.

(a)

▸ *Mercenary* people are (a) ruthlessly grasping, (b) altruistic. ( )

(a)

▸ *Meticulous* craftsmen are (a) careful and precise, (b) sloppy. ( )

meticulous

▸ Staining these cells under the microscope requires _____ technique.

mercenary

▸ Mike's religion was money, and he was completely *mer*_____.

meticulous
mercenary

▸ Uncle Marmaduke became a _____ dresser; for he was determined, in his _____ way, to marry a rich widow, if he could find one.

15. **myopic** (mī-op′ik): nearsighted.
16. **naive** (na-ēv′): childlike; artless; lacking in worldly wisdom.

myopic	▶ Nearsighted people are _____ [myopic / hyperopic].
naive	▶ Anyone who thinks that concert artists don't have to practice is pretty _____ [naive / astute].
myopic	▶ Elmer sat in the front row and strained to see the movie—he was quite *my_____*.
naive	▶ College freshmen range from the very sophisticated to the very _____.
myopic naive	▶ Without his contact lenses Wilmer is very *m_____*, and so he dived into the dry swimming pool. He will not make that *n_____* error again.

17. **nebulous** (neb′yoo-ləs): cloudy; vague; indefinite.
18. **nostalgic** (nos-tal′jik): homesick; yearning for what is past or far away.

(b)	▶ *Nebulous* plans are (a) clearly detailed, (b) vague. ( )
(b)	▶ A *nostalgic* line is (a) "Brevity is the soul of wit," (b) "Gone, gone, are the lovely lasses of yesteryear." ( )
nostalgic	▶ Recalling his three happy years in the fifth grade, Grandpa became *no_____*.
nebulous	▶ Through the Los Angeles smog we could make out the *neb_____* outline of the city hall.
nostalgic nebulous	▶ Dad sings "When You and I Were Young, Maggie" and other _____ songs; meanwhile his prospects for finding a job are _____.

19. **occult** (ə-kult′): beyond human understanding; mysterious.
20. **ominous** (om′ə-nəs): threatening; menacing.

(b)	▶ *Occult* subjects include (a) geometry, (b) astrology. ( )

occult

▶ Telepathy and reincarnation belong to those puzzling areas known as the *oc_____*.

(b)

▶ An *ominous* gesture is (a) friendly, (b) threatening. ( )

ominous

▶ Over the ball park hung dark and _____ clouds.

occult
ominous

▶ A spiritualist with *oc_____* powers evoked a baritone ghost—it made *om_____* predictions that curled our hair.

Quiz

Write the letter that indicates the best definition.

1. (f)	( ) 1. lucid	a. unsophisticated; foolishly simple
2. (d)	( ) 2. lunar	b. supernatural; beyond understanding
3. (e)	( ) 3. mercenary	c. vague; misty
4. (j)	( ) 4. meticulous	d. of the moon
5. (i)	( ) 5. myopic	e. done for payment only; greedy
6. (a)	( ) 6. naive	f. easy to understand; clear
7. (c)	( ) 7. nebulous	g. sentimental about the past
8. (g)	( ) 8. nostalgic	h. menacing; sinister
9. (b)	( ) 9. occult	i. nearsighted
10. (h)	( ) 10. ominous	j. careful about minute details

21. **opaque** (ō-pāk′): not letting light through; obscure; unintelligent.
22. **ostentatious** (os′tən-tā′shəs): showy and pretentious so as to attract attention.

(a)

▶ *Opaque* glass is sometimes used in (a) bathrooms, (b) automobile windshields. (a)

(b)

▶ An *ostentatious* living room seems to say, (a) "I'm simple and comfortable," (b) "Look, look—see how grand and expensive I am!" (b)

103

ostentatious (a)	▶ It was a bit *ost*entatious of Mrs. Schmaltz to go shopping for groceries (a) in her pink Cadillac with chauffeur, (b) on her Schwinn bicycle. (a)
opaque	▶ Such a dolt! His mind is absolutely *op*aque.
opaque ostentatious	▶ My dusty glasses were practically *op*aque, yet I saw that Diamond Jim was wearing six or eight sparkling rings. Hm-m, somewhat *ost*entatious, I thought.

23. **petulant** (pech′oo-lənt): peevish; fretful.
24. **phlegmatic** (fleg-mat′ik): sluggish; slow to move or become excited.

(a)	▶ A *phlegmatic* fellow tends to move and react somewhat like (a) a tired elephant, (b) a scared rabbit. (a)
phlegmatic	▶ Our postman is probably faster than a glacier, but in our impatient eyes he is slow-moving and *ph*legmatic.
(b)	▶ A *petulant* infant says things like (a) "M-m-mm, good!," (b) "Don't wanna!" (b)
petulant	▶ When the delegate could not have his way he stamped out of the UN meeting like a *petulant* child.
phlegmatic petulant	▶ Mr. Fleisch, fat and *ph*legmatic, loves to sit in his easy chair; while his wife keeps whining in a *petulant* voice: "You never take me out, you slob."

25. **picayune** (pik′ē-yoon′): petty; trivial; contemptible.
26. **prolific** (prō-lif′ik): fruitful; fecund; producing many works.

prolific	▶ Agatha Christie, who wrote mystery novels by the dozen, was obviously very *prolific* [phlegmatic / prolific].
picayune	▶ Charging extra for toothpicks in a restaurant is pretty *picayune* [picayune / petulant].

104

prolific	▸ Rats multiply fast—they are pr_olific_.
picayune	▸ Mike stabbed his brother for four cents, or some such pi_cayune_ amount.
prolific picayune	▸ Your fat batch of poems proves that you are pr_olific_ and my criticism of the spelling in your inspired poetry will seem _picayune_.

27. **pusillanimous** (pū′sə-lan′ə-məs): cowardly; fainthearted.
28. **raucous** (rô′kəs): rough-sounding; hoarse; boisterous.

raucous	▸ The foghorn that awakened me was merely the sergeant's _raucous_ [pusillanimous / raucous] voice.
(a)	▸ On the battlefield the braggart Falstaff was actually timid—in fact, (a) pusillanimous, (b) raucous. (_a_)
pusillanimous	▸ Pancho is shy—he wants to marry Rosa but he is too p_usillanimous_ to pop the question.
raucous	▸ One distrusts car salesmen who are pushy and r_aucous_.
raucous pusillanimous	▸ A bumblebee chased me out of the park, and I heard r_aucous_ laughter from those who thought me p_usillanimous_.

29. **sacrilegious** (sak′ri-lij′əs): impious; profaning what is held sacred.
30. **sagacious** (sə-gā′shəs): shrewd; sound in judgment.

(a)	▸ A _sagacious_ decision is (a) wise, (b) stupid. (_a_)
(b)	▸ A _sacrilegious_ act shows (a) respect for religion, (b) disrespect for religion. (_b_)
sacrilegious	▸ Drawing cartoons in his prayer book is certainly sac_rilegious_.
sagacious	▸ Advertising your umbrellas for sale just before the rainy season was _sagacious_.

sagacious
sacrilegious

▶ Galileo's discovery that the earth moves was *sag_acious_*, yet his theory seemed to contradict the Bible and it was therefore condemned by the church as _sacriligious_

Quiz

Write the letter that indicates the best definition.

1. (h)	(h)	1. opaque	a. insulting to a religion
2. (f)	(f)	2. ostentatious	b. trivial; petty; cheap; worthless
3. (j)	(j)	3. petulant	c. timid; cowardly
4. (g)	(g)	4. phlegmatic	d. having sound judgment
5. (b)	(b)	5. picayune	e. harsh; rough-sounding
6. (i)	(i)	6. prolific	f. showy to attract attention
7. (c)	(c)	7. pusillanimous	g. sluggish; slow to act
8. (e)	(e)	8. raucous	h. not transparent
9. (a)	(a)	9. sacrilegious	i. producing in abundance
10. (d)	(d)	10. sagacious	j. irritable and annoyed

31. **sanctimonious** (sangk'tə-mō'ni-əs): pretending to be very holy.
32. **sardonic** (sär-don'ik): sarcastic; cynical.

(b)
▶ A *sanctimonious* churchgoer is (a) very sincere, (b) somewhat smug and hypocritical. (b)

(b)
▶ A *sardonic* tone is (a) admiring, (b) scornful. (b)

sardonic
▶ The old cynic gave a bitter, *sar_donic_* laugh.

sanctimonious
▶ When Mr. Higgins was not chasing his typist around the office, he was greeting customers with a *san_ctimonious_* smile.

sanctimonious
sardonic
▶ As Henry gave *san_ctimonious_* advice to the Sunday school class, his girl friend Patty threw him a *sar_donic_* grin.

33. **secular** (sek'yə-lər): worldly, not churchly or spiritual.
34. **sedentary** (sed'ən-ter'i): involving sitting; physically inactive.

(a)
▶ *Sedentary* work is done by (a) bookkeepers, (b) bricklayers. (a)

106

sedentary

▸ The cowboy did not want office work or any other sed_*entary*_ job.

(b)

▸ An example of *secular* music is (a) Handel's *Messiah*, (b) "The Beer Barrel Polka." (*b*)

secular

▸ John Donne's poetry dealt at first with woman's love and other sec_*ular*_ themes, later with religious themes.

secular
sedentary

▸ Pedro will get a practical sec_*ular*_ education at Yale, but he may find the academic life to be rather sed_*entary*_.

35. **senile** (sē′nīl): aged and infirm; showing the mental and bodily weaknesses of old age.
36. **sinister** (sin′is-tər): hinting of imminent danger; threatening harm.

(a)

▸ *Senile* people are often cared for in a home for (a) the aged, (b) wayward girls. (*a*)

senile

▸ The day Grandpa wandered away from home in his jockey shorts we felt he was getting _*senile*_.

(b)

▸ If you were confronted by *sinister* strangers, you would probably be (a) amused, (b) worried. (*b*)

sinister

▸ The conspirators hatched a si_*nister*_ plot.

senile
sinister

▸ The druggist, who was old and se_*nile*_, saw nothing _*sinister*_ in Beulah's purchase of a quart of arsenic.

37. **sinuous** (sin′ū-əs): winding; curving in and out; serpentine.
38. **spurious** (spyoor′i-əs): false; not genuine.

spurious

▸ I may be wrong, madam, but your three-dollar bill looks _*spurious*_ [sinuous / spurious].

(a)

▸ A *sinuous* movement is characteristic of (a) snakes, (b) cockroaches. (*a*)

sinuous	▶ The hula dancers went through their graceful and _sinuous_ motions.
spurious	▶ Only fifty dollars! I should have known that the Rembrandt he sold me was *spurious*.
sinuous spurious	▶ Tom followed the twisting, _sinuous_ path to a swamp, for he had been given a _spurious_ address.

39. **stoical** (stō′i-kəl): indifferent to pain or pleasure.
40. **succinct** (sək-singkt′): concise; terse; brief and meaningful.

succinct	▶ Cablegrams at three dollars a word should be _succinct_ [succinct / redundant].
succinct	▶ Wordiness is boring, so be _succinct_.
(a)	▶ Even during childbirth she was *stoical:* she was (a) calm and uncomplaining, (b) screaming her head off. (a)
stoical	▶ The Indian endured the ritual of torture with _stoical_ calm.
stoical succinct	▶ Mr. Koltz sat quiet and *stoical* during most of Buster's birthday party, but finally he made a *succinct* announcement: "Shut up!"

108

Quiz

Write the letter that indicates the best definition.

1. (i)	(i) 1. sanctimonious	a. curving in and out
2. (j)	(j) 2. sardonic	b. repressing the emotions
3. (f)	(f) 3. secular	c. old and feeble
4. (d)	(d) 4. sedentary	d. involving sitting
5. (c)	(c) 5. senile	e. ominous; threatening
6. (e)	(e) 6. sinister	f. dealing with nonreligious subjects
7. (a)	(a) 7. sinuous	g. counterfeit
8. (g)	(g) 8. spurious	h. concise; brief
9. (b)	(b) 9. stoical	i. making a show of holiness
10. (h)	(h) 10. succinct	j. bitterly ironical; sneering

41. **taciturn** (tas′i-tûrn′): not inclined to talk; uncommunicative.
42. **therapeutic** (ther′ə-pū′tik): healing; curative.

▶ *Taciturn* people tend to (a) be silent; (b) talk your arm off. (a)

(a)

▶ *Therapeutic* waters will presumably make you (a) sick, (b) healthier. (b)

(b)

▶ The Chinese doctors believe that certain herbs have
therapeutic   th*erapeutic* qualities.

taciturn   ▶ Chess players are inclined to be reflective and tac*iturn*.

therapeutic   ▶ "Do you think the fresh air of New England is *therapeutic*?"
taciturn   I asked a *taciturn* native, and he said, "H-m-mp."

43. **toxic** (tok′sik): poisonous.
44. **vacuous** (vak′ū-əs): empty; stupid.

(b)   ▶ A *vacuous* mind is (a) full of ideas, (b) empty. (b)

▶ The candidate won our hearts but told us nothing—his speech
vacuous   was v*acuous*.

toxic   ▶ Pesticides are usually *toxic* [toxic / therapeutic].

toxic	▸ Willie said he wasn't afraid of ___toxic___ fumes—we bury him tomorrow.
vacuous toxic	▸ Whiskey to cure snakebite?—that's a va_cuous_ suggestion, since both whiskey and snake venom are __toxic__.

45. **venerable** (ven'ər-ə-bəl): worthy of reverence; revered.
46. **verbose** (vər-bōs'): wordy; long-winded.

venerable	▸ Ulysses was a wise and __venerable__ [venerable / venereal] warrior.
(b)	▸ *Verbose* statements contain too many (a) ideas, (b) words. (b)
verbose	▸ Trim your theme; it is __verbose__.
venerable	▸ We gazed at the ven__erable__ statue of Abraham Lincoln.
venerable verbose	▸ Every evening my white-haired and __venerable__ military friend gave me a __verbose__ account of how he won the war.

47. **verdant** (vûr'dənt): green; covered with grass; unsophisticated.
48. **vicarious** (vī-kâr'i-əs): participating by imagination in another's experience.

(a)	▸ *Verdant* fields are (a) grassy, (b) covered with boulders. (a)
vicarious	▸ By identifying yourself with your movie hero you have __vicarious__ [venerable / vicarious] pleasure.
verdant	▸ William Wordsworth trod these ver__dant__ meadows.
vicarious	▸ From the adventures of D'Artagnan, Jane Eyre, and Martin Arrowsmith we derive a vi__carious__ thrill.
verdant vicarious	▸ Novels take us from foamy seas to __verdant__ hills; they let us live a thousand __vicarious__ lives.

49. **vindictive** (vin-dic′tiv): revengeful; spiteful.
50. **zealous** (zel′əs): ardently devoted to a cause; enthusiastic.

vindictive	▶ To spite me, Mary bored a hole in my rowboat—it was a _vindictive_ [vindictive / venerable] act.
vindictive	▶ One who burns your garage in order to get even with you has a v_indictive_ nature.
(b)	▶ A *zealous* reader reads with (a) reluctance, (b) enthusiasm. (b)
zealous	▶ A town orchestra or museum exists only because of a few _zealous_ supporters.
zealous vindictive	▶ My roommate, a z_ealous_ musician, played his violin all night until a v_indictive_ neighbor threw a can of beans through our window.

Quiz

Write the letter that indicates the best definition.

1. (h)	(h)	1. taciturn	a. inclined to revenge; spiteful
2. (e)	(e)	2. therapeutic	b. wordy; talkative
3. (j)	(j)	3. toxic	c. without content; empty
4. (c)	(c)	4. vacuous	d. fervent; ardently active
5. (g)	(g)	5. venerable	e. tending to cure disease
6. (b)	(b)	6. verbose	f. sharing the feelings of others
7. (i)	(i)	7. verdant	g. commanding respect because of age
8. (f)	(f)	8. vicarious	h. not talkative
9. (a)	(a)	9. vindictive	i. green with vegetation
10. (d)	(d)	10. zealous	j. poisonous

Review Test

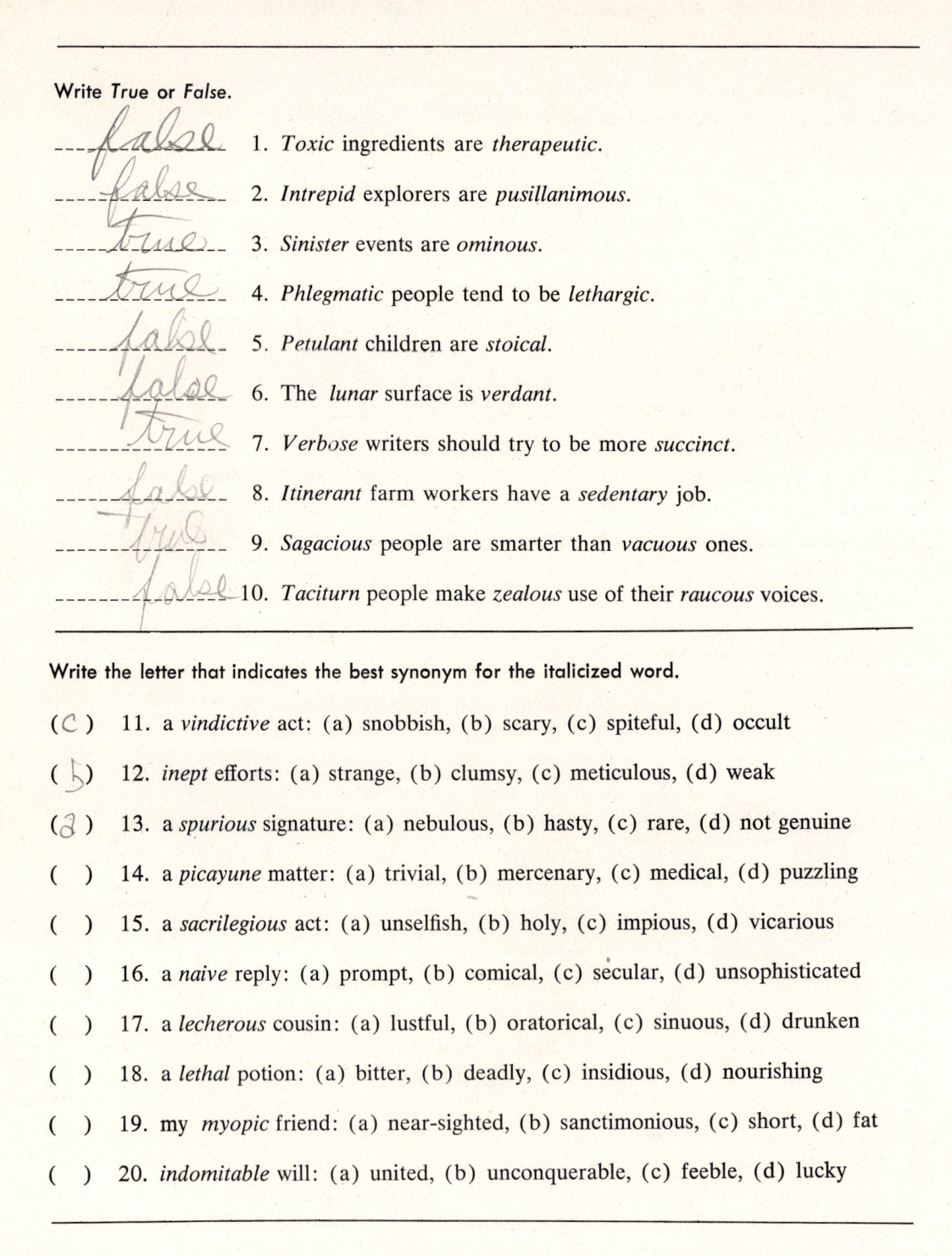

Write *True* or *False*.

false 1. *Toxic* ingredients are *therapeutic*.

false 2. *Intrepid* explorers are *pusillanimous*.

true 3. *Sinister* events are *ominous*.

true 4. *Phlegmatic* people tend to be *lethargic*.

false 5. *Petulant* children are *stoical*.

false 6. The *lunar* surface is *verdant*.

true 7. *Verbose* writers should try to be more *succinct*.

false 8. *Itinerant* farm workers have a *sedentary* job.

true 9. *Sagacious* people are smarter than *vacuous* ones.

false 10. *Taciturn* people make *zealous* use of their *raucous* voices.

Write the letter that indicates the best synonym for the italicized word.

(c) 11. a *vindictive* act: (a) snobbish, (b) scary, (c) spiteful, (d) occult

(b) 12. *inept* efforts: (a) strange, (b) clumsy, (c) meticulous, (d) weak

(d) 13. a *spurious* signature: (a) nebulous, (b) hasty, (c) rare, (d) not genuine

( ) 14. a *picayune* matter: (a) trivial, (b) mercenary, (c) medical, (d) puzzling

( ) 15. a *sacrilegious* act: (a) unselfish, (b) holy, (c) impious, (d) vicarious

( ) 16. a *naive* reply: (a) prompt, (b) comical, (c) secular, (d) unsophisticated

( ) 17. a *lecherous* cousin: (a) lustful, (b) oratorical, (c) sinuous, (d) drunken

( ) 18. a *lethal* potion: (a) bitter, (b) deadly, (c) insidious, (d) nourishing

( ) 19. my *myopic* friend: (a) near-sighted, (b) sanctimonious, (c) short, (d) fat

( ) 20. *indomitable* will: (a) united, (b) unconquerable, (c) feeble, (d) lucky

Matching. Write the letter that indicates the best definition.

( ) 21. lucid
( ) 22. venerable
( ) 23. sardonic
( ) 24. ostentatious
( ) 25. opaque

a. showy in order to impress
b. clear
c. resembling a fish
d. not transparent
e. a type of triangle
f. aged and respected
g. lacking money
h. ironic; sarcastic

Write the word studied in this chapter that will complete the sentence.

26. She could not read his face—it was *in_____*.
27. Lisa was born talented; her gifts are *in_____*.
28. Scott wrote two dozen novels; he was *pr_____*.
29. Old Oscar lost his teeth and his memory; he was becoming *se_____*.
30. Such sweet memories! Mamma makes *nos_____* references to the past.
31. Colleges do not teach astrology, spiritualism, and such *oc_____* subjects.
32. Junior won a gold medal, giving Dad a *vi_____* thrill.
33. Hayden wrote church music as well as the *se_____* variety.

Key to Review Test

Check your test answers by the following key. Deduct 3% per error from a possible 100%.

1. False
2. False
3. True
4. True
5. False
6. False
7. True
8. False
9. True
10. False
11. (c)
12. (b)
13. (d)
14. (a)
15. (c)
16. (d)
17. (a)
18. (b)
19. (a)
20. (b)
21. (b)
22. (f)
23. (h)
24. (a)
25. (d)
26. inscrutable
27. innate
28. prolific
29. senile
30. nostalgic
31. occult
32. vicarious
33. secular

Score: _____%

Supplementary List

Exercise 6

Fill in the blanks at the left with the descriptive words that fit the definitions. Although these words were not defined in this chapter, you should recognize most of them. Check your answers with the key at the end of the exercise. Use your dictionary to study any unknown words.

inclement, indolent, indefatigable, insipid, luminous

1. _____ without flavor; tasteless; dull
2. _____ stormy; without leniency
3. _____ shining; clear; bright
4. _____ tireless
5. _____ lazy; idle

nomadic, morbid, ornate, precocious, ruthless

6. _____ overdecorated; flowery
7. _____ wandering
8. _____ cruel; pitiless
9. _____ maturing early; bright for its age
10. _____ excessively interested in gruesome matters

salutary, scurrilous, skeptical, spasmodic, squalid

11. _____ doubting; questioning; not easily convinced
12. _____ occurring now and then; fitful
13. _____ wretched; poverty-stricken in appearance
14. _____ foul-mouthed; grossly abusive
15. _____ beneficial; having a good effect

squeamish, staid, stalwart, suave, subtle

16. _____ strong; valiant; unyielding
17. _____ smoothly pleasant and polite; urbane

18. _____ oversensitive; prudish, easily disgusted

19. _____ cunning; crafty; delicately skillful

20. _____ sedate and settled

sullen, surreptitious, tepid, terse, voracious

21. _____ secret; stealthy; sneaky

22. _____ gloomy and resentful; glum; morose

23. _____ concise; to the point

24. _____ greedy; gluttonous; insatiable

25. _____ lukewarm

Key

1. insipid
2. inclement
3. luminous
4. indefatigable
5. indolent
6. ornate
7. nomadic
8. ruthless
9. precocious
10. morbid
11. skeptical
12. spasmodic
13. squalid
14. scurrilous
15. salutary
16. stalwart
17. suave
18. squeamish
19. subtle
20. staid
21. surreptitious
22. sullen
23. terse
24. voracious
25. tepid

7

Action Words

1. abscond
2. acquit
3. adulterate
4. alienate
5. authenticate
6. bicker
7. blaspheme
8. bungle
9. canonize
10. canvass
11. cauterize
12. condone
13. decimate
14. deify
15. disconcert
16. disparage
17. disseminate
18. elucidate
19. emasculate
20. espouse
21. exhume
22. exorcise
23. expurgate
24. extradite
25. gawk
26. grapple
27. haggle
28. heckle
29. immobilize
30. impeach
31. intimidate
32. laud
33. maim
34. malinger
35. orient
36. ostracize
37. pander
38. procrastinate
39. prognosticate
40. rant
41. raze
42. recant
43. reconcile
44. sabotage
45. simulate
46. slander
47. smirk
48. supersede
49. vacillate
50. vegetate

The verb is the beating heart of the sentence. A strong verb often lets you cut out prepositional phrases that clutter and suffocate a sentence. One student writes, "The temperatures were now at a much lower level than during the previous period." Another writes, "The temperatures plunged." The good writer gets considerable mileage from vigorous, well-selected verbs.

Chapter 7 presents fifty action words, plus a supplementary list. The drill technique is the same as in Chapters 5 and 6. Study carefully the words and definitions at the top of each frame; then fill in the blanks without looking back unless necessary.

Exercises

COVER-THIS STRIP

1. **abscond** (ab-skond'): to depart hastily and secretly, especially to escape the law.
2. **acquit** (ə-kwit'): to declare innocent; to absolve.

▶ If *acquitted* of a crime you are legally (a) guilty, (b) innocent. (b)

(b)

▶ The female prisoner was so pretty that the Yukon jury voted unanimously to ac_quit_____ her.

acquit

▶ A company clerk known as Honest Jim has _absconded_ [absconded / abdicated] with our money.

absconded

▶ The bank teller who ___abscond___ed was five feet tall and ten thousand dollars short.

absconded

▶ Although the treasurer did _abscond___ one night with the union funds, his lawyer managed later to get him _acquitt___ed.

abscond
acquitted

3. **adulterate** (ə-dul'tə-rāt'): to cheapen by adding inferior ingredients; to corrupt.
4. **alienate** (āl'yə-nāt'): to make unfriendly; to estrange.

▶ Adding sawdust to sausage meat _adulterates_ [fortifies / adulterates] it.

adulterates

▶ Insulting your friends in public is usually a good way to _alienate___ [alienate / captivate] them.

alienate

▶ If Linus flirts with everybody, he'll soon al_ienate____ his girl friend.

alienate

▶ Chemical additives often _adulterate_ our food.

adulterate

117

adulterate
alienate

▶ Many bakeries add generous amounts of artificial preservative to their bread and thus *adulterate* it; such practices *alienate* thoughtful customers.

5. **authenticate** (ô-then'ti-kāt'): to confirm; to prove to be true or genuine.
6. **bicker** (bik'ər): to squabble; to have a petty dispute.

(a)

▶ To *authenticate* a Titian painting is to verify that it was really painted by (a) Titian, (b) an imitator. (*a*)

authenticate

▶ This Handel manuscript may not be genuine—we must *authenticate* it.

bicker

▶ The cranky old couple would often *bicker* [bicker / bamboozle] over petty details.

bicker

▶ Small-minded people argue and bi*cker* endlessly.

bicker
authenticate

▶ The landlord claimed that George Washington—or his horse—had slept in the bed; we began to bi*cker* as to how to *authenticate* the claim.

7. **blaspheme** (blas-fēm'): to speak profanely of God or sacred things; to curse.
8. **bungle**: to botch; to perform clumsily.

bungled

▶ If her surgeon had been sober, he would not have *bungled* [bungled / misfired] that operation.

(a)

▶ Those who *blaspheme* are (a) cursing, (b) praying. (*a*)

blaspheme

▶ The priest shuddered to hear the atheist bl*aspheme* the Creator.

bungle

▶ If you bu*ngle* your baking, the upside-down cake may come out rightside-up.

bungle
blaspheme

▶ The clumsy carpenter had to cut only one board but managed to *bungle* the job; then he began to bl*aspheme*.

9. **canonize** (kan'ə-nīz'): to declare a dead person to be a saint.
10. **canvass** (kan'vəs): to go through a district asking for votes, opinions, or orders.

▶ We'll get Dooley elected even if we have to _canvass_ [canvas / canvass] the whole town.

canvass

▶ The Catholic Church has *canonized* (a) Columbus, (b) Saint Joan of Arc. (b)

(b)

▶ Live like a saint and maybe the church will can_onize_ you.

canonize

▶ "To sell tickets for—pardon the expression—*Gotterdammerung*," said Silas, "we had to can_vass_ the county."

canvass

▶ When Bobo hit that grand slam home run, he became an instant saint; you didn't have to _canvass_ the crowd to know they would practically _canonize_ him.

canvass
canonize

Quiz

Write the letter that indicates the best definition.

1. (e)	(e) 1. abscond	a. to botch; to do something awkwardly
2. (h)	(h) 2. acquit	b. to add impure elements
3. (b)	(b) 3. adulterate	c. to solicit votes or opinions
4. (j)	(j) 4. alienate	d. to argue over trivia
5. (g)	(g) 5. authenticate	e. to evade the law
6. (d)	(d) 6. bicker	f. to raise to sainthood
7. (i)	(i) 7. blaspheme	g. to verify genuineness
8. (a)	(a) 8. bungle	h. to declare not guilty
9. (f)	(f) 9. canonize	i. to speak irreverently; to curse
10. (c)	(c) 10. canvass	j. to make hostile

11. **cauterize** (ko'tə-rīz'): to sear with a hot iron, as to cure wounds.
12. **condone** (kən-dōn'): to pardon or overlook a fault.

▶ Infected wounds can be *cauterized* by (a) burning, (b) ice cubes. (a)

(a)

condone

▶ When a father shrugs off his son's vandalism, he is said to _condone_ [condone / canonize] it.

cauterize

▶ A white-hot needle was used to c_auterize_ the ugly scratch.

condone

▶ Though Gauguin was an inspired artist, many cannot c_ondone_ his desertion of his family.

cauterize
condoned

▶ The army surgeon's failure to c_auterize_ Fenwick's bullet wound cannot be _condon_ed.

---

13. **decimate** (des′ə-māt′): to kill many of.
14. **deify** (dē′ə-fī′): to make a god of; to exalt and idealize.

deify

▶ We tend to _deify_ [decimate / deify] our top athletes.

deify

▶ A heavyweight champion is not a god, and we should not d_eify_ him.

decimate

▶ With the hydrogen bomb any two nations can _decimate_ [decimate / deify] each other more efficiently.

decimate

▶ We gave the South Sea natives the benefits of our modern syphilization and managed to d_ecimate_ them.

deify
decimate

▶ It was the habit of the ancient Greeks to d_eify_ the sun, the moon, and the winds; it was also their habit to _decimate_ their enemies.

---

15. **disconcert** (dis′kən-sûrt′): to embarrass; to confuse; to upset.
16. **disparage** (dis-par′ij): to belittle; to speak of with contempt.

disparage

▶ To belittle a man's efforts is to _disparage_ [condone / disparage] them.

disconcert

▶ Jeering at a speaker tends to _disconcert_ [deify / disconcert] him.

disconcert

▶ Finding half a worm in my apple was enough to *dis_concert_* me.

disparage

▶ Don't *dis_parage_* the restaurant coffee; you, too, may be old and weak some day.

disparage
disconcert

▶ The clarinet duet sounded like cats fighting, but let's not *_disparage_* it or we may *_disconcert_* the young artists.

---

17. **disseminate** (di-sem′ə-nāt′): to scatter everywhere; to spread, as if sowing.
18. **elucidate** (i-lōō′si-dāt′): to make clear; to explain.

(b)

▶ To *elucidate* a literary passage is (a) to disparage it, (b) to clarify its meaning. (b)

(b)

▶ To *disseminate* propaganda is (a) to stifle it, (b) to spread it. (b)

elucidate

▶ This poem sounds like jabberwocky. Please *el_ucidate_* it, Sheldon.

disseminate

▶ A helicopter was used to drop and *dis_seminate_* circulars advertising Anti-Litter Week.

disseminate
elucidate

▶ In December the Internal Revenue Service will *dis_seminate_* among common citizens a tax form that only a genius can *_elucidate_*.

---

19. **emasculate** (i-mas′kyoo-lāt′): to castrate; to deprive of vigor and virility; to weaken.
20. **espouse** (i-spouz′): to adopt or support as a cause.

(b)

▶ To *espouse* women's liberation is (a) to fight it, (b) to support it.

(a)

▶ To *emasculate* a horse—or, say, a critical report—is (a) to weaken it, (b) to strengthen it.

emasculate

▸ Government censorship of the press will em_*asculate*_ an author's creativity.

espouse

▸ John Greenleaf Whittier hated slavery and was quick to es_*pouse*_ the Abolitionist movement.

espouse
emasculate

▸ We es_*pouse*_ a strong reform bill, but our opposition is pushing through several amendments to _emasculate_ it.

Quiz

Write the letter that indicates the best definition.

1. (h)	(h) 1. cauterize	a. to discredit; to show little respect for
2. (f)	(f) 2. condone	b. to advocate
3. (d)	(d) 3. decimate	c. to rob of vigor
4. (j)	(j) 4. deify	d. to take many lives
5. (e)	(e) 5. disconcert	e. to upset or embarrass
6. (a)	(a) 6. disparage	f. to forgive a fault
7. (g)	(g) 7. disseminate	g. to scatter like seeds
8. (i)	(i) 8. elucidate	h. to burn with a hot iron
9. (c)	(c) 9. emasculate	i. to clarify; to explain
10. (b)	(b) 10. espouse	j. to look upon as a god

21. **exhume** (iks-hūm′): to dig out of the earth; to disinter; to unearth; to reveal.
22. **exorcise** (ek′sôr-sīz′): to cast out an evil spirit.

(b)

▸ Prohibitionists tried to *exorcise* the demon rum from our midst, that is, (a) to spread its influence, (b) to cast it out. (b)

(a)

▸ To *exhume* ancient scrolls is (a) to dig them up, (b) to translate them. (a)

exhume

▸ Sometimes grave robbers, known as ghouls, would _exhume_ a corpse.

exorcise

▸ Puritans often "beat the devil" out of a child—they tried, that is, to _exorcise_ [exercise / exorcise] the demon in him.

exhume
exorcise

▶ We dug away and managed to _exhume_ a religious parchment that told us how to _exorcise_ our evil desires.

---

23. **expurgate** (ek'spər-gāt'): to remove obscene or objectionable matter; to purge.
24. **extradite** (ek'strədīt'): to return a fugitive to another state or nation.

(a)

▶ The PTA *expurgated* our class play—that is, they (a) cleaned it up, (b) added a few dirty words. (_a_)

(b)

▶ France promised to *extradite* Killer McGee—in other words, he will be (a) executed there, (b) shipped back to us. (_b_)

extradite

▶ Argentina was requested by Israel to ex_tradite_ a Nazi war criminal.

expurgate

▶ Censors used a blue pencil to ex_purgate_ the naughty lines.

extradite
expurgate

▶ Some countries refuse to ex_tradite_ political refugees; some show Hollywood films but will ex_purgate_ the kissing scenes.

---

25. **gawk** (gôk): to stare stupidly; to gape.
26. **grapple**: to come to grips; to struggle; to seize.

(a)

▶ To *gawk* at the bathing beauties is (a) to stare at them, (b) to flirt with them. (_a_)

(b)

▶ To *grapple* with an intruder is (a) to argue, (b) to struggle. (_b_)

grapple

▶ Philosophers *grapple* with cosmic issues, whereas I g_rapple_ with practical issues, such as how to pay the landlord.

gawk

▶ Farm boys g_awk_ at the Empire State Building.

grapple
gawk

▶ At the county fair we saw two wrestlers g_rappling_ with each other and we stopped to g_awk_ at the fat lady.

123

27. **haggle:** to argue in petty fashion about terms and prices.
28. **heckle:** to harass with questions and sarcastic remarks.

▶ Those who *haggle* at a garage sale are probably discussing (a) politics, (b) prices. (b)

(b)

▶ To *heckle* the chairman is to shower him with words of (a) sarcasm, (b) praise. (a)

(a)

▶ Natives in the marketplace would sometimes h__aggle__ ten minutes over the price of a fish.

haggle

▶ Spectators in Hyde Park who disagree with any speakers will mercilessly __heckle__ them.

heckle

▶ The crowd began to h__eckle__ the orator; meanwhile, the peddler and the hippie continued to h__aggle__ for the overripe cantaloupe.

heckle
haggle

---

29. **immobilize** (i-mō′bə-līz′): to make unable to move; to fix in place.
30. **impeach:** to accuse an official of wrongdoing.

▶ President Andrew Johnson was *impeached;* this means that he was (a) guilty, (b) accused. (b)

(b)

▶ If the governor has misued the funds, we should __impeach__ him.

impeach

▶ To *immobilize* a broken leg is (a) to exercise it; (b) to keep it from moving. (b)

(b)

▶ The policeman pulled Nick's arms back so as to __immobilize__ him.

immobilize

▶ One columnist predicts that we will __impeach__ Senator Swindle, convict him, and send him to a prison cell to __immobilize__ him.

impeach
immobilize

124

Quiz

Write the letter that indicates the best definition.

1. (f)
2. (j)
3. (a)
4. (c)
5. (d)
6. (b)
7. (h)
8. (e)
9. (i)
10. (g)

(f)	1. exhume	a. to delete obscenities
(j)	2. exorcise	b. to grab and struggle
(a)	3. expurgate	c. to send back a fugitive
(c)	4. extradite	d. to stare stupidly
(d)	5. gawk	e. to taunt a public speaker
(b)	6. grapple	f. to dig out of the earth
(h)	7. haggle	g. to charge an official with misconduct
(e)	8. heckle	h. to argue about prices
(i)	9. immobilize	i. to prevent movement
(g)	10. impeach	j. to drive out a devil

31. **intimidate** (in-tim′i-dāt′): to make timid; to control action by inducing fear.
32. **laud** (lôd): to praise.

intimidate

▶ Bugsy's scowl and brass knuckles were enough to *intimidate* [intimate / intimidate] me.

(a)

▶ If the critics *laud* your performance, they are (a) praising it, (b) knocking it. (a)

laud

▶ Some artists have to die before anyone will *laud* them for their accomplishments.

intimidate

▶ Drive a compact car in heavy traffic and the huge trucks will *intimidate* you.

laud
intimidate

▶ Belinda saved the hikers' lives, and our newspapers all *laud* her bravery. She did not let the grizzly bears *intimidate* her.

33. **maim:** to cripple; to mutilate; to disable.
34. **malinger** (mə-ling′gər): to pretend to be ill so as to escape duty.

(b)

▶ The employee who *malingers* is (a) working, (b) shirking. (b)

(a)

▶ To *maim* is (a) to cripple, (b) to rob. (a)

maim

▶ A young shark can bite your leg and __maim__ you for life.

malinger

▶ When term papers are due, an epidemic of the flu always hits the class—for students will mal__inger__.

maim
malinger

▶ Captain Yossarian distrusted grenades, which could __maim__ a man; he preferred to __malinger__ among the pretty hospital nurses.

---

35. **orient** (ōr′ē-ent′): to adjust to a situation.
36. **ostracize** (os′trə-sīz′): to exclude from society; to banish.

ostracized

▶ When a person is shunned by others, he is said to be __ostracized__ [extradited / ostracized].

orient

▶ In your first days of work at the stock exchange, you will try to __orient__ [alienate / orient] yourself.

oriented

▶ The new clerk at the department store didn't know a lace curtain from a lace panty—he was not yet __orient__ed.

ostracize

▶ Jasper was a sneak and a tattletale, so his fellow workers began to os__tracize__ him.

orient
ostracized

▶ Every year this college must __orient__ a new class of freshmen and must hope that each newcomer will be accepted, not __ostraciz__ed, by campus groups.

---

37. **pander:** to help satisfy the base desires of others.
38. **procrastinate** (prō-kras′tə-nāt′): to delay, to postpone action.

pander

▶ Dope pushers, bootleggers, and prostitutes __pander__ [pander / don't pander] to the vices of others.

pander

▶ No lust or desire is so low but that someone will pa__nder__ to it.

(b)

▶ Elmer *procrastinates,* repeating, (a) "Let's do it now," (b) "Let's wait." (b)

126

procrastinate

▶ Huge term reports are due soon, so don't *procrastinate*.

procrastinate
pander

▶ Our town drunkard gets up early; he does not *procrastinate*. By nine a.m. he has found a bartender to *pander* to his thirst.

---

39. **prognosticate** (prog-nos′tə-kāt′): to predict; to foretell.
40. **rant:** to speak wildly; to rave.

(a)

▶ Every day the newspaper *prognosticates* (a) the weather, (b) accidents and crimes. (*a*)

(b)

▶ To *rant* is to speak (a) logically, (b) loudly and wildly. (*b*)

rant

▶ Julius mounted the soapbox and began to fling his arms around and *rant*.

prognosticate

▶ Madame Zaza used a crystal ball to *prognosticate* the misfortunes ahead.

rant
prognosticate

▶ Professor Schluck would glare at us and *rant* about our lack of discipline; then he would *prognosticate* our final reward—on the gallows.

Quiz

Write the letter that indicates the best definition.

1. (e)	(e)	1. intimidate	a. to talk wildly and loudly
2. (d)	(d)	2. laud	b. to shut out from society
3. (j)	(j)	3. maim	c. to postpone; to delay
4. (i)	(i)	4. malinger	d. to praise
5. (g)	(g)	5. orient	e. to overawe; to make fearful
6. (b)	(b)	6. ostracize	f. to satisfy the vices of others
7. (f)	(f)	7. pander	g. to adjust to a situation
8. (c)	(c)	8. procrastinate	h. to predict
9. (h)	(h)	9. prognosticate	i. to feign illness and loaf
10. (a)	(a)	10. rant	j. to mutilate or injure

41. **raze** (rāz): to tear to the ground; to demolish.
42. **recant** (ri-kant'): to renounce formally one's previous statements.

▶ To *recant* is (a) to add overwhelming evidence, (b) to take back one's words. (*b*)

(b)

▶ To improve our city we should first ___raze___ [raise / raze] more condemned tenements.

raze

▶ Galileo asserted that the earth revolved around the sun, but he was forced by the church to r___ecant___.

recant

▶ Let's r___aze___ the old barn, Hiram, and build a new-fangled garage.

raze

▶ Governor Gronk promised that he would ___raze___ all school buildings that might be unsafe in an earthquake, but he has had to ___recant___.

raze
recant

43. **reconcile** (rek'ən-sīl'): to bring into harmony; to make compatible.
44. **sabotage** (sab'ə-täzh'): to do malicious damage, as to machinery or to a war effort.

▶ The befuddled bookkeeper was unable to rec___oncile___ his figures.

reconcile

▶ Igor blew up an electric plant to sab___otage___ the military preparations.

sabotage

▶ Aaron Burr and Alexander Hamilton could not rec___oncile___ their differences, except with pistols.

reconcile

▶ A strike at the bazooka factory would ___sabotage___ our war effort.

sabotage

▶ When the third bridge collapsed, we had to ___reconcile___ ourselves to the fact that somebody was trying to ___sabotage___ our military work.

reconcile
sabotage

128

45. **simulate** (sim′yoo-lāt′): to pretend; to imitate; to counterfeit.
46. **slander:** to utter falsehoods injuring someone's reputation.

▶ "Real simulated pearls," recently advertised for $4.95, are (a) genuine pearls, (b) imitations. (*b*)

(b)

▶ Death and agony, says Emily Dickinson, are genuine and not easy to *sim*___ulate___.

simulate

▶ To print damaging lies about somebody is to libel; to speak such lies is to ___slander___.

slander

▶ Call the tax assessor a "bribe-happy reptile" and he'll sue you for ___slander___.

slander

▶ Thomas Paine had many enemies, and when he died a few tried to *sim*___ulate___ grief and others continued to *sl*___ander___ him.

simulate
slander

47. **smirk:** to smile in a conceited or affected manner.
48. **supersede** (soo′pər-sēd′): to take the place of; to replace; to supplant.

▶ As a news reporter you would be insulting the guest of honor if you wrote that he (a) smiled, (b) smirked. (*b*)

(b)

▶ If Plan X *supersedes* Plan W, then (a) both plans are in effect, (b) only Plan X is in effect. (*b*)

(b)

▶ Yesterday's orders are void because today's orders ___supercede___ them.

supersede

▶ Posing for the camera, most tourists will stand in front of a museum and *s*_____.

smirk

▶ When Dora told Moose, the big fullback, that he was going to *su*_____ everybody else in her affections, he could only scratch his ear and *s*_____.

supersede
smirk

129

49. **vacillate** (vas′ə-lat′): to waver in mind; to fluctuate; to hesitate.
50. **vegetate** (veg′ə-tāt′): to live in a dull, passive way.

▶ Women often *vacillate* when (a) they are choosing a dress, (b) their child is about to eat rat poison. ( ) (a)

▶ To *vegetate* is to live a life (a) of furious activity, (b) somewhat like that of a vegetable. ( ) (b)

▶ A talented symphony conductor would probably ve_____ in solitary confinement. vegetate

▶ The time to invest is now, so don't va_____. vacillate

▶ You want to enter law school? Then you must not va_____ any longer. Otherwise you will ve_____ forever in the village with your regrets. vacillate / vegetate

---

Quiz

Write the letter that indicates the best definition.

1. (b)	( ) 1. raze	a. to pretend; to imitate
2. (h)	( ) 2. recant	b. to tear down; to demolish
3. (j)	( ) 3. reconcile	c. to say false, malicious things
4. (g)	( ) 4. sabotage	d. to exist in sluggish fashion
5. (a)	( ) 5. simulate	e. to smile conceitedly
6. (c)	( ) 6. slander	f. to waver indecisively
7. (e)	( ) 7. smirk	g. to interfere with production
8. (i)	( ) 8. supersede	h. to take back what one has said
9. (f)	( ) 9. vacillate	i. to replace
10. (d)	( ) 10. vegetate	j. to end opposition; to harmonize

Review Test

Write *True* or *False*.

_____ 1. To *reconcile* is to *alienate*.

_____ 2. Countries often *extradite* those who *abscond*.

_____ 3. To *impeach* means to remove from office.

_____ 4. To *haggle* is to *bicker* over prices.

_____ 5. To *blaspheme* is to *espouse* a religion.

_____ 6. Those who *heckle* a speaker are likely to *disconcert* him.

_____ 7. To *exhume* a body is to bury it.

_____ 8. To *laud* is to *disparage*.

_____ 9. To *vacillate* and *procrastinate* will delay action.

_____ 10. To *maim* an athlete will improve his performance.

Write the letter that indicates the best synonym for the italicized word.

( ) 11. *elucidate* a passage: (a) clarify, (b) expurgate, (c) read, (d) correct

( ) 12. *ostracize* a neighbor: (a) orient, (b) entertain, (c) shun, (d) annoy

( ) 13. *exorcise* the devil: (a) canonize, (b) cast out, (c) idolize, (d) fight

( ) 14. *disseminate* falsehoods: (a) oppose, (b) write, (c) speak, (d) spread

( ) 15. *simulate* passion: (a) arouse, (b) feel, (c) imitate, (d) stifle

( ) 16. *raze* a structure: (a) lecorate, (b) demolish, (c) build, (d) pay for

( ) 17. *decimate* the troops: (a) kill many of, (b) count, (c) expand, (d) train

( ) 18. *condone* her sins: (a) slander, (b) sabotage, (c) forgive, (d) recant

( ) 19. *prognosticate* a victory: (a) foretell, (b) prevent, (c) bungle, (d) aid

( ) 20. *deify* a hero: (a) emasculate, (b) treat as a god, (c) authenticate, (d) acquit

Matching. Write the letter that indicates the best definition.

( ) 21. adulterate   a. to stare; to gape
( ) 22. cauterize   b. to share secrets
( ) 23. gawk   c. to make impure by admixture
( ) 24. intimidate   d. to talk wildly
( ) 25. rant   e. to burn a wound
                          f. to sin
                          g. to smile stupidly
                          h. to inspire with fear

Write the word studied in this chapter that will complete the sentence.

26. Don't move his fractured neck. We must im_____ it.
27. Joe managed to trip the burglar and began to gr_____ with him.
28. This soldier is healthy—don't let him ma_____ in the hospital.
29. Dooley needs more votes. Let us ca_____ the town.
30. Spend ten years in Dullsville? We would only ve_____ there.
31. These new rules will replace the old ones—that is, su_____ them.
32. What a conceited grin! Look at him sm_____ at the women.
33. The Mafia traffics in drugs and prostitutes—it pa_____ to the weaknesses of citizens.

Key to Review Test

Check your test answers by the following key. Deduct 3% per error from a possible 100%.

1. False	8. False	15. (c)	22. (e)	29. canvass
2. True	9. True	16. (b)	23. (a)	30. vegetate
3. False	10. False	17. (a)	24. (h)	31. supersede
4. True	11. (a)	18. (c)	25. (d)	32. smirk
5. False	12. (c)	19. (a)	26. immobilize	33. panders
6. True	13. (b)	20. (b)	27. grapple	
7. False	14. (d)	21. (c)	28. malinger	

Score: _____%

Supplementary List

Exercise 7

Fill in the blanks at the left with the verbs that fit the definitions. Although these verbs were not defined in this chapter, you should recognize most of them. Check your answers with the key at the end of the exercise. Use your dictionary to study any unknown words.

atrophy, belie, browbeat, corroborate, covet

1. _____ to bully; to intimidate
2. _____ to confirm; to make more certain
3. _____ to prove false
4. _____ to desire what belongs to another
5. _____ to wither; to waste away

decry, deploy, dismantle, edify, emulate

6. _____ to instruct; to enlighten spiritually
7. _____ to imitate so as to equal or excel
8. _____ to spread out forces according to plan
9. _____ to denounce; to condemn; to disparage
10. _____ to strip of equipment; to disassemble

epitomize, equivocate, implicate, impoverish, jettison

11. _____ to represent the essence of
12. _____ to be ambiguous purposely; to hedge; to mislead
13. _____ to make poor; to reduce to poverty
14. _____ to throw cargo overboard in an emergency
15. _____ to show to be involved; to entangle

mollify, osculate, rankle, retaliate, retrench

16. _____ to kiss

17. _____ to cause resentment; to fester; to irritate

18. _____ to pay back injury for injury; to revenge

19. _____ to make less angry; to soothe; to appease

20. _____ to cut expenses; to economize

scrutinize, skulk, swelter, thwart, tipple

21. _____ to prevent from accomplishing a purpose; to hinder

22. _____ to drink liquor frequently

23. _____ to move about furtively; to lurk; to shirk

24. _____ to examine carefully; to look at closely

25. _____ to suffer or perspire from oppressive heat

Key

1. browbeat	6. edify	11. epitomize	16. osculate	21. thwart
2. corroborate	7. emulate	12. equivocate	17. rankle	22. tipple
3. belie	8. deploy	13. impoverish	18. retaliate	23. skulk
4. covet	9. decry	14. jettison	19. mollify	24. scrutinize
5. atrophy	10. dismantle	15. implicate	20. retrench	25. swelter

8
Words Often Misused

1. a
2. an
3. accept
4. except
5. affect
6. effect
7. amount
8. complexioned
9. conscience
10. conscious
11. consensus
12. enthusiastic
13. etc.
14. feature
15. funny
16. hanged
17. hung
18. have
19. imply
20. infer
21. its
22. it's
23. leave
24. let
25. less
26. liable
27. likely
28. loose
29. lose
30. lots of

Common, trivial words—these are a disaster area for many college students. If English professors earned a nickel every time they red-penciled *it's*, *too*, and *their*, they could retire at forty. Are you anxious to learn *ambivalence*, *denouement*, and *existentialism*? Be patient—you will master them later. First be sure that you are not misusing *affect*, *than*, and *whose*. Your thoughts may be profound, yet your composition will look amateurish if it is speckled with flaws. Your ploy should be to keep your teachers happy and in a generous mood—and so your aim number one must be to use basic words correctly. Demonstrate in themes that you understand the difference in meaning between *its* and *it's* and your teacher will want to embrace you.

To write *loose* when one means *lose* is usually classed as an error in spelling rather than in vocabulary, but actually it is both kinds of error. Look at it this way: Students can easily write *loose* and *lose*—they just aren't always sure which word means what. So spelling fault or vocabulary fault, the quibble is pointless. Words are being misused. And whatever one calls the disease, it has to be cured.

Most words in Chapters 8 and 9 look deceptively easy. But one should not be overconfident. These words are demons. Be sure to write the correct answers in full—either in the blanks provided or on a separate sheet of paper—before you check the answer columns. Your fingers are an extension of your brain; they must learn to do the right thing automatically. Thus, the act of writing and rewriting these demons correctly is vital.

Exercises

COVER THIS STRIP

1. **a:** one (used before a consonant sound: "a girl, a historian, a mark, a fat ox").
2. **an:** one (used before a vowel sound: "an itch, an honor, an easy mark, an ox").

▶ The words *city, year,* and *pretty* begin with a _____ [vowel / consonant] sound so we use the word _____ [a / an] immediately in front of each of them.

consonant
a

▶ The words *apple, ear,* and *idiotic* begin with a _____ [vowel / consonant] sound so we use the word _____ [a / an] immediately in front of each of them.

vowel
an

▶ Write *a* or *an:*
Jenks is _____ absent-minded man. He dictated _____ letter to his dog and tried to give his secretary _____ bath.

an
a
a

▶ Such magic! The guest flicks _____ ancient cigar and turns _____ Persian rug into _____ ashtray.

an
a
an

▶ I remember _____ evening when my roommate typed thirty words _____ hour and erased twenty words _____ minute.

an
an
a

3. **accept** (ak-sept'): to take or receive. "*Accept* the lemons of life, and make lemonade."
4. **except** (ik-sept'): all but; excluding. "This singer has everything *except* talent." *Except* has to do with an *exception*.

accept
except

▶ The church will ac_____ all your paintings ex_____ the nude.

except accept	▶ Every teacher _____ Smedley will _____ the 2 percent raise.
accept except	▶ The opera singer was glad to _____ the gift package, which was quite ordinary _____ for its ticking sound.
except accept except	▶ Flem had no coins _____ a wooden nickel, yet he would never _____ a free drink—_____ when he was awake.

5. **affect** (ə-fect′): *Verb*—to produce a change; to influence. "The damp air may *affect* Joe's lungs."
6. **effect** (i-fect′): *Noun*—result. "Physicists study cause and *effect*." *Verb*—to cause or bring about. "Dad tried to *effect* a change in my study habits."

affect	▶ Marriage will _____ Tony's career. [Verb: means "to influence."]
effect	▶ Marriage will have an excellent _____ on Tony. [Noun: means "result."]
effect	▶ Marriage will _____ an improvement in Tony's habits. [Verb: means "to bring about."]
affect effect	▶ The concussion did not _____ my academic grades, which were low anyhow, and seemed to have no lasting _____.
effect effect	▶ Baseball representatives can probably _____ a compromise, but they must consider the _____ on the box-office.
effect affect	▶ Drugs had a tragic _____; his hallucinations still _____ him day and night.

7. **amount:** quantity; mass (not to be confused with *number,* which refers to countable objects). "Joe ate a huge *amount* of ice cream and a small *number* [not *amount*] of doughnuts."

137

▶ Write *amount* or *number:*

number — Sheila collected an unusual _____ of mosquito bites.

number
amount — The mugger separated me from a large _____ of credit cards and a small _____ of cash.

number — The sink had no drainpipe, so I washed a great _____ of dishes and my feet at the same time.

number
amount — St. Patrick chased a vast _____ of snakes out of Ireland, but they return to those who drink a certain _____ of whiskey.

---

8. **complexioned** (kəm-plek′shənd): having a specified skin color (preferable to the colloquial *complected*).

(a) — ▶ The Rose Bowl queen is rosy- (a) complexioned, (b) complected. ( )

complexioned — ▶ When the blond visitor finally came out of the dusty coal mine, he was dark-*com*_____.

complexioned
complexioned — ▶ Phineas claimed that his skin ointment was as good for light-*c*_____ people as for dark-*c*_____ people, and it probably was.

complexioned — ▶ The word *complected* is considered colloquial or dialectal, and most good writers prefer to use the word _____.

---

9. **conscience** (kon′shəns): a moral sense steering toward right action.
10. **conscious** (kon′shəs): aware; able to feel and think.

conscience — ▶ *Science* means "knowledge," and your so-called knowledge of right and wrong is your *c*_____.

conscious — ▶ At age twelve Manuel became *c*_____ of girls—he had always thought they were soft boys.

138

conscience
conscious

▶ The big employers must develop their c_____ as well as their investments; they must become c_____ of the needs of employees.

conscious
conscience

▶ The mutilated dog was now _____ again; and the researchist, feeling a pang of _____ at the sight, put on his dark glasses.

Quiz

Write the letter that indicates the best definition.

1. (i)
2. (e)
3. (g)
4. (c)
5. (h)
6. (a)
7. (d)
8. (j)
9. (f)
10. (b)

( ) 1. a   a. result
( ) 2. an   b. aware
( ) 3. accept   c. all but
( ) 4. except   d. quantity
( ) 5. affect   e. one (used before vowels)
( ) 6. effect   f. sense of right and wrong
( ) 7. amount   g. to take
( ) 8. complexioned   h. to influence
( ) 9. conscience   i. one (used before consonants)
( ) 10. conscious   j. having a certain facial appearance

11. **consensus** (kən-sen′səs): a general opinion.

wordiness
avoid

▶ Since *consensus* means "a general opinion," the phrase "consensus of opinion" is an example of the _____ [crispness / wordiness] that careful writers usually _____ [avoid / favor].

consensus

▶ We are due for an earthquake soon, according to a _____ [consensus / consensus of opinion] of experts.

consensus

▶ More women should enter politics, according to a _____ of congressional leaders.

of opinion

▶ News item: "The consensus of opinion of fashion designers is that dresses will be shorter next summer." What must be cut in that sentence (not counting dresses)? _____

12. **enthusiastic:** eager; ardent. (Avoid using the colloquial *enthused*.)

▶ The strip teaser performed before a seedy throng of _____ [enthused / enthusiastic] old men.

enthusiastic

▶ The Englishman _____ [enthused / was enthusiastic] about the house with two bathrooms.

was enthusiastic

▶ We were all _____ [enthused / enthusiastic] when Tom Mix untied his girl from the railroad tracks.

enthusiastic

▶ In formal writing the use of *enthused* is generally (a) acceptable, (b) undesirable. ( )

(b)

---

13. **etc.:** et cetera (et set′rə); and others; and so forth. (The abbreviation *etc.* is usually avoided in formal writing. Use its English equivalent.)

▶ Poe later wrote "The Tell-Tale Heart," "The Black Cat," (a) etc., (b) and other horror stories. ( )

(b)

▶ If accepted at Harvard, I will take courses in physics, chemistry, (a) etc., (b) and mathematics. ( )

(b)

▶ To pronounce and spell *etc.* correctly, you should think of the first three letters of *et cetera*—they give us the abbreviation _____.

etc.

▶ *Etc.* means "and so forth"—thus to write "and etc.," with its additional "and," is (a) incorrect, (b) correct. ( )

(a)

---

14. **feature** (fē′chər): *Noun*—a distinct quality; part of the face; a motion picture. *Verb*—to make prominent; to make a specialty of. (Avoid the informal use of *feature* to mean "imagine" or "to conceive of.")

▶ I cannot _____ [feature / imagine] a world without music.

imagine

140

comprehend
▶ The average, well-fed American can hardly _____ [feature / comprehend] the utter poverty of Calcutta.

feature
▶ The Hilton dining room will _____ lobster thermidor this evening.

imagine
feature
▶ Can you _____ [imagine / feature] what Aunt Fanny would think of that shocking double _____ at the Pussycat Theater?

---

15. **funny:** comical; laughable; humorous. (Avoid *funny* in formal writing when you mean "strange, peculiar, odd.")

strange
▶ We thought it was _____ [funny / strange] that our low-salaried sheriff could buy a yacht.

unusual
▶ When Hilda found the letters from John's three other wives, she realized that something _____ [funny / unusual] was going on.

funny
▶ Mark Twain's lectures were extremely f_____.

mournful
▶ The widow sat near the casket with a _____ [mournful / funny] look on her face.

---

16. **hanged:** suspended by the neck until dead.
17. **hung:** fastened or supported from above (preferably not referring to death by hanging).

hung
▶ We h_____ our clothes on a hickory limb.

hanged
hung
▶ The posse h_____ Wee Willie, and the rest of us h_____ our heads in shame.

hung
▶ Nancy h_____ the mistletoe above her typewriter.

hanged
▶ The prisoner had a choice: he could be shot or _____.

hanged
hung

▶ Nathan Hale was _____, but we have _____ his picture in our hall of fame.

---

18. **have:** to possess. (Use *have* as an auxiliary verb in phrases like "should *have*," "could *have*," "might *have*," and AVOID the nonstandard "should of," "could of," . . . .)

▶ Write *have* or *of* in the sentences that follow:

have

The lost aviator should _____ stayed in bed.

have
of

The material might _____ cost ten dollars a yard, but none _____ the bathers wore twenty cents worth.

have
of
of

Junior must _____ reached for the hammer instead _____ the swatter when he saw the fly on the top _____ the baby's head.

have
have

You should _____ warned me that Ambrose would sing here, so that I could _____ gone to the ball game instead.

of
have

Olaf washed the top windows _____ the building and must _____ stepped back to admire his work.

---

19. **imply** (im-plī′): to hint at; to suggest without stating; to signify.
20. **infer** (in-fûr′): to draw a conclusion.

imply
infer

▶ These bloodstains im_____ that the victim may have been knifed. What do you in_____?

imply

▶ Her high grades i_____ unusual intelligence.

infer
imply

▶ From various evidence I i_____ that the baseball fans no longer admire Lefty Smeeby. Their jeers i_____ that they have lost confidence in him.

imply
infer

▶ Melvin's smiles _____ success. We can _____ that Betty has accepted his marriage proposal.

142

inferred

▶ Hot tar was spilled at the intersection, from which the police _____ed that there was dirty work at the crossroads.

Quiz

Write the letter that indicates the best definition.

1. (d)
2. (g)
3. (a)
4. (i)
5. (c)
6. (b)
7. (j)
8. (h)
9. (f)
10. (e)

( ) 1. consensus   a. and so forth
( ) 2. enthusiastic   b. strangled on a gallows
( ) 3. etc.   c. humorous
( ) 4. feature   d. the general opinion
( ) 5. funny   e. to conclude
( ) 6. hanged   f. to suggest
( ) 7. hung   g. eager
( ) 8. have   h. to own (auxiliary verb)
( ) 9. imply   i. to make prominent
( ) 10. infer   j. supported from above, as on a hook

21. **its** (possessive): "The basset hound stepped on *its* ear."
22. **it's** (contraction): it is. "Frankly, *it's* a hot dog."

it's
its

▶ Surely _____ no fun for a rabbit to be held by _____ ears. (Hint: Write *it's* only if "it is" can be substituted for it.)

it's
its

▶ As for this camel, _____ a poor specimen; it has bumps on _____ back.

its
its

▶ The baby was so ugly at _____ birth that the doctor slapped _____ mother.

its
its

▶ I bravely stroked the old lion's head, _____ nose, _____ gums.

it's
it's

▶ Truly _____ lucky to own a shiny penny—if _____ wrapped in fifty-dollar bills.

its
it's

▶ Our child has a silver spoon in _____ mouth, but _____ better to have teeth.

23. **leave:** to depart. "We will *leave* at dawn."
24. **let:** to allow. "Please *let* us help."

▶ Society must l_____ women develop to their full potential.

let

▶ Before we l_____, l_____ us come to an understanding.

leave
let

▶ The hostess will _____ you kiss her when you _____.

let
leave

▶ The pacifist would not _____ his son _____ for the front.

let
leave

---

25. **less:** a smaller quantity (but use *fewer* when referring to a smaller number). "We used *less* fertilizer and harvested *fewer* tomatoes."

▶ Write *less* or *fewer*:

Although given _____ time, the girls made _____ mistakes.

less
fewer

Eat _____ hot fudge sundaes, and you will weigh _____.

fewer
less

As their romance cooled, they exchanged _____ letters and made _____ telephone calls.

fewer
fewer

This year I have _____ bees, and that means _____ honey, _____ money, and _____ stings.

fewer
less
less
fewer

---

26. **liable** (li′ə-bəl): legally responsible; exposed to a risk or danger. "Parents will be held *liable*. . . . The professor identified a new disease to which infants are *liable*." Do not use *liable* to mean "probable."
27. **likely:** probable; to be expected. "It is *likely* to rain."

144

likely	▶ Edith is *li*_____ to be valedictorian.
likely liable	▶ A crash is *li*_____ to occur on this one-lane country road, and one of us will be *li*_____.
likely	▶ This old frog is _____ to croak during the night.
likely liable	▶ The patient with the rubber gloves in his stomach is _____ to hold the hospital _____ for negligence.
liable likely	▶ If I am _____ for that million-dollar loss, you are _____ to collect about four dollars.

28. **loose** (rhymes with *goose*): not tight; unfastened.
29. **lose:** to suffer a loss.

loose lose	▶ The goose is *l*_____! We must not *l*_____ it.
loose lose	▶ In time of war a *l*_____ tongue can cause us to *l*_____ a troopship.
lose loose	▶ When I _____ weight, my pants hang _____.
lose lose loose	▶ Not only did I _____ the fight, but I may also _____ this _____ tooth.
loose	▶ The word *goose* rhymes with the word *l*_____.

30. **lots of; a lot of:** many; a great deal. (The informal phrases "lots of" and "a lot of" are acceptable but tend to be used far too frequently; they should be avoided in formal writing. Incidentally, "a lot" is two words, not one.)

numerous	▶ Shakespeare wrote _____ [a lot of / numerous] sonnets.

Many
considerable

▸ _____ [Lots of / Many] farms were struck by the hailstorm and _____ [lots of / considerable] damage was done.

many

▸ Grandpa bought a few lots near the garbage dump and made _____ [lots of / many] other bad investments.

informal
sparingly

▸ The phrases "lots of" and "a lot of" are considered _____ [formal / informal] and should therefore be used _____ [sparingly / lots of times] in your research papers.

Quiz

Write the letter that indicates the best definition.

1. (c)	( ) 1. its	a. to permit
2. (h)	( ) 2. it's	b. legally responsible
3. (e)	( ) 3. leave	c. possessive form of *it*
4. (a)	( ) 4. let	d. to suffer a loss
5. (f)	( ) 5. less	e. to depart; to go
6. (b)	( ) 6. liable	f. a smaller amount
7. (i)	( ) 7. likely	g. many; a great deal
8. (j)	( ) 8. loose	h. contraction for "it is"
9. (d)	( ) 9. lose	i. probable
10. (g)	( ) 10. lots of	j. unfastened; not tight

Review Test

Write Correct, if the italicized word is used correctly. Otherwise, write the word that should be used.

_____ 1. Brutus is *a* honorable man.

_____ 2. We have *an* orange cat that watches mice—just watches them.

_____ 3. In honor of the moon landing, please *except* this gift of green cheese.

_____ 4. Would sudden wealth *affect* me? I'll never find out.

_____ 5. Sunshine will bring out a greater *amount* of voters.

_____ 6. Throwing your parakeet to the cat! Have you no *conscious*?

_____ 7. Some comedians can be *funny* without a script.

_____ 8. Even Gloomy Gus, our coach, was *enthused* about our prospects.

_____ 9. On Christmas Eve we *hanged* our stockings on the mantel.

_____ 10. His high fever may *imply* serious illness.

_____ 11. Try not to *lose* that fat wallet.

_____ 12. It's *liable* to rain tomorrow.

_____ 13. The funeral director, like the corpse, was dark-*complected*.

_____ 14. The big tip to the waiter had a marvelous *effect*.

_____ 15. The factory belched *its* smoke into the sleeping city.

Write the better choice.

16. What will be the _____ [affect / effect] of another tax raise?
17. Surprisingly, our teacher does have a _____ [conscious / conscience].
18. The cattle thief was _____ [hanged / hung] from the apple tree.
19. Scarface won't talk, and we must _____ [imply / infer] that he is protecting someone.
20. During the classical period Beethoven composed _____ [lots of / a number of] symphonies.
21. Better highway signs will result in _____ [fewer / less] accidents.
22. Please _____ [leave / let] Tina plant the watermelon seeds.
23. Cooper wrote *The Leatherstocking Tales* _____ [and other novels / etc.].

24. Dorothea Fry should _____ [have / of] been our college president.
25. Like the Whiffenpoofs, many of us _____ [lose / loose] our way.

Key to Review Test

Check your test answers by the following key. Deduct 4% per error from a possible 100%.

1. an	10. Correct	19. infer
2. Correct	11. Correct	20. a number of
3. accept	12. likely	21. fewer
4. Correct	13. complexioned	22. let
5. number	14. Correct	23. and other novels
6. conscience	15. Correct	24. have
7. Correct	16. effcct	25. lose
8. enthusiastic	17. conscience	
9. hung	18. hanged	

Score: _____%

9
Words Often Misused

1. majority
2. nice
3. passed
4. past
5. principal
6. principle
7. prejudiced
8. supposed to
9. used to
10. really
11. reason
12. regardless
13. so
14. suspicion
15. than
16. then
17. themselves
18. their
19. there
20. they're
21. this
22. to
23. too
24. try
25. unique
26. which
27. who's
28. whose
29. your
30. you're

Chapter 9 continues our study of words often misused. Follow the same procedure as in Chapter 8.

Exercises

COVER THIS STRIP

1. **majority:** more than half of the total number; the excess over all the rest of the votes. (A *plurality,* however, refers to the excess of votes received by the leading candidate over the second of three or more candidates. Do not use *majority* to refer to most of a single thing. WRONG: "Bill ate the majority of the watermelon.")

▶ The elderly couple were sick during _____ [most / the majority] of the trip on the pleasure cruiser.

most

▶ Myrtle did _____ [most / the majority] of the engine design.

most

▶ Anna had 80 votes; Ben, 40 votes; Clarence, 30 votes. Anna _____ [did / did not] receive a majority of the votes. She won the election by a majority of _____ [10 / 40 / 80].

did
10

▶ In another election, Alice had 95 votes; Bill, 89 votes; Chester, 72 votes. Alice _____ [did / did not] receive a majority of the votes. She won the election by a plurality of _____ [6 / 13 / 95] votes.

did not
6

▶ Mr. Grunt has cut down twelve of his twenty pine trees. He has, therefore, cut a *ma*_____ of his trees. He will spend _____ [most / the majority] of the money he earns on a hernia operation.

majority
most

2. **nice:** pleasant; agreeable; satisfying; refreshing; comfortable; cordial; amiable; genial; dainty; delicate; delicious; attractive; engaging; fascinating; seductive; enchanting; delightful; charming; gratifying; cheerful. (Avoid overuse of *nice.* Try to use a more precise word in its place.)

▶ The phrase "a nice trip" expresses approval in a _____ [vague / precise] way.

vague

150

(b)

(b)

Examples:
  expensive
  refreshing
  smogless

passed

past

past
passed

past
passed
passed

past
passed

▶ Which gives a clearer description? (a) a nice room, (b) a comfortable room. ( )

▶ Which gives a clearer description? (a) a nice clerk, (b) an amiable clerk. ( )

▶ Substitute a more precise word for "nice":
nice car _____ car
nice drink _____ drink
nice weather _____ weather

---

3. **passed:** went by (verb, past tense of *pass*). "The smoky truck *passed* the joggers."
4. **past:** beyond; earlier; an earlier period. (*Past* is not a verb.) "During the *past* minute, six smoky trucks have gone *past* the joggers."

▶ Write *passed* or *past:*

Tony _____ the tavern. (Here *Tony* is the subject of a missing verb, and the verb ends in *ed*.)

Tony walked _____ the tavern. (Here *Tony* is the subject of the verb *walked,* and the missing word is not a verb.)

In the dim _____ Tom wanted to be a barber. He took a licensing test and _____ by a hair.

The bullet screamed _____ my ear, and I heard it twice; first, when it _____ me, and then when I _____ it.

At half-_____ ten Mary bid six spades, and I _____.

---

5. **principal:** main; head of a school; chief actor or doer; a capital sum. " 'Spend the interest and save the *principal*'—that was the *principal* lesson that the school *principal* taught us."
6. **principle:** a rule of action or conduct. (Note that *principle* and *rule* both end in *le*.) "Isaac Newton worked out the *principle* of gravitation."

151

principle	▶ The professor explained a basic *prin*_____ of thermodynamics. (Refers to a ru*le*.)
principal	▶ The *prin*_____ cause of divorce is marriage.
principal principal	▶ The high school _____ played the _____ role in the faculty play.
principle principal	▶ Jane Pittman was a woman of lofty _____, and that is a _____ reason we honor her.
principal principle	▶ My _____ objection is to speech courses that stress the questionable _____, "Say it with sincerity, whether you believe it or not."

Be sure to include the final *d*, as shown, in the following words:

7. **prejudiced:** biased. "Tom was *prejudiced*" (not "was prejudice").
8. **supposed to:** "We are *supposed* to study" (not "suppose to").
9. **used to:** "I *used* to be a dog-sitter" (not "use to").

▶ Write the missing word in full:

used	Joe u_____ to pass the crematorium and ask, "What's cooking?"
supposed	Students are s_____ to write compositions weekly, not weakly.
used prejudiced	I u_____ to be *pr*_____ against pigeons —but they're delicious.
supposed used	You are not s_____ to loaf. Even God u_____ to put in a six-day week.
prejudiced supposed	Smart shoppers are *pre*_____ against chemical preservatives. We are s_____ to read food labels carefully.
used prejudiced	Whenever the Miltown Misfits lost a baseball game, their coach u_____ to say that the umpires were p_____.

152

10. **really:** actually; genuinely; in fact. (Avoid overuse of *really* in your compositions. The word can usually be deleted without loss.)

▸ Cross out every useless *really* in the following passage:

I was really anxious for school to begin this fall. I have always really enjoyed studying and meeting people, and I really believe that the opportunities here at Knockwurst College are really outstanding.

▸ In the foregoing passage the word *really* can be cut _____ times without loss; in fact, these deletions have resulted in a more _____ [wordy / mature] style.

four
mature

▸ Choose the fresher, more effective modifier:

Interpretations of Beckett's play (a) differ significantly, (b) really differ. ( ) Yet critics do agree that the play is _____ [really / strangely] provocative.

(a)
strangely

Really is _____ [really / perfectly] grammatical, but constant repetition of the word is _____ [really / certainly] inadvisable.

perfectly
certainly

Quiz

Circle the choice which results in the more acceptable sentence.

1. letters
2. sparkling
3. passed
4. past
5. principle
6. principal
7. prejudiced
8. supposed
9. used
10. remarkably generous

1. Fay wrote the majority of the (letters / correspondence).
2. Patrick had a kindly face and (nice / sparkling) eyes.
3. The years (passed / past) like falling leaves.
4. History is a thing of the (passed / past).
5. Live by the (principal / principle) of the golden rule.
6. The (principal / principle) influence on a man is a woman.
7. All human beings are (prejudice / prejudiced) in some way.
8. An actor is (suppose / supposed) to be a jack of all traits.
9. Bread (use / used) to be ten cents a loaf.
10. His sponsor was (remarkably generous / really nice) to him.

11. **reason:** cause; purpose. (Avoid "the reason is because," since that phrase says in effect: "the cause is because.")

BAD: The reason Sam shot the dog is because it had rabies.
ACCEPTABLE: The reason Sam shot the dog is that it had rabies.
ACCEPTABLE: Sam shot the dog because it had rabies.

▶ A possible reason for Shaw's longevity is _____ [that / because] he was a vegetarian.

that

▶ The main reason my great-grandmother was late for her tennis lesson today is _____ [that / because] she had a miscarriage.

that

▶ Choose the better sentence:

a. Sue smiles because she loves her job.
b. The reason Sue smiles is because she loves her job.
( )

(a)

a. The reason Max got a ticket is because he hit a police car.
b. Max got a ticket because he hit a police car.
( )

(b)

---

12. **regardless:** heedless; in spite of; anyway. (Do not use the nonstandard term *irregardless*.)

▶ Use correct English _____ [regardless / irregardless] of how it may shock a few illiterate friends.

regardless

▶ Americans must have equal opportunities, _____*less* of sex, color, or creed.

regardless

▶ In the word *regardless,* the suffix *less* expresses a negative; therefore, the addition of the negative prefix *ir*—creating a double negative—is (a) logical, (b) illogical. ( )

(b)

▶ Adding the prefix *ir* to the word *regardless* would create _____ [a correct / an incorrect] expression, _____*less* of who used it.

an incorrect
regardless

154

13. **so:** therefore; as indicated. (Avoid the overuse of *so* to mean "very," in formal writing.)

▶ The view of the sea from Malibu is _____ [so / extremely] beautiful.

extremely

▶ After a hard day of banquets and toasts, the mayor is usually _____ [so / very] tired.

very

▶ "Americans have admired their war generals; *so* we have elected several to the presidency." Here the word *so* is used in its acceptable formal sense to mean (a) "very," (b) "therefore." ( )

(b)

---

14. **suspicion:** distrust; doubt. (Avoid using the noun *suspicion* when the verb *suspect* is called for.)

▶ When the bank teller saw her customer holding a gun, she _____ [suspected / suspicioned] that he would request instant cash.

suspected

▶ The young couple often flung dishes and pounded heads against the wall, and we _____ [suspicioned / suspected] that they were solving some minor marital problems.

suspected

▶ In a detective story the butler was usually the first person to be (a) suspected, (b) suspicioned. (.)

(a)

▶ *Suspected* is a verb; *suspicion* is (a) a noun, (b) a verb. ( )

(a)

---

15. **than** (used in comparisons). "Fido bites harder *than* Rover."
16. **then:** at that time. "We were younger and thinner *then*."

▶ Now and _____ Junior loses a tooth.

then

▶ The wrestler's nose was flatter _____ a bicycle seat.

than

▶ Our government operated on a smaller budget _____ _____ now.

then
than

155

then than	▶ The shepherd saw her sweater and _____ realized that the wool looked better on the girl _____ on the sheep.
than *then*	▶ The word _____ suggests a comparison; the word _____ suggests time.

17. **themselves** (reflexive and emphatic form of *them*). (Do not use nonstandard variations such as *theirselves* or *themselfs*.)

themselves	▶ Teachers don't fail students; students fail _____ [themselves / theirselves].
themselves	▶ Talented women must move th_____ from the kitchen to the public arena.
themselves	▶ The salesmen th_____ had more crust than a pie factory.
themselves themselves	▶ The ministers th_____ tell us that God helps those that help th_____.

18. **their** (possessive). "*Their* dog has fleas."
19. **there**: in that place. "Sit *there* and wait."
20. **they're**: they are. "*They're* sleeping."

their they're	▶ The dentist will have to straighten _____ teeth, because _____ not going to straighten themselves.
there their	▶ Soon the three wise men arrived _____ on _____ camels.
there their their	▶ The weather was so hot _____ that the boys wanted to take off _____ skin and sit around in _____ bones.
they're their	▶ The old couple say _____ happy in _____ merry Oldsmobile.

156

there
they're
their

▸ The incubator babies are over _____—and some day on Mother's Day _____ going to be sending _____ flowers to an oven.

Quiz

Circle the choice which results in the more acceptable sentence.

1. that
2. regardless
3. extremely
4. suspected
5. there
6. themselves
7. then
8. their
9. than
10. they're

1. The reason Tom speeds is (because / that) he wants attention.
2. Buy the bagels (regardless / irregardless) of price.
3. The leading man was (extremely / so) handsome.
4. The swimmer (suspicioned / suspected) that the sharks were looking for lunch.
5. All my friends were (their / there / they're)—both of them.
6. Writers must learn to criticize (theirselves / themselves).
7. Let us go (than / then), you and I.
8. After a meal my friends picked (their / there / they're) teeth.
9. Linda's diamond looks bigger (than / then) a tennis ball.
10. The parents admit that (their / there / they're) to blame.

21. **this.** (Refers to something nearby or just mentioned. Avoid the vague use of *this*, particularly in reference to something not yet mentioned.)

▸ Write *Right* or *Wrong*, depending on whether the word *this* is used correctly. Assume that each sentence is the opening line of a theme.

Wrong

_____ This poem is about this Viking who elopes with this princess.

Right

_____ Longfellow's "A Skeleton in Armor" is about a Viking who elopes with a princess; the poem describes the fate of this pair in America.

Wrong

_____ I still remember this boy in our schoolyard who threw this big snowball at me.

Right

_____ To this day I remember the boy in our schoolyard who threw a big snowball at me.

Wrong	_____ This friend of mine has this hobby of collecting Avon bottles.

22. **to:** toward; until; also used before a verb, as in "*to* fly." "Gus threatened *to* sing *to* us."
23. **too:** more than enough; also. "He's *too* skinny, *too*."

too to	▶ The bronco was _____ nervous for me _____ ride it.
to to	▶ The guests began _____ stagger _____ the bathroom.
too to too	▶ Edna was only _____ happy _____ be given tuba lessons, and I was, _____.
to too to	▶ Soldiers have _____ get up much early—no wonder they are ready _____ kill.
to too too	▶ Hazel said _____ the salesman: "You are asking _____ much for a car that has been hit by a truck and by lightning, _____."

24. **try:** to attempt. (Write "try to" instead of the informal "try and.")

to	▶ I will try _____ [to / and] analyze how James Fenimore Cooper portrays women in his novels.
to	▶ The marriage vows should suggest that a couple try _____ [to / and] live within their income.
(b)	▶ Careful writers prefer the phrase (a) "try and," (b) "try to." ( )
to to	▶ Gunther will try _____ [to / and] do the triple somersault, and tomorrow I will try _____ [to / and] visit him in the hospital.

25. **unique:** the only one of its kind; peerless. "Poe's 'Ulalume' is unique." (Avoid the somewhat illogical "more unique" and "most unique.")

unique
▸ The world has only one Taj Mahal; that beautiful building is u_____.

impossible
▸ Your right thumbprint is unique, the only one of its kind. It is, therefore, _____ [possible / impossible] for any other fingerprint to be more one-of-its-kind than that one.

exotic
▸ Sandra's Hawaiian muumuu is more _____ [unique / exotic] than her J. C. Penney dress.

rare
unique
▸ Only two copies of Franklin's original *Almanack* are known to exist. Each copy is extremely _____ [unique / rare], but it is not _____ [unique / rare].

unique
▸ Suppose you had the only 1807 dollar of its kind in the world; that coin would be _____.

26. **which.** (Reference to a thing previously mentioned. But use *who* or *that*, not *which*, when referring to a person.) "A man *who* saw me coming sold me this horse *which* just died."

who
▸ This is the little boy _____ [who / which] hit a home run through our window.

which
▸ Our cat is one creature _____ [who / which] never cries over spilt milk.

who
which
▸ The man _____ [who / which] lives in the apartment above us wears shoes _____ [who / which] are made of wood.

which
▸ Alvin owns a parrot _____ [who / which] doesn't talk but is a good listener.

who
▸ Boris is a barber _____ [who / which] will take a big load off your mind.

159

27. **who's:** who is. "Who's calling, please?"
28. **whose** (possessive). "Whose shoes are these?"

whose / who's
▶ Find out _____ car was smashed and _____ to blame. (Hint: Write *who's* only if "who is" would fit into the blank.)

whose / who's
▶ The aged alumni, _____ class reunion this is, are getting together to see _____ falling apart.

who's / whose
▶ Mr. Bigmouth wants to know _____ marrying _____ daughter.

who's
▶ A girl _____ fit as a fiddle should have a beau.

who's / whose
▶ "I'd like to catch the actor _____ careless," said Hamlet, "and _____ spear keeps jabbing me in the third act."

whose / *who's*
▶ The word _____ is possessive; the word _____ means "who is."

29. **your** (possessive). "Put on *your* gas mask."
30. **you're:** you are. "*You're* beautiful."

your / you're
▶ Hold _____ horses—_____ traveling too fast.

you're
▶ Until April 15 _____ deep in the heart of taxes.

your / you're
▶ Wilhelm, _____ poems are so sweet that _____ giving us diabetes.

you're / your
▶ When _____ famous, the public takes an interest in _____ sins.

You're / your
▶ Y_____ old only if you feel that _____ future is behind you.

160

you're
your
your

▶ "Listen," said Barnum to Tom Thumb, "_____ so little that you have to stand on _____ chair to brush _____ teeth."

Quiz

Circle the choice which results in the more acceptable sentence.

1. your
2. rare
3. Whose
4. too
5. to
6. who's
7. to
8. an
9. you're
10. which

1. This is (your / you're) life.
2. A snowstorm in Pasadena is extremely (rare / unique).
3. (Whose / Who's) cat has been eating my tropical fish?
4. Mr. Brunk jumped when the fire became (to / too) hot.
5. Try (to / and) impress your teacher by reading extra books.
6. Joe sang, "I wonder (whose / who's) kissing her now."
7. The batter swung like a fence and fell (to / too) the ground.
8. Ten years ago I had (an / this) unforgettable accident.
9. Read constantly, or (your / you're) wasting time in college.
10. The donkey is a small beast (who / which) carries a big load.

Review Test

Write *Correct*, if the italicized word is used correctly. Otherwise, write the word that should be used.

_____ 1. My boss never hits a fellow *which* is down—he kicks him.

_____ 2. Kate's companion was harder to get rid of *than* malaria.

_____ 3. The reason our coach succeeds is *that* he pays high salaries.

_____ 4. Smedley believes in the *principle,* "Love thy neighbor."

_____ 5. Officials should keep *their* campaign promises.

_____ 6. David started at the bottom and stayed *there*.

_____ 7. Stay out until midnight and your mother *suspicions* the worst.

_____ 8. The doctor advised Ned to try *and* give up spicy foods.

_____ 9. Big Rufus grunted and *passed* the turnips to his sister.

_____ 10. People on juries should not be *prejudice*.

_____ 11. Frank *use* to have a million-dollar figure, but inflation set in.

_____ 12. The blood bank found *too* much alcohol in his blood.

_____ 13. If *they're* your friends, they will respect your privacy.

_____ 14. Do what is right, *irregardless* of public opinion.

_____ 15. Find out *whose* toupee fell from the balcony.

Write the better choice.

16. Take off _____ [your / you're] shoes at the temple door.

17. Malone delivered _____ [a nice / an impressive] speech.

18. The hippies disguised _____ [themselves / theirselves] to look like Republicans.

19. Lack of money is the _____ [principle / principal] root of evil.

20. For some incredible reason a farmer's wife was _____ [supposed / suppose] to slave in the kitchen.

21. You are happiest when _____ [your / you're] in love.

22. Rossini spent _____ [most / a majority] of the winter in an asylum.

23. My job is perfect for someone _____ [who's / whose] able to work thirty hours a day.

24. Betty practiced law for the _____ [past / passed] few years.

25. The trained seal was _____ [highly / so] intelligent.

Key to Review Test

Check your test answers by the following key. Deduct 4% per error from a possible 100%.

1. who	6. Correct	11. used	16. your	21. you're
2. Correct	7. suspects	12. Correct	17. an impressive	22. most
3. Correct	8. to	13. Correct	18. themselves	23. who's
4. Correct	9. Correct	14. regardless	19. principal	24. past
5. Correct	10. prejudiced	15. Correct	20. supposed	25. highly

Score: _____%

Supplementary List

Exercise 9

WORDS OFTEN CONFUSED. Use each word correctly in a sentence. When in doubt about the meaning of a word, consult your desk dictionary.

1. adapt, adopt
2. addition, edition
3. advice, advise
4. aisle, isle
5. alley, ally
6. allowed, aloud
7. allusion, illusion
8. altar, alter
9. anecdote, antidote
10. angel, angle
11. ascent, assent
12. assistance, assistants
13. bare, bear
14. base, bass
15. beach, beech
16. beat, beet
17. berth, birth
18. beside, besides
19. board, bored
20. boarder, border
21. brake, break
22. breath, breathe
23. bridal, bridle
24. capital, capitol
25. censor, censure
26. cereal, serial
27. choose, chose
28. chord, cord
29. cite, sight, site
30. close, clothes, cloths
31. coarse, course
32. complement, compliment
33. consul, council, counsel
34. costume, custom
35. dairy, diary
36. dammed, damned
37. dear, deer
38. deceased, diseased
39. decent, descent
40. desert, dessert
41. device, devise
42. dual, duel
43. dyeing, dying
44. emigrate, immigrate
45. eminent, imminent
46. envelop, envelope
47. fair, fare
48. flea, flee
49. flour, flower
50. foreword, forward
51. forth, fourth
52. foul, fowl
53. heal, heel
54. hear, here
55. hoarse, horse
56. hole, whole
57. holey, holy
58. incidence, incidents
59. instance, instants
60. knew, new
61. later, latter
62. lead, led
63. lessen, lesson
64. liable, libel
65. mantel, mantle
66. marital, martial
67. meat, meet
68. medal, metal
69. miner, minor
70. moral, morale
71. naval, navel
72. pail, pale
73. peace, piece
74. peak, peek
75. pedal, petal
76. personal, personnel
77. picture, pitcher
78. plain, plane
79. pole, poll
80. pore, pour
81. presence, presents
82. profit, prophet

83. prophecy, prophesy
84. quiet, quite
85. respectfully, respectively
86. ring, wring
87. road, rode
88. role, roll
89. sail, sale
90. shone, shown
91. shudder, shutter
92. stake, steak
93. stationary, stationery
94. steal, steel
95. summary, summery
96. threw, through
97. vain, vein
98. waist, waste
99. weak, week
100. weather, whether

10
Name Derivatives

1. aphrodisiac
2. boycott
3. chauvinism
4. cynic
5. Darwinism
6. Frankenstein monster
7. herculean
8. jabberwocky
9. laconic
10. lilliputian
11. machiavellian
12. maudlin
13. maverick
14. mentor
15. nimrod
16. odyssey
17. Pyrrhic victory
18. quixotic
19. robot
20. solon
21. spoonerism
22. stentorian
23. tantalize
24. utopian
25. vandal

The names of people and places are imbedded in our language. The commonest forms are simple adjectives like "Shakespearean" or "Siamese." But when someone like Louis Pasteur or John L. McAdam discovers or develops something of wide use, we get words like "pasteurize" or "macadamize." From literature and mythology come a horde of words such as "cereal" (from "Ceres," goddess of the grain), "jovial" (from "Jove"), and "yahoo" (from Jonathan Swift's *Gulliver's Travels*, 1726).

The name words in Chapter 10 are a cultural heritage and are sure to turn up in your reading. Learning their source will make it easier to remember their meaning. Four supplementary exercises on name words are included at the end of the chapter.

Exercises

COVER THIS STRIP

1. **aphrodisiac** (af′rə-diz′i-ak): arousing sexual desire. An *aphrodisiac* is any drug, food, or agent which excites lust; it is named after *Aphrodite*, the goddess of love.
2. **boycott:** to refuse to deal or associate with, in order to coerce or punish. Captain Charles *Boycott* was shunned by the Irish Land League in 1880 for refusing to reduce land rents.

▸ An *aphrodisiac* increases one's (a) beauty, (b) sexual desire. ( )

(b)

▸ Any music, perfume, or food which increases sexual desire is an _____.

aphrodisiac

▸ When Aldous Huxley refers to a certain juice as "tart and *aphrodisiac*," he means the drink will arouse (a) hostility, (b) lustfulness. ( )

(b)

▸ To *boycott* is to _____ [trade with / shun].

shun

▸ Those who *boycott* a restaurant (a) avoid the place, (b) hold luncheon meetings there. ( )

(a)

▸ Grandfather claims that most so-called adult movies merely act as an aph_____; obviously he should stay away from such motion pictures—that is, he should _____ them.

aphrodisiac
boycott

3. **chauvinism** (shō′vin-iz′əm): fanatical or blind patriotism. Nicolas *Chauvin* became ridiculous with bragging about his superloyalty to Napoleon and France.
4. **cynic** (sin′ik): one who has a sneering disbelief in human sincerity and goodness. The *Cynics* were ancient Greek philosophers who maintained that virtue was the goal of life and who in result became very critical of other people and their motives.

chauvinism	▸ The Nazi conviction that Hitler and Germany could do no wrong was c_____.
(a)	▸ The patriotism of a *chauvinist* is (a) extreme, (b) moderate. ( )
chauvinism (b)	▸ The intense national spirit known as _____ is manifested in most countries by (a) impartial criticism of national policy, (b) much flag-waving. ( )
(a)	▸ A *cynical* person is (a) suspicious and sarcastic, (b) agreeable and innocent. ( )
(b)	▸ The *Cynic* Diogenes, who kept looking for an honest man, obviously thought that most people are (a) virtuous, (b) lacking in virtue. ( )
cynic chauvinism chauvinism	▸ One who sneers at our motives is a c_____, and such a person would have a low opinion of fanatical patriotism, known as national c_____, or, possibly, of the delusion that males are the superior sex, known as male _____.

5. **Darwinism:** the theory of evolution that plants and animals transmit slight hereditary variations to future generations and that those forms survive and develop that are best suited to their environment. *Darwinism* involves, in brief, the concepts of natural selection and of the survival of the fittest.

Darwinism (a)	▸ According to the theory of evolution, known as D_____, species of plants and animals (a) have been changing and developing from earlier species, (b) have always been as they are now. ( )
(b)	▸ Nature permits a species to survive, according to *Darwinism*, if that species (a) has moral goodness, (b) adapts itself to its environment. ( )
Darwinism (b)	▸ Those species that have the necessary claws or fins or teeth, according to _____ism, will (a) be punished, (b) survive. ( )

168

Quiz

Write the letter that indicates the best definition.

( ) 1. aphrodisiac   a. fanatical patriotism
( ) 2. boycott   b. a suspicious, sarcastic pessimist
( ) 3. chauvinism   c. refuse to deal with
( ) 4. cynic   d. tending to excite lust
( ) 5. Darwinism   e. evolution of species through the survival of the fittest

---

6. **Frankenstein monster** (frank′ən-stīn′): anything that becomes a danger to its creator. In Mary Shelley's novel *Frankenstein* (1818) a natural philosopher named *Frankenstein* creates a repulsive monster which gets out of control and murders him.

▶ A *Frankenstein monster* becomes (a) a threat to its inventor, (b) a faithful, useful servant. ( )

▶ The monster gets out of control and kills F_____; one must remember that *Frankenstein* is the name of (a) the treacherous monster, (b) the scientist who created the monster. ( )

▶ A _____ monster among us today, threatening its creators, is (a) the thermonuclear bomb, (b) the bicycle. ( )

---

7. **herculean** (hur′kyoo-lē′ən): very powerful and courageous. *Hercules*, son of Zeus, performed twelve tremendous labors which Hera imposed on him.

▶ A *herculean* task demands (a) power and courage, (b) wit and grace. ( )

▶ The job of digging the Panama Canal was h_____; another tremendous, h_____ job was construction of (a) Hoover Dam, (b) Mabel's new earrings. ( )

▶ Like all *herculean* heroes, steel-drivin' John Henry was courageous and (a) highly educated, (b) powerful. ( )

Answers (margin):
1. (d)
2. (c)
3. (a)
4. (b)
5. (e)

(a)

Frankenstein
(b)

Frankenstein
(a)

(a)

herculean
herculean
(a)

(b)

169

8. **jabberwocky:** nonsensical talk. "Jabberwocky" is an amusing nonsense poem in Lewis Carroll's *Through the Looking Glass* (1872).

jabberwocky
(b)

▸ Nonsense talk is called j_____. To understand *jabberwocky* is (a) easy, (b) almost impossible. ( )

(b)

▸ Which of the following lines is *jabberwocky*?—(a) "He did not wear his scarlet coat," (b) " 'Twas brillig, and the slithy toves. . . ." ( )

jabberwocky
(a)

▸ To accuse a congressman of *jab_____* is to imply that his talk is (a) meaningless, (b) unpatriotic. ( )

---

9. **laconic** (lə-kon′ik): brief; pithy. The *Laconians* were thrifty with words; they replied to an enemy ultimatum with one word: "If."
10. **lilliputian** (lil′ə-pū′shən): very small; a tiny person. On the island of *Lilliput,* described in Swift's *Gulliver's Travels* (1726), the men and women are six inches tall.

laconic

▸ Most classified ads are _____ [laconic / prolix].

brief

▸ A *laconic* answer is _____ [verbose / brief].

lilliputian
(a)

▸ To say that a presidential candidate is "*lil_____* in talents" is (a) insulting to him, (b) flattering to him. ( )

tiny

▸ A *lilliputian* house is _____ [huge / tiny].

laconic

▸ Political candidates tend to be wordy rather than _____.

Lilliputians

▸ Gulliver meets the Brobdingnagians, a race of highly intelligent giants who are quite the opposite of the tiny _____s.

Quiz

Write the letter that indicates the best definition.

1. (d)
2. (e)
3. (b)
4. (a)
5. (c)

( ) 1. Frankenstein monster   a. brief; concise
( ) 2. herculean   b. gibberish; doubletalk
( ) 3. jabberwocky   c. tiny
( ) 4. laconic   d. a threat to its own inventor
( ) 5. lilliputian   e. powerful; requiring great strength and bravery

---

11. **machiavellian** (mak'i-ə-vel'i-ən): crafty and deceitful in political strategy. In *The Prince* (1513) Niccolo *Machiavelli,* a Florentine diplomat, describes ways to grasp and maintain political power.

12. **maudlin** (môd'lin): tearfully emotional or sentimental; foolishly drunk. Mary *Magdalen* was depicted by medieval painters with her eyes red and swollen from weeping.

▶ Sentimental people often revel in their tearful memories and become m_____.

maudlin

▶ One who is *maudlin* is emotionally _____ [stable / unstable] and perhaps inclined to _____ [dissect / weep over] a dead bird.

unstable
weep over

▶ Bribes, double dealing, and false promises are common to m_____ diplomacy.

machiavellian

▶ The *machiavellian* politician is hard-boiled and _____ [honorable / unscrupulous] with no time for tearful loyalties and _____ sentiment.

unscrupulous
maudlin

▶ The woman who weeps softly into her beer is _____.

maudlin

▶ The diplomat who thinks "Anything goes" is _____.

machiavellian

13. **maverick** (mav′ẽr-ik): a person of unorthodox ideas who tends to act independently of parties and factions. Samuel *Maverick* (circa 1850), a Texas rancher, would not brand his calves and they were called *mavericks*.

maverick

▸ An independent-minded congressman who can't be counted on to vote with his party is sometimes called a _____.

(b)

▸ A *maverick* is (a) a conformist, (b) a nonconformist. ( )

maverick

▸ Henry David Thoreau, who defied his government by refusing to pay his poll tax, was a m_____.

defend
maverick

▸ Ralph Waldo Emerson believed in self-reliance and genuine individualism, and so his essays tend to _____ [defend / attack] a man's right to be a m_____.

---

14. **mentor** (men′tər): a wise and loyal adviser; a trusted teacher. In Greek legend, *Mentor* gives wise counsel to Odysseus and his son Telemachus.

mentor

▸ A head football coach is sometimes referred to as a _____ [monitor / mentor].

counselor

▸ A *mentor* is a trusted _____ [wife / counselor].

mentor
(a)

▸ You might refer to your English professor as your m_____. After all, *Mentor* was Telemachus' (a) wise teacher, (b) mortal enemy. ( )

---

15. **nimrod:** a hunter. *Nimrod,* the grandson of Ham, is described as a mighty hunter in *Genesis,* 10:8.

(a)

▸ A store for *nimrods* sells (a) shotguns, (b) women's purses. ( )

Nimrod
hunter

▸ The Bible mentions N_____ who was a mighty _____ [drinker / hunter].

172

nimrods

▶ Our western elk have been decimated by _____ [nimrods / hotrods].

Quiz

Write the letter that indicates the best definition.

1. (b)
2. (a)
3. (e)
4. (c)
5. (d)

( ) 1. machiavellian   a. weakly or tearfully emotional
( ) 2. maudlin   b. politically crafty; unscrupulous
( ) 3. maverick   c. a counselor
( ) 4. mentor   d. a hunter
( ) 5. nimrod   e. a nonconformist

16. **odyssey** (od′ə-si): a long eventful journey. Homer's *Odyssey* describes ten adventurous years of wandering by *Odysseus* on his homeward voyage after the fall of Troy.

odyssey

▶ In Steinbeck's *The Grapes of Wrath* (1939) the Joads make an adventurous o_____ from Oklahoma to California.

odyssey (b)

▶ A long journey, such as was made by Lewis and Clark, is called an o_____ if it is (a) quick and direct, (b) wandering and with unexpected delays. ( )

odyssey (a)

▶ Colorful wanderings such as those of Odysseus are known as an _____—and you would probably use the word *odyssey* to describe your (a) two-year trip across Asia by donkey, (b) overnight flight to Chicago. ( )

17. **Pyrrhic victory** (pir′ik): a too costly victory. *Pyrrhos* defeated the Romans at Asculum, 279 B.C., but lost so many men that he exclaimed, "One more such victory and we are undone!"

Pyrrhic (b)

▶ A *Pyr*_____ victory is (a) an overwhelming success, (b) extremely expensive. ( )

Pyrrhic

▶ A baseball team which wins a practice game but loses its shortstop and its star pitcher in a bone-breaking collision has won a _____ *victory*.

173

victory hollow	▶ A nation which drains its resources to win a small military objective has won a *Pyrrhic* _____, that is, a rather _____ [wonderful / hollow] triumph.

18. **quixotic** (kwik-sot′ik): idealistic but ridiculously impractical. Don *Quixote*, the hero of a novel by Cervantes (1615), is a romantic visionary, a tilter at windmills, but one of God's fools.

quixotic (b)	▶ Idealists like Don Quixote are *qu*_____; they tend to be (a) level-headed and conventional, (b) impulsive and romantic. ( )
quixotic (a)	▶ Critics condemned Woodrow Wilson's plan for a League of Nations as *qu*_____, that is, (a) visionary, (b) cynical. ( )
quixotic impractical	▶ The American Transcendentalists were full of visionary and _____ schemes, such as the Brook Farm experiment, a truly _____ [practical / impractical] undertaking.

19. **robot** (rō′bət): a man-like machine or a machine-like man. *R.U.R., Rossum's Universal Robots* (1923), a satiric play by Karel Kapek, introduced the word *robot* into our language.
20. **solon** (sō′lən): a wise lawmaker. *Solon* is referred to in Plato's "The Symposium" as "the revered father of Athenian Laws."

solons	▶ Legislators are often called *s*_____.
robots	▶ Automatons are *r*_____.
Congress factories	▶ Normally one might expect to see *solons* in _____ [factories / Congress] and *robots* in _____ [factories / Congress].
robot	▶ A person who must perform the same simple mechanical operation day after day becomes a kind of _____.
(b)	▶ *Robots* have (a) passions and free will, (b) only mechanical reactions. ( )

solons

▸ Our laws are formulated by _____.

▸ The word *solon* has traditionally suggested a _____
wise
[wise / feather-headed] lawmaker.

Quiz

Write the letter that indicates the best definition.

1. (d)   ( ) 1. odyssey   a. a wise lawmaker
2. (b)   ( ) 2. Pyrrhic victory   b. a costly triumph
3. (c)   ( ) 3. quixotic   c. visionary; impractical
4. (e)   ( ) 4. robot   d. a wandering journey
5. (a)   ( ) 5. solon   e. an automaton

21. **spoonerism:** an accidental transposition of sounds in adjacent words. The Rev. W. A. *Spooner* of New College, Oxford, used to make comic blunders like "our queer old dean" for "our dear old queen."

▸ *Spoonerisms* like "nosey little cook" for "cozy little nook" involve
(a)
(a) transposed sounds, (b) gross exaggerations. ( )

spoonerism
▸ "It is kistumary to cuss the bride" is a s_____.

spoonerism
▸ Another _____ism is "half-warmed fish" for (a) "half-
(a)
formed wish," (b) "half-hearted kiss." ( )

▸ The phrase "tons of soil" is a *spoonerism* for "sons of toil," and
spoonerism
"well boiled icicle" is a _____ for "well _____
oiled bicycle
_____."

22. **stentorian:** extremely loud. *Stentor* is described by Homer in *The Iliad* as a Greek herald with the voice of fifty men.

▸ Challenging the Trojans in the distance required a _____
stentorian
voice.

(b)
▸ A *stentorian* voice is like (a) a whisper, (b) a bellow. ( )

175

stentorian
(a)

▶ Of course, st_____ tones are quite acceptable in (a) a football stadium, (b) a college library. ( )

was not

▶ The Greek herald named Stentor _____ [was / was not] silent as a sphinx.

---

23. **tantalize:** to tease and torment by withholding what is offered. *Tantalus* was tormented in Hades by water and fruit that he could never quite reach.

smell

▶ A hungry cat is *tantalized* when it is allowed to _____ [eat / smell] a roast chicken.

tantalize
(b)

▶ We usually tease, or t_____, by (a) giving gifts, (b) withholding satisfactions. ( )

tantalized
(b)

▶ A famished beggar is _____zed as he walks (a) through a forest, (b) past a bakery. ( )

---

24. **utopian** (ū-tō′pi-ən): impossibly ideal, especially in social organization. Sir Thomas More's *Utopia* (1516) describes a flawless government and society—imaginary, of course.

utopian

▶ A nation without wars, without crime, without poverty? That would be ut_____.

utopian
(b)

▶ Dreamers envision a _____ social order in which everything will be (a) lousy, (b) practically perfect. ( )

utopian
(a)

▶ Edward Bellamy's *Looking Backward* (1887) describes a ut_____ society of the year 2000, wherein conditions will presumably be vastly (a) improved, (b) worse. ( )

(b)

▶ Ivor Brown speaks of H. G. Wells' "charting of Utopias," meaning that Wells explored (a) African jungles, (b) plans for ideal societies. ( )

---

25. **vandal:** a person who willfully or ignorantly mars or destroys property, especially what is beautiful or valuable. The *Vandals* were a Germanic people who ravaged Gaul and Spain and, under Genseric, in A.D. 455 sacked Rome.

176

vandals
(b)

▸ Window smashers and tire slashers are v_____; in short, they are public (a) benefactors, (b) menaces. ( )

vandal

▸ Whoever painted those vulgar words all over our elementary school is a v_____, and a poor speller, too.

vandal
(b)

▸ A beauty-defacing rascal, or _____, might be found (a) drawing a famous ruin, (b) ruining a famous drawing. ( )

vandal

▸ Were Venus de Milo's arms broken off by a _____, or did she chew her fingernails too much?

Quiz

Write the letter that indicates the best definition.

1. (e)
2. (d)
3. (a)
4. (c)
5. (b)

( ) 1. spoonerism   a. to tease and torment
( ) 2. stentorian   b. a destroyer of property
( ) 3. tantalize   c. ideal; existing only in theory
( ) 4. utopian   d. loud as a trumpet
( ) 5. vandal   e. turned-around syllables

Review Test

Supply the missing word in each sentence. The first letter of each answer is given.

1. A voice of Homeric loudness is s_____.
2. A hunter is sometimes called a n_____.
3. A slip of the tongue involving transposed syllables is a s_____.
4. A general refusal to deal with somebody is a b_____.
5. Winning a contest at tremendous cost is a P_____ v_____.
6. To be tearfully, drunkenly sentimental is to be m_____.
7. A drug or other agent which excites lust is an a_____.
8. An automaton or mechanical man is a r_____.
9. One who maliciously defaces public property is a v_____.
10. A lawmaker is a s_____.
11. A device which becomes a threat to its own creator is a F_____ m_____.
12. Patriotism carried to a fanatical extreme is c_____.
13. A long wandering journey is an o_____.
14. A nonconformist acting independently of party is a m_____.
15. The concepts of natural selection and of the survival of the fittest are basic to D_____.

Write *True* or *False*.

_____ 16. A *Lilliputian* would probably be an effective basketball center.

_____ 17. A *herculean* task requires great strength and endurance.

_____ 18. *Jabberwocky* is clear, standard English.

_____ 19. A *mentor* is a wise counselor or teacher.

_____ 20. A *cynic* tends to distrust people's motives.

Write the letter that indicates the best completion.

( ) 21. A *utopian* plan is (a) economical, (b) practical, (c) democratic, (d) visionary.
( ) 22. A *machiavellian* leader is (a) unscrupulous, (b) honorable, (c) self-sacrificing, (d) naive.
( ) 23. A *laconic* comment is (a) flattering, (b) windy, (c) short, (d) amusing.
( ) 24. A *quixotic* undertaking is (a) expensive, (b) impractical, (c) popular, (d) dull.
( ) 25. To *tantalize* is (a) to inoculate, (b) to tickle, (c) to tease, (d) to eat.

Key to Review Test

Check your test answers by the following key. Deduct 4% per error from a possible 100%.

1. stentorian	6. maudlin	11. Frankenstein monster	16. False	21. (d)
2. mentor	7. aphrodisiac	12. chauvinism	17. True	22. (a)
3. spoonerism	8. robot	13. odyssey	18. False	23. (c)
4. boycott	9. vandal	14. maverick	19. True	24. (b)
5. Pyrrhic victory	10. solon	15. Darwinism	20. True	25. (c)

Score: _____%

Supplementary Lists

Exercise 10-A

1. **argosy** (är′gə-sē): a merchant ship or fleet of ships (from *Ragusa*, a Dalmatian port).
2. **Boswell:** a friend and biographer (from James *Boswell,* who wrote *The Life of Samuel Johnson,* 1791).
3. **behemoth** (bi-hē′məth): a huge animal (alluded to in *Job,* 40:15–24).
4. **derrick:** crane; hoist (from Derrick, a seventeenth-century London hangman).
5. **draconian** (drā-kō′nē-ən): harsh, cruel (from Draco, a Greek lawmaker).
6. **galvanize:** to startle; to excite; to electrify (from L. Galvani, an Italian physicist).
7. **hector:** to browbeat; to bully; to pester (from Hector, the Trojan hero of Homer's *Iliad*).
8. **jezebel** (jez′ə-bel′): a shameless, wicked woman (from the wife of King Ahab, in *II Kings,* 9:7, 30).

Quiz

Write the letter that indicates the best definition.

1. (e)
2. (c)
3. (h)
4. (d)
5. (g)
6. (b)
7. (a)
8. (f)

( ) 1. argosy — a. to bully; to annoy
( ) 2. Boswell — b. to electrify; to startle
( ) 3. behemoth — c. a biographer
( ) 4. derrick — d. a crane
( ) 5. draconian — e. a fleet of merchant ships
( ) 6. galvanize — f. a shameless woman
( ) 7. hector — g. cruel; inhumanly severe
( ) 8. jezebel — h. a hippopotamus-like animal

Exercise 10-B

1. **martinet** (mär′tə-net′): a very strict disciplinarian (from General Jean Martinet, a seventeenth century French drillmaster).
2. **masochism** (mas′ə-kiz′əm): the obtaining of pleasure, particularly sexual pleasure, from being hurt (from Leopold von Sacher-Masoch, an Austrian author).
3. **mecca:** a place attracting many people; a goal (from Mecca, a holy city of the Moslems).
4. **mesmerize:** to hypnotize (from Franz Mesmer, a German physician).
5. **panjandrum** (pan-jan′drəm): an exalted official (from a character invented by Samuel Foote, English dramatist).
6. **pharisaical** (far′i-sā′i-kəl): self-righteous; hypocritical (from the Pharisees in the New Testament).

7. **pickwickian:** benevolent, naive, and blundering (from Mr. Samuel Pickwick in Dickens' *Pickwick Papers,* 1836).
8. **Portia** (pôr'shə): a female lawyer (from the heroine of Shakespeare's *The Merchant of Venice,* 1596).

Quiz

Write the letter that indicates the best definition.

1. (f)	( ) 1. martinet	a. the goal of many travelers
2. (d)	( ) 2. masochism	b. an official of lofty importance
3. (a)	( ) 3. mecca	c. a lady lawyer
4. (e)	( ) 4. mesmerize	d. the enjoyment of being hurt
5. (b)	( ) 5. panjandrum	e. to hypnotize
6. (h)	( ) 6. pharisaical	f. a rigid disciplinarian
7. (g)	( ) 7. pickwickian	g. good-hearted, naive, muddled
8. (c)	( ) 8. Portia	h. self-righteous, censorious

Exercise 10-C

1. **protean** (prō'ti-ən): changeable; readily taking on different shapes (from Proteus in Greek mythology).
2. **rodomontade** (rod'ə-mon-tād'): bragging; blustering (from Rodomonte, a boastful king in Ariosto's *Orlando Furioso,* 1516).
3. **sadism** (sad'iz-əm): the obtaining of pleasure, particularly sexual pleasure, from hurting others (from the author Count de Sade, who describes brutal sexual aberrations).
4. **sardonic** (sär-don'ik): scornful; sneering; cynical (from a poisonous Sardinian plant causing laughter-like convulsions).
5. **serendipity** (ser'ən-dip'i-tē): a knack for making lucky discoveries by accident (from the story, "The Three Princes of Serendip," whose heroes made lucky finds).
6. **Shylock:** a relentless creditor (from the usurer in Shakespeare's *The Merchant of Venice,* 1597, who wants his pound of flesh).
7. **titian** (tish'ən): auburn; reddish yellow (from the artist Titian, who often painted women's hair this shade).
8. **yahoo** (yä'hoo): a crude or vicious person (from the brutish Yahoos in *Gulliver's Travels*).

Quiz

Write the letter that indicates the best definition.

1. (f)
2. (h)
3. (a)
4. (g)
5. (e)
6. (b)
7. (c)
8. (d)

( ) 1. protean — a. the enjoyment of inflicting pain
( ) 2. rodomontade — b. a hard-fisted creditor
( ) 3. sadism — c. reddish yellow
( ) 4. sardonic — d. a bestial person
( ) 5. serendipity — e. a knack for lucky finds
( ) 6. Shylock — f. changeable in form
( ) 7. titian — g. cynical; scornful
( ) 8. yahoo — h. boasting; blustering

Exercise 10-D

1. **Adonis** (ə-don′is): an extremely handsome young man (from Adonis, who was loved by Aphrodite but was killed by a wild boar).
2. **Amazon:** any tall, strong, or athletic woman (from the Amazon women who helped the Trojans fight the Greeks).
3. **Babbitt:** a smug, conventional, uncultured businessman (from George Babbitt, a character in a Sinclair Lewis novel).
4. **bacchanalia** (bak′ə-nā′li-ə): drunken parties; orgies (from Bacchus, god of wine).
5. **bedlam** (bed′ləm): a scene of noisy confusion (from Bethlehem, a lunatic asylum in London).
6. **gargantuan** (gär-gan′choo-ən): huge; gigantic (from Gargantua, the enormous prince in Rabelais' *Gargantua and Pantagruel*).
7. **micawberish**: ever optimistic and cheerful (from the Dickens character Micawber, who keeps saying, "Something will turn up").
8. **Spartan:** brave, hardy, stoical (from the Spartan soldiers who practiced austerity and self-discipline).

Quiz

Write the letter that indicates the best definition.

1. (c)
2. (f)
3. (g)
4. (d)
5. (a)
6. (e)
7. (h)
8. (b)

( ) 1. Adonis — a. mad, noisy disorder
( ) 2. Amazon — b. hardy; lacking luxury
( ) 3. Babbitt — c. a handsome male
( ) 4. bacchanalia — d. drunken orgies
( ) 5. bedlam — e. enormous; very large
( ) 6. gargantuan — f. a female warrior
( ) 7. micawberish — g. a middle-class conformist
( ) 8. Spartan — h. optimistic

PART TWO

11

Figures of Speech

alliteration, 3
allusion, 13
antithesis, 10
apostrophe, 7
hyperbole, 5

irony, 14
litotes, 6
metaphor, 2
metonymy, 8
onomatopoeia, 4

oxymoron, 9
pathetic fallacy, 12
personification, 11
simile, 1
symbol, 15

   Abraham Lincoln said that a man should preach "like a man fighting off a swarm of bees" (simile); that "we must save the good old ship of the Union on this voyage" (metaphor); that we must "bind up the nation's wounds" (personification). Figures of speech are a trademark of the imaginative writer. A random survey of William Shakespeare, Emily Dickinson, Herman Melville, or Jim Murray would reveal a galaxy of similes, metaphors, hyperboles, oxymorons. Your familiarity with such terms can help you in two ways: As an analyst of literary passages you can more ably identify and appreciate the stylistic devices used; as a creative writer you can gain sparkle and vigor by using a greater variety of figures of speech.

Exercises

COVER THIS STRIP

1. **simile** (sim'ə-lē): a figure of speech comparing two unlike things, usually with "like" or "as"; for example, "She has a figure like an hourglass—and not a minute of it wasted."
2. **metaphor** (met'ə-fôr'): a figure of speech in which one thing is said to be another thing, without "like" or "as," or in which a likeness is implied; for example, "All the world's a stage"; "My boss barked out his orders."

▸ After each example write *simile* or *metaphor:*

"Boston was a beehive"—_____.

metaphor   "Orville has a head like a granite block"—_____.

simile   "Teacher's heart is as big and soft as an overripe pumpkin"—

simile   _____.

metaphor   "My mother-in-law sailed into the room"—_____.

▸ An expressed comparison between unlike things, with "like" or

simile   "as," is a _____; an implied comparison is a _____.

metaphor

▸ Write *simile* or *metaphor:*

metaphor   "Mabel was a dynamo, but she got short-circuited"—_____.

simile   "He looks like a dishonest Abe Lincoln"—_____.

metaphor   "The Buick purred down the freeway"—_____.

3. **alliteration:** the repetition of an initial sound in words or accented syllables close together. *Alliteration* abounds in the big brutal battles of *Beowulf*.
4. **onomatopoeia** (on'ə-mat'ə-pē'ə): the use of words whose pronunciation suggests their meaning. *Onomatopoeic* words are common: *boom, hiss, murmur, zoom, moan, hum, chug, sizzle, cuckoo, glug*.

onomatopoeia   ▸ Using words that sound like what they mean is o_____.

alliteration   ▸ Using the same initial letter in neighboring words is a_____.

▶ Which line of poetry by Robert Herrick contains *alliteration*?— (a) "The liquefaction of her clothes," (b) "I sing of brooks, of blossoms, birds and bowers." (   )

(b)

▶ After each example write *alliteration* or *onomatopoeia:*
"The locomotive snorted and hissed—then went chug-ah!"— _____.

onomatopoeia

"What a tale of terror now their turbulency tells!"—_____.

alliteration

"That lazy, lovable lunatic"—_____.

alliteration

"He dived on his belly—plop, splash"—_____.

onomatopoeia

---

5. **hyperbole** (hī-pûr′bə-lē): a gross exaggeration for rhetorical effect; for example, "The new blonde typist made errors by the barrel, but nobody noticed."

6. **litotes** (lī′tə-tēz′): a figure of speech in which a point is made by a denying of its opposite; a kind of understatement; for example, "It's no small matter"; "Rockefeller was no pauper"; "The prisoner approached the gallows without enthusiasm."

▶ Denying the opposite of what you mean is _____.

litotes

▶ Gross exaggeration is _____.

hyperbole

▶ A *hyperbole* might say that the village boozer (a) drank several bottles of beer, (b) made the local brewery go on a twenty-four hour shift. (   )

(b)

▶ An example of *litotes* is (a) "The mackerel had a bad odor," (b) "The mackerel did not smell like Chanel No. 5." (   )

(b)

▶ After each example write *hyperbole* or *litotes:*
"The mosquitoes were rangy and enterprising, and they'd siphon a quart of blood before you noticed them"—_____.
"There's enough poetry on the boys' washroom walls to put Shakespeare out of business"—_____.

hyperbole
hyperbole

"Gangster Al Capone did not exactly win the Best Citizen award" —_____.

litotes

"Helen of Troy was no hag, you know"—_____.

litotes

1. (c)
2. (e)
3. (f)
4. (d)
5. (b)
6. (a)

Quiz

Write the letter that indicates the best example.

( ) 1. alliteration   a. a hairdo like an unmade bed
( ) 2. hyperbole   b. the *bar-r-room* of the trombones
( ) 3. litotes   c. lively lads and lasses
( ) 4. metaphor   d. Alice was sugar and cream.
( ) 5. onomatopoeia   e. Lulu has an army of suitors.
( ) 6. simile   f. Caruso was not a bad singer either.

7. **apostrophe** (ə-pos′trə-fē): addressing a personified object, or an absent person as though present; example from Francis Thompson: "O world invisible, we view thee."
8. **metonymy** (mi-ton′ə-mē): a figure of speech in which the name of a thing is used for something else associated with it; virtually synonymous with *synecdoche;* for example, "The sailor was warned to stay away from the skirts."

▸ In *apostrophe* the poet is emotionally involved with some absent person or some personified object and speaks directly _____ [to it / of it].

to it

metonymy

(a)

▸ "He was addicted to the bottle" is m_____ because "bottle" is associated with (a) liquor, (b) glassware. ( )

▸ After each example write *apostrophe* or *metonymy:*
   "Dinner is $2.95 a plate"—_____.
   "Melvin has read Tennessee Williams"—_____.
   Robert Burns: "O Scotia! my dear, my native soil!"—_____.
   "The White House announces . . ."—_____.

metonymy
metonymy
apostrophe
metonymy

(a)

▸ Which line involves *apostrophe?*—(a) William Wordsworth: "Milton! thou shouldst be living at this hour," (b) John Masefield: "Oh London Town's a fine town." ( )

9. **oxymoron** (ok′si-mōr′on): a combination of two apparently contradictory words; for example, "dazzling darkness," "devout atheism," "lively corpse."
10. **antithesis** (an-tith′i-sis): the strong contrast of expressions, clauses, sentences, or ideas within a balanced grammatical structure; for example, "Life is short; art is long," "Give me liberty or give me death."

oxymoron	▶ A seeming contradiction like "clever idiot" is an _____.
antithesis does	▶ "We must all hang together, or assuredly we shall all hang separately." This famous utterance by Franklin in 1776 illustrates *ant_____*, since it _____ [does / does not] present a contrast of ideas in a balanced pattern.
(b)	▶ Which ending results in *antithesis*?—"Johnny was in the church basement making taffy, and (a) wondering if Jimmy ever had so much fun," (b) Jimmy was in the theater balcony making love." ( )
oxymoron oxymorons	▶ "Militant pacifism" is an *ox_____*, and Sir Philip Sidney's reference to "living deaths, dear wounds, fair storms, and freezing fires" includes four *ox_____*.
noisy attractive	▶ An *oxymoron* might refer to a "_____ [strange / noisy] silence" or to an "_____ [attractive / unusual] repulsiveness."
antithesis	▶ A contrast of ideas expressed as a balanced sentence is known as *ant_____*.
(b)	▶ An example of *antithesis* is (a) "You do not have to cut off your fingers to write shorthand," (b) "A cat has its claws at the end of the paws; a comma has its pause at the end of the clause." ( )

---

11. **personification** (pər-son′ə-fə-kā′shən): the giving of human qualities to something that is not human; for example, "stern-faced Duty" and "the murmuring pines."
12. **pathetic fallacy** (fal′ə-sē): attributing human feelings to inanimate things: an aspect of personification. In *Modern Painters* (1856) John Ruskin objects to the *pathetic fallacy,* or falseness, in phrases like "the cruel crawling foam" or "weeping skies."

(b)	▶ *Personification,* like "the brow of the hill," gives human qualities to (a) people, (b) non-human things. ( )

fallacy
(a)

(a)

(a)

pathetic
(b)

▶ *Personification* is referred to as the *pathetic* _____ when trees or skies are not merely likened to humans but are even endowed with (a) human feelings, (b) divine qualities. ( )

▶ Which line involves *personification*?—(a) Samuel Coleridge: "The one red leaf, the last of its clan, / That dances as often as dance it can," (b) Alfred Tennyson: "Comrades, leave me here a little, while as yet 'tis early morn." ( )

▶ Which line involves *personification*?—(a) William Shakespeare: "Blow, winds, and crack your cheeks," (b) Christina Rossetti: "This Advent moon shines cold and clear." ( )

▶ The type of *personification* which attributes feelings to things, known as the _____ *fallacy,* is suggested by (a) "in the teeth of the wind," (b) "the wailing wind." ( )

Quiz

Write the letter that indicates the best example.

1. (d)
2. (b)
3. (c)
4. (a)
5. (f)
6. (e)

( ) 1. apostrophe   a. her bold shyness
( ) 2. antithesis   b. Man proposes; God disposes.
( ) 3. metonymy   c. The farmer hired three hands.
( ) 4. oxymoron   d. Here's to thee, oh Alma Mater!
( ) 5. pathetic fallacy   e. the eye of the storm
( ) 6. personification   f. the groaning branches of fruit (special type of personification)

13. **allusion** (ə-lōō′zhən): a passing reference to something; an indirect mention. Milton's poetry is peppered with classical *allusions,* that is, references to passages in world literature.

allusion

▶ Mentioning Achilles or Sancho Panza or Blake's "The Tiger" would be a literary al_____.

(a)

▶ A man makes a Biblical *allusion* if he refers to his wife as his (a) "rib," (b) "ball and chain." ( )

allusion

▶ "Everything that Tanya touches turns to gold"—here the writer has made a passing reference, or _____, to the story of King Midas.

allusion
(a)

▶ "Well, I'll be a monkey's cousin!"—this comment embodies an indirect reference, or _____, to (a) Darwinism, (b) Jeffersonian democracy. ( )

---

14. **irony** (i′rə-nē): saying the opposite of what is meant, by way of mockery: known as *verbal irony;* in general, the implying of a contrast between an obvious attitude or condition and a possible one; see also *irony of fate* (Chapter 15, frame 16), *Socratic irony* (Chapter 12, frame 24), *dramatic irony* (Chapter 16, frame 12). The modern poet tends to avoid the simple expression of love or indignation, preferring the complex, self-critical attitude of *ironic* statement.

(b)

▶ When peace-loving Stephen Crane says, "War is kind," he is probably (a) serious, (b) ironic. ( )

irony
(b)

▶ "That's right," says your father, "have a good time, forget your homework, become a bum!" His advice is an example of i_____ because he really means (a) exactly what he says, (b) the opposite of what he says. ( )

irony

▶ In "A Modest Proposal" (1729) Jonathan Swift urges with tongue in cheek, or with i_____, that Englishmen should eat Irish infants.

(a)

▶ Verbal *irony* is a form of (a) sarcasm, (b) eulogy. ( )

(b)

▶ The baseball coach uses *irony* when he says, "You struck out five times—(a) such rotten luck!" (b) such a marvelous athlete!" ( )

---

15. **symbol** (sim′bəl): an object or a story element which has a basic meaning yet which also has another meaning; for example, a dove is a bird of the pigeon family yet it also stands for peace. In Hawthorne's *The Scarlet Letter,* the minister keeps putting his hand to his heart, a natural gesture but also a *symbol* of hidden guilt.

symbol

▶ A flag, a cross, or a handclasp may stand for something beside themselves and thus each may be a s_____.

(a)

(b)

symbol
(a)

▶ Appropriate *symbols* to suggest old age might be (a) withered leaves and dry ashes, (b) budding flowers and gushing waters. ( )

▶ *Symbolism* in fiction can exist (a) only in concrete objects such as an ivory leg, a livid scar, a white whale, (b) in objects, characters, gestures, situations, etc. ( )

▶ As the Hemingway hero lies mortally wounded, he sees the buzzards circle closer and closer. The buzzards are a s_____ of (a) death, (b) hope. ( )

Quiz

Write the letter that indicates the best definition.

1. (c)
2. (a)
3. (b)

( ) 1. allusion   a. mockery by expressing opposites
( ) 2. irony   b. that which stands for something else
( ) 3. symbol   c. a casual reference to something

Review Test

Supply the missing word in each sentence. The first letter of each answer is given.

1. A gross exaggeration is a h_____.
2. The repetition of initial letters in words is a_____.
3. Saying the opposite of what is really meant, in order to ridicule, is known as i_____.
4. A comparison using "like" or "as" is a s_____.
5. Use of words that sound like what they mean is o_____.
6. Addressing the absent as though present is known as a_____.
7. Naming of a thing to represent something closely associated with it is m_____.
8. "I was a stricken deer"—Cowper's figure of speech is a m_____.
9. "The sun peered at me"—this figure of speech is p_____.
10. "Darkness visible"—Milton's contradictory phrase is an o_____.

Name the figure of speech in each example. The first letter of each answer is given.

11. lovely Lulu from Laredo   a_____
12. a head shaped like a Persian melon   s_____
13. Eat another plate.   m_____
14. a beach not without its beer cans and litter   l_____
15. Boom, crash, clang went the drum section.   o_____
16. Her brain is a storage vault.   m_____
17. The bitter sweetness of farewell   o_____
18. Kay's wardrobe closet is about fifty yards long.   h_____
19. The pansies closed their little eyes.   p_____
20. O Eve, Eve, why did you eat the forbidden fruit?   a_____
21. He generously gave the church all of two cents.   i_____
22. Sam spends much; he earns little.   a_____

23. Respect the sceptre, the sword, the flag.   s_____

24. We spoke of Plato, Chartres, Waterloo, Einstein's theory, and the art of Chaplin.   a_____

25. the grieving, melancholy clouds   p_____ f_____

Key to Review Test

Check your test answers by the following key. Deduct 4% per error from a possible 100%.

1. hyperbole	10. oxymoron	19. personification
2. alliteration	11. alliteration	20. apostrophe
3. irony	12. simile	21. irony
4. simile	13. metonymy	22. antithesis
5. onomatopoeia	14. litotes	23. symbols
6. apostrophe	15. onomatopoeia	24. allusions
7. metonymy	16. metaphor	25. pathetic fallacy
8. metaphor	17. oxymoron	
9. personification	18. hyperbole	

Score: _____%

12

Rhetoric

acronym, 6
ad hominem, 19
analogy, 23
antonym, 7
bandwagon device, 21
begging the question, 17
cliché, 5
comma splice, 26
concreteness, 9
connotation, 10

ellipsis, 16
euphemism, 4
exposition, 12
faulty dilemma, 22
fragment, 25
homonym, 8
idiom, 30
infinitive, 27
malapropism, 3
non sequitur, 20

parallelism, 29
paraphrase, 15
participle, 28
plagiarism, 14
post hoc, 18
précis, 13
prose, 11
redundancy, 2
rhetoric, 1
Socratic irony, 24

When you write English, you are like a G.I. crawling through a mined field. You have to recognize and avoid the traps and snares—clichés, redundancy, plagiarism, logical fallacies. You have to know and use the helpful devices, too—concreteness, analogy, parallelism, ellipsis, idioms. As a resourceful writer you study your craft to survive.

Chapter 12 defines terms that deal with writing. Most frames present two definitions and the usual choices and completions. As in previous chapters, choose the right words to fill the blanks. But you can do more than learn word meanings. You can, perhaps—without damage to your creativity—apply some concepts behind these terms to your own writing.

Exercises

COVER THIS STRIP

1. **rhetoric** (ret′ə-rik): the art of using words persuasively and effectively in writing and speaking. *Rhetoric* involves grammar, logic, style, and figures of speech.
2. **redundancy** (ri-dun′dən-sē): wordiness; needless repetition; tautology; for example, "visible to the eye," "each and everyone," "7:00 p.m. in the evening," "Jewish rabbi."

▶ The art of composition is called _____ [rhetoric / redundancy].

rhetoric

▶ Padded phrases like "red in color" are examples of re_____.

redundancy

▶ The phrase "necessary essentials" also illustrates _____ and is poor rh_____.

redundancy
rhetoric

▶ Mere *rhetoric* without sound ideas usually results in (a) empty eloquence, (b) a literary masterpiece. ( )

(a)

▶ Terms like *tautology, pleonasm, verbiage, verbosity, circumlocution, diffuseness, periphrasis,* and *prolixity* refer to various aspects of wordiness, or re_____.

redundancy

▶ The master of effective writing, or rh_____, avoids *redundant* phrases such as (a) "a hot pastrami sandwich," (b) "edible food to eat." ( )

rhetoric
(b)

3. **malapropism** (mal′ə-prop-iz′əm): ridiculous misuse of a word for another one that sounds like it. Mrs. *Malaprop* in Richard Sheridan's play *The Rivals* (1775) spoke of "an allegory on the banks of the Nile."

▶ The misuse of a word for another one that sounds like it, as in "they won the world serious," is a _____.

malapropism

(b)	▶ Which of these two blunders involves a *malapropism*? (a) "Us boys went," (b) "a lecher course in history." ( )
malapropism	▶ "Every morning my mother exercises her abominable muscles"—this sentence contains a m_____.
malapropism	▶ Cross out each ridiculous misuse, known as a m_____, and write the correct word above it:
incandescent	Thomas Edison invented the indecent lamp.
frankincense	The wise men brought gifts of myrrh and frankfurters.
reservations	Our government put the Indians into reservoirs.
monarchy	The government of England is a limited mockery.
an imaginary line	The equator is a menagerie lion that runs around the middle of the earth.

4. **euphemism** (yōō′fə-miz′əm): a mild expression substituted for a distasteful one, for example, "a morals charge" for "rape," "resting place" for "grave," "stylishly stout" for "fat."
5. **cliché** (klē-shā′): a trite phrase; a stale expression, for example, "sigh of relief," "sadder but wiser," "fair sex," "reigned supreme," "bouncing baby boy."

euphemism	▶ A mild, indirect expression to avoid a blunt, painful one is a e_____.
euphemism	▶ A phrase like "a lung condition" for "lung cancer" is a e_____.
cliché	▶ A trite phrase like "last but not least" or "without further ado" is a c_____.
(a)	▶ Such *clichés* as "nipped in the bud" should be (a) nipped, (b) used often in themes. ( )

euphemism

▸ A substitute expression—like "by golly" for "by God," "goldarn" for "God damn," or "cripes" for "Christ"—is a e_____.

stale
cliché

▸ A phrase like "doomed to disappointment" or "conspicuous by his absence" is _____ [fresh / stale]; therefore it is called a c_____.

euphemism
cliché

▸ An expression like "passed away" or "went to his reward" is a mild substitute for "died," and trite, too; therefore, it is both a e_____ and a c_____.

Quiz

Write the letter that indicates the best definition.

1. (e)
2. (a)
3. (d)
4. (b)
5. (c)

( ) 1. rhetoric   a. tautology; wordiness
( ) 2. redundancy   b. a mild substitute expression
( ) 3. malapropism   c. a much-overused phrase
( ) 4. euphemism   d. a ridiculous word blunder
( ) 5. cliché   e. art of effective communication

6. **acronym** (ak′rə-nim): a word made up from the initial letters or syllables of a title or phrase, for example, "CARE," "ASCAP," and "snafu."

acronym

▸ A word like "WAC," made up from the initials of "Women's Army Corps," is an a_____.

initial
acronym

▸ The word "AWOL" is made up basically from the _____ [initial / final] letters of "absent without leave" and is therefore called an a_____.

▸ Write the *acronym* for each of the following titles or phrases:

UFO
radar
UNESCO

_____ unidentified flying object
_____ radio detecting and ranging
_____ United Nations Educational, Scientific, and Cultural Organization

197

7. **antonym** (an′tə-nim): a word of opposite meaning; for example, "tall" and "short," "fast" and "slow," "smart" and "stupid" are pairs of *antonyms*.
8. **homonym** (hom′ə-nim): a word that sounds like another word but has a different meaning and usually a different spelling; for example, "air" and "heir," "past" and "passed," "site" and "cite" are *homonyms*.

homonyms	▸ Pairs of words like "principle" and "principal," "block" and "bloc," are called h_____.
antonyms	▸ Pairs of words like "beautiful" and "ugly," "rich" and "poor," are called a_____.
antonyms homonyms	▸ "Dear" and "hateful" are _____; "dear" and "deer" are _____.
homonyms antonyms	▸ "Bare" and "bear" are _____; "bare" and "clothed" are _____.

9. **concreteness:** quality of being specific and of referring to particular things. *Concreteness* adds clarity and power to writing.
10. **connotation:** the suggestiveness and emotional associations of a word, apart from its denotation, or literal meaning. Propagandists often use words that seem honest but which, by their *connotations*, arouse prejudice.

concreteness	▸ Clarity of detail is called *conc*_____.
(b)	▸ Choose the *concrete* phrase: (a) "some young fellow," (b) "a shambling newsboy." ( )
(b)	▸ Choose the *concrete* phrase: (a) "an interesting animal," (b) "a blue-bottomed ape." ( )
connotation	▸ The feeling that surrounds a word is its *conn*_____.
steadfast staunch unflinching	▸ Underline three words with favorable *connotations* to describe an ancestor who absolutely refused to change his opinions about anything: obstinate, pig-headed, steadfast, hidebound, bigoted, staunch, unflinching.

(b)

▶ Which news headline has unfavorable *connotations*? (a) "Mayor and Wife Invite Friends to Housewarming," (b) "Facts Bared About Mayor's New Love-Nest." ( )

Quiz

Write the letter that indicates the best definition.

1. (d)
2. (e)
3. (b)
4. (a)
5. (c)

( ) 1. acronym   a. exactness; specificness
( ) 2. antonym   b. word with same sound
( ) 3. homonym   c. suggestive qualities; overtones
( ) 4. concreteness   d. word made from initials
( ) 5. connotation   e. word with opposite meaning

---

11. **prose:** writing or speech which is not poetry. Most communication—whether of newspapers, magazines, or conversation—is *prose*.

(a)

▶ *Prose* is the language of (a) ordinary conversation and writing, (b) Longfellow's "The Village Blacksmith." ( )

prose

▶ All of your life you have been talking in _____ [poetry / prose].

prose

▶ Essays by Michael Montaigne, Charles Lamb, and Robert Benchley are all written in _____ [poetry / prose].

(b)

▶ A *prose* composition requires (a) rhyming, (b) no rhyming. ( )

---

12. **exposition:** writing which explains or informs. *Exposition* is one of four traditional types of discourse, the others being *description, narration,* and *argumentation*.
13. **précis** (prā′sē): a short condensed version of a piece of writing. The *précis* is shorter than the original but it maintains something of the same phrasing, tone, order, and proportion of ideas.

exposition

▶ Writing that is explanatory is called _____ [narration / exposition].

précis

▶ Summarizing a composition but preserving the original phrasing and tone results in a *p*_____.

(a)

▶ The *précis* of a magazine article or essay (a) shortens it, (b) expands it. ( )

exposition
(b)

▶ To set forth information is the function of *ex_____*; so the natural language of *exposition* is (a) poetry, (b) prose. ( )

(a)

▶ A good subject for *exposition* might be (a) symbolism in Melville's *Billy Budd,* (b) an imaginary dialogue between two love-smitten Eskimos. ( )

(a)

▶ Although the *précis* of a composition is much shorter than the original, it usually retains (a) some of the original phrasing and tone, (b) only the restated main ideas. ( )

---

14. **plagiarism** (plā′jə-riz′əm): copying the language or ideas of another author and presenting them as one's own; includes the lifting of phrases and sentences from research sources without using quotation marks. *Plagiarism* results in severe penalties at most colleges.
15. **paraphrase** (par′ə-frāz′): to restate a passage in different words. The researcher must *paraphrase* borrowed material or place it within quotation marks, and must credit the source in either case.

plagiarism

▶ Copying somebody else's writing without giving proper credit is called _____.

paraphrase

▶ To restate a borrowed passage in one's own words is to _____.

credit

▶ Whether one *paraphrases* a passage or quotes it, he should _____ [credit / ignore] the original source.

(a)

▶ *Plagiarism* is (a) literary theft, (b) permissible borrowing. ( )

plagiarism
(b)

▶ To avoid the serious offense of _____, one might (a) change a word now and then in borrowed material, (b) use quotes around each borrowed passage and credit the original writer. ( )

(b)
plagiarism

▶ If a line is too individual or clever for easy *paraphrasing* the researcher should (a) steal it, (b) place it in quotation marks. ( ) Then, if he also credits the source, he will avoid _____.

Quiz

Write the letter that indicates the best definition.

1. (d)
2. (e)
3. (b)
4. (c)
5. (a)

( ) 1. prose   a. a restatement in one's own words
( ) 2. exposition   b. a condensation; a shortened version
( ) 3. précis   c. literary theft
( ) 4. plagiarism   d. ordinary nonpoetic language
( ) 5. paraphrase   e. informative writing; one type of essay

16. **ellipsis** (i-lip'sis): the omission of words, as from quoted material, usually indicated by three dots or asterisks. *Ellipsis* may be used to shorten a quoted passage but not so as to change the meaning or to remove surgically any damaging evidence.

(a)

▶ "But, in a larger sense, we cannot dedicate . . . this ground"—here the three dots indicate (a) an ellipsis, (b) a pause while Lincoln took a drink. ( )

ellipsis

▶ The omission of words from a quoted passage is called an _____.

three

▶ The *ellipsis* is indicated by _____ [three / seven] dots.

improper
ellipsis

▶ If your research source says, "Poe drank, although very infrequently, during this period" and you write it as "Poe drank . . . during this period," you are making _____ [proper / improper] use of _____.

17. **begging the question:** assuming what has yet to be proved. *Begging the question* is a fallacy of logic, as when we say, "Shouldn't all those crooks at City Hall be turned out of office?" or "It's a waste of money to give that murderer a trial—just string 'im up!"

201

18. **post hoc** (pōst hok'): assuming that one thing caused another merely because it happened earlier. This term for a fallacy of logic is from the Latin phrase *post hoc, ergo propter hoc,* which literally means "after this, therefore because of this."

begging	▶ To take something for granted without proof is called _____ *the question*.
question "useless"	▶ "Why must a useless course like history be made compulsory?" —here the word that *begs the* _____ and needs proving is _____ ["useless" / "course"].
post hoc	▶ When an Indian dance gets credit for causing the rain that falls the next day, the reasoning behind such credit is called p_____ h_____.
post hoc	▶ The fallacy of assuming that two events that follow each other must have a cause-effect relationship is called _____ _____.
begs (b)	▶ "We must not permit a pornographic book like *The Catcher in the Rye* to be kept in our library"—here the word that _____ *the question* and needs proving is (a) "permit," (b) "pornographic." ( )
(a)	▶ A young pugilist wearing a certain bathrobe scored a knockout in one round; thereafter he insisted on wearing that same robe, never cleaned, to every fight of his career—he believed in (a) *post hoc* reasoning, (b) hygiene. ( )

19. **ad hominem** (ad hom'ə-nəm): appealing to a person's prejudices or selfish interests rather than to his reason; attacking an opponent rather than sticking to the issue. The Latin phrase *argumentum ad hominem* means "argument at or to the man."

20. **non sequitur** (non sek'wi-tər): a conclusion that does not follow from the evidence presented. The Latin phrase *non sequitur* means "it does not follow."

hominem	▶ In a debate about state lotteries, an attack on your moral character is *ad* _____.

(a)

▶ *Ad hominem* implies that the real issue of the argument gets (a) overlooked, (b) close attention. ( )

▶ "My husband loves Italian motion picture films, so I think he'll enjoy the chicken cacciatora I am going to cook for him"—the reasoning here involves a *non* _____.

sequitur

▶ In a *non sequitur* the conclusion _____ [does / does not] follow from the evidence presented.

does not

▶ "Schopenhauer was very pessimistic and nobody should read his essays"—the conclusion is not justified by the evidence, and we have a _____ _____.

non sequitur

▶ "Better vote against this school bill, Smedley; your kids have graduated already and you'll just get soaked for more taxes"—the argument here is a _____ h _____.

ad hominem

Quiz

Write the letter that indicates the best definition.

1. (c)   ( ) 1. ellipsis   a. appeal to prejudice
2. (d)   ( ) 2. begging the question b. an illogical conclusion
3. (e)   ( ) 3. *post hoc*   c. omission of words
4. (a)   ( ) 4. *ad hominem*   d. assuming without proof
5. (b)   ( ) 5. *non sequitur*   e. after this, therefore because of this

21. **bandwagon device:** persuasion to join the popular or winning side. "To climb aboard the bandwagon" means to shift one's vote to the apparent winner.

▶ "Three out of four smoke Hempos!"—such ads that suggest that we join the majority use the _____ *device*.

bandwagon

▶ The *bandwagon device* tells us to vote for Jim Snurd because he is going to _____ [lose / win] by a landslide.

win

203

bandwagon (b)	▶ "Three million sold already!"—whether this pitch refers to Klunker cars, to horseburgers, or to albums by the Five Lunatics, it uses the _____ device and it urges you to do (a) the rational thing, (b) what the crowd is doing. ( )

22. **faulty dilemma** (di-lem′ə): the offering of only two alternatives when more than two exist. "We must wipe out the Pootzians or we will perish"—such talk illustrates the *faulty dilemma*, since it ignores the possibility of peaceful coexistence.

23. **analogy** (ə-nal′ə-jē): an extended comparison to clarify an idea; a comparison of things which are alike in certain ways and therefore presumably alike in other ways. *Analogies* can illustrate an idea but they do not prove it.

dilemma	▶ "Either the man is boss in a home or the woman will rule"—such logic presents a *faulty* _____.
analogy	▶ Comparing man to an eagle that must rule its own nest is an a_____.
illustrate	▶ *Analogies* _____ [prove / illustrate] ideas.
analogy	▶ "The early bird catches the worm, so I'll be up at dawn and find a job"—this is reasoning by _____.
faulty dilemma	▶ "Don't touch alcohol or you'll end up in the looney bin"—this choice is the f_____ d_____.
two	▶ The *faulty dilemma* forces one to choose from _____ [two / all of the] possibilities.
analogy	▶ Bede's *Ecclesiastical History* (eighth century) likens our life to the quick flight of a sparrow through a lighted hall at night—this is an _____.

24. **Socratic irony** (sə-krat′ik): the device of pretending to be ignorant and asking questions in order to trap the opponent into obvious error. Socrates uses *Socratic irony,* for instance, to refute a husky Athenian who argues that might makes right.

▶ The man who uses *Socratic irony* asks a series of innocent-sounding questions (a) because he is stupid, (b) because he is leading his opponent into self-contradiction. ( )

▶ To employ S_____ irony one must (a) ask adroit questions to draw out the other fellow's ignorance, (b) talk constantly in an opinionated fashion. ( )

▶ If falsely accused of plagiarism you might use *Socratic* _____ to clear yourself by saying, (a) "I'm innocent, teacher; I swear I'm innocent!" (b) "Very interesting—now where is this passage which I have stolen?" ( )

(b)

Socratic
(a)

irony
(b)

Quiz

Write the letter that indicates the best definition.

( ) 1. bandwagon device   a. an extended comparison
( ) 2. faulty dilemma   b. argument for joining the popular side
( ) 3. analogy
( ) 4. Socratic irony   c. refuting by means of clever but innocent-sounding questions
   d. offering two alternatives when more exist

1. (b)
2. (d)
3. (a)
4. (c)

25. **fragment:** an incomplete sentence. *Fragments* are often considered the unpardonable sin in freshman themes, though they are acceptable in exclamations, dialogue, and certain types of informal writing.

26. **comma splice:** the use of a comma between main clauses where a period or semicolon should be used; for example, "Jack London wrote about supermen and superdogs, he became a rich socialist."

205

▶ After each of the following write *fragment, comma splice,* or *correct:*

comma splice

H. L. Mencken was pungent and opinionated, I never thought he was dull. _____

fragment

Alexandre Dumas being about the most imaginative novelist I had ever read. _____

fragment

Because the *Bhagavad* teaches complete unselfishness, humility, and goodness. _____

correct

O. Henry fled. _____

▶ After each of the following write *fragment, comma splice,* or *correct:*

comma splice

The British loved Kipling, however, he was never poet laureate. _____

fragment

A scholarly analysis, which reads like a detective story, of the Shakespeare sonnets, particularly those dealing with the Dark Lady. _____

correct

My brother can't write like Chaucer, but he spells like him. _____

---

27. **infinitive** (in-fin′i-tiv): a verbal form that consists usually of "to" plus a verb, as "to walk." The *infinitive* can do the work of a noun, adjective, or adverb.
28. **participle** (pär′ti-sip′əl): a verbal adjective. "Flying in a battered plane, I had some frightening moments"—here "flying," "battered," and "frightening" are *participles*.

infinitive

▶ A phrase like "to paint" is an i_____.

participle

▶ A verbal adjective—like "honking" in "honking geese"—is a p_____.

participle
infinitive
participle

▶ "Attacking his critics, James Fenimore Cooper began to waste valuable writing time"—here "Attacking" is a _____, "to waste" is an _____, and "writing" is a _____.

infinitives

▶ "To strive, to seek, to find, and not to yield"—this final line of Tennyson's poem "Ulysses" (1842) contains four _____.

▶ Inserting words between "to" and the verb in an *infinitive* results in a *split infinitive,* a phrasing which often sounds awkward. Which phrase has a split infinitive?—(a) "to as soon as possible analyze Chekhov's play," (b) "to analyze Chekhov's play as soon as possible. ( )

(a)

▶ "Shakespeare was able to find several gripping themes in the chronicles of Holinshed"—here "to find" is an _____ and "gripping" is a _____.

infinitive
participle

▶ A *participle* that does not clearly modify the right word is a *dangling participle.* After each of the following write *dangler* or *correct:*
Becoming six years old, my mother got a divorce. _____
Echoing Emerson, Walt Whitman spoke of man's divinity. _____
If stewed, you will enjoy these prunes. _____

dangler

correct

dangler

---

29. **parallelism** (par′ə-lel′iz-əm) : similarity of grammatical structure given to similar ideas. *Parallelism* in phrasing brings out *parallelism* in ideas.

▶ Consider the sentence "Fritz loves fishing, climbing, and to yodel"—it has faulty *par_____* but would become acceptable if the phrase "to yodel" were changed to the word y_____.

parallelism
yodeling

▶ "Gunder has vowed to work, to save money, and that he will succeed in business"—this sentence has _____ [acceptable / faulty] *parallelism.*

faulty

▶ Which has better *parallelism*?—(a) "I came and after I saw the enemy they were conquered by me," (b) "I came, I saw, I conquered." ( )

(b)

▶ Lincoln referred to "government of the people, by the people, _____ [for / to help] the people" and achieved structural _____.

for
parallelism

207

30. idiom: an accepted phrase that is contrary to the usual language pattern. *Idioms* are natural, supple, and often very informal, for example, "catch cold," "give in," "hint at," "knock off work," "pick a fight."

idioms

▶ Phrases like "comes in handy" and "takes after his father" are i_____.

(a)

▶ Although *idioms* violate normal language construction they are (a) proper and acceptable, (b) colorful but unusable. ( )

idiom
(b)

▶ Another peculiar English phrasing, known as an _____, is (a) "walk with me," (b) "angry with me." ( )

(b)

▶ Which is an *idiom*?—(a) "became a loafer," (b) "went to the dogs." ( )

idiomatic

▶ Ernest Hemingway achieved vigor and naturalness in his stories by using _____ [formal / idiomatic] English.

Quiz

Write the letter that indicates the best example.

1. (e)
2. (c)
3. (a)
4. (d)
5. (f)
6. (b)

( ) 1. fragment
( ) 2. comma splice
( ) 3. infinitive
( ) 4. participle
( ) 5. parallelism
( ) 6. idiom

a. "*To err* is human."
b. We grabbed a bite.
c. "Here comes Lulu, get the hymn book."
d. " 'The Lottery' is a *terrifying* story."
e. "Whereas Irving knew the Catskills."
f. He lived; he loved; he died.

Review Test

Supply the missing word in each sentence. The first letter of each answer is given.

1. Copying material without giving proper credit is p_____.
2. The ridiculous misuse of a word for another that sounds like it is a m_____.
3. A word like "WAVE," made up from the initials of a title, is an a_____.
4. A mild word substituted for a blunt one is a e_____.
5. Prose composition that explains or sets forth is e_____.
6. Ordinary writing that is not poetry is called p_____.
7. A word of opposite meaning is an a_____.
8. A word with the same sound but different meaning is a h_____.
9. A conclusion which "does not follow" from the evidence is a n_____ s_____.
10. Needless repetition or wordiness is r_____.
11. An accepted phrase that defies normal language patterns is an i_____.
12. The verbal "grinning" in "grinning faces" is a p_____.
13. An incomplete sentence is a f_____.
14. Propaganda urging one to follow the crowd is the b_____ device.
15. An omission of words, indicated by three dots, is an e_____.

Write *True* or *False*.

_____ 16. *Concreteness* refers to the use of clear, specific detail.

_____ 17. *Post hoc* logic is considered valid in science.

_____ 18. *Begging the question* means assuming without proof.

_____ 19. An argument *ad hominem* sticks to the main issue.

_____ 20. *Clichés* add color and vigor to one's style.

_____ 21. To use *Socratic irony* means to argue and fall into one's own trap.

209

_____ 22. In the *faulty dilemma* one must choose from an incomplete set of alternatives.

_____ 23. *Comma splice* refers to the omission of a comma.

_____ 24. The following contains *parallelism:* "We will fight with guns, with bombs, and with fists."

_____ 25. *Rhetoric* is the art of persuasive writing and speaking.

Write the letter that indicates the best completion.

( ) 26. An *analogy* is (a) a proof, (b) an exaggeration, (c) a comparison, (d) a stale expression.
( ) 27. An example of an *infinitive* is (a) "the critic Mencken," (b) "criticizing," (c) "to criticize," (d) "to critics."
( ) 28. A *précis* is (a) an explanation, (b) an expansion, (c) a quotation, (d) a condensation.
( ) 29. A *paraphrase* is (a) a restatement, (b) a quotation, (c) a line of poetry, (d) a wordy passage.

Match each word with its definition.

( ) 30. participle   a. a worn-out phrase
( ) 31. cliché   b. suggestiveness
( ) 32. connotation   c. verbal adjective
( ) 33. plagiarism   d. literary theft

Key to Review Test

Check your test answers by the following key. Deduct 3% per error from a possible 100%.

1. plagiarism	12. participle	23. False
2. malapropism	13. fragment	24. True
3. acronym	14. bandwagon	25. True
4. euphemism	15. ellipsis	26. (c)
5. exposition	16. True	27. (c)
6. prose	17. False	28. (d)
7. antonym	18. True	29. (a)
8. homonym	19. False	30. (c)
9. *non sequitur*	20. False	31. (a)
10. redundancy	21. False	32. (b)
11. idiom	22. True	33. (d)

Score: _____%

13
Psychology

ambivalence, 1
aptitude, 2
claustrophobia, 3
compensation, 4
dipsomania, 5
ego, 7
extrasensory perception (ESP), 10
free association, 11
hallucination, 13
hypochondria, 14
id, 8
kleptomania, 6
narcissism, 16
Oedipus complex, 17
paranoia, 19
psychoanalysis, 12
psychosis, 18
psychosomatic, 15
rationalization, 21
regression, 22
schizophrenia, 20
sibling, 23
superego, 9
trauma, 24
voyeur, 25

A cynic has said that psychology "tells us what everybody knows, in language that nobody understands." His comment is more witty than accurate. Actually, psychology, which is the study of human behavior, tells us many things we don't know about ourselves and in language we can learn to understand quite well. In fact, the terms of psychology must be understood if we are to qualify in such diverse areas as social work, law, and medicine; or if we are to analyze the fiction of Faulkner, the poetry of Jeffers, the dramas of O'Neill.

Chapter 13 stresses twenty-five basic terms of psychology, and presents fifty more definitions in a supplementary list. As you fill in the frames, try to relate the terms to people you have known or read about. Can you think of anyone with a *neurosis*, a *psychosomatic* illness, or a trace of *narcissism*? Have you yourself had a *traumatic* experience? Are you a *sibling* (or would you knock a person down for calling you that)? Words become more meaningful when you see how they apply to the life around you.

Exercises

COVER THIS STRIP

1. **ambivalence** (am-biv′ə-ləns): conflicting feelings, such as love and hate, toward the same person or thing. You may have a deep affection for your parents and yet be angry because they interfere with your decisions—your attitude toward them, then, is one of *ambivalence*.

▶ A child wants to pet a strange "doggie" but is fearful. The conflict of feelings is called am__bivalence__.

ambivalence

▶ Felix wants to order the giant hot fudge sundae but he doesn't want to get fat. His attitude toward the sundae is one of am__bivalence__.

ambivalence

▶ A star basketball player has *ambivalent* feelings toward his coach. This means that the athlete (a) can shoot with either hand, (b) has contradictory emotions. (b)

(b)

▶ Wilmer wants to ask Alice for a date but worries that she will turn him down; Alice loves Jerry but has fits of jealousy when he talks to other girls; Jerry craves alcohol but realizes that it can ruin him. These conflicting attitudes illustrate am__bivalence__.

ambivalence

▶ It is __possible__ [possible / impossible] for a person to be both attracted and repelled by something. The condition is called __ambivalence__.

possible
ambivalence

2. **aptitude** (ap′tə-tōōd′): the natural ability to acquire a skill or type of knowledge. A test of musical *aptitude*, for example, does not measure achievement but predicts future performance.

▶ A high score in a mechanical-*aptitude* test means (a) that you have unusual ability as a mechanic, (b) that you could be trained to be a good mechanic. (b)

(b)

212

aptitude	▸ An achievement test measures what you can do now; an *aptitude* test predicts what you will be able to do with training.
aptitude	▸ Glenna is extremely athletic, and although she has never played tennis she probably has an *aptitude* for it.
does aptitude	▸ Harvey is an excellent speller and scores high in a finger-dexterity test; apparently he *does* [does / doesn't] have an *aptitude* for typewriting.

3. **claustrophobia** (klô'strə-fō'bē-ə): morbid fear of being in enclosed or narrow places.

claustrophobia	▸ Linus feels stifled and fearful in an elevator or a closet. He has *claustrophobia*.
(a)	▸ *Claustrophobia* manifests itself in an abnormal fear of (a) small rooms, (b) heights. (*a*)
claustrophobia	▸ A phobia involves excessive fear in the absence of real danger. The excessive fear and anxiety of a clerk who must work in a small, windowless office may be due to *claustrophobia*.
(a)	▸ A person with *claustrophobia* would probably feel comfortable (a) in a meadow, (b) in a trunk. (*a*)

4. **compensation:** an attempt to make up for an undesirable trait by exaggerating a socially approved one.

compensation	▸ A student who is weak in academic courses may try to excel in athletics—an example of *compensation*.
inferiority	▸ *Compensation* is an effort to excel in one activity in order to make up for a feeling of *inferiority* [inferiority / accomplishment] in another.
compensation	▸ Napoleon, Hitler, and Stalin were of short stature, and their drive for political power was probably a form of *compensation*.

success
compensation

▶ Igor was embarrassingly poor in athletics, so he tried doubly hard to become a _success_ [success / failure] as a debater, an effort known as c_ompensation_.

---

5. **dipsomania:** an abnormal craving for alcoholic liquors.
6. **kleptomania:** an abnormal tendency to steal.

kleptomania
dipsomania

▶ An irresistible impulse to steal is k_leptomania_; an insatiable desire for alcohol is d_ipsomania_.

drink
steal

▶ Emotional disturbances have been cited as a cause of *dipsomania*, or the tendency to _drink_ [steal / drink], and *kleptomania*, or the tendency to _steal_ [steal / drink].

dipsomania

▶ Alcoholics Anonymous is an excellent organization for those whose problem is d_ipsomania_.

kleptomania

▶ "Stealing lingerie?" said the judge. "Looks like a case of k_leptomania_. Ten days should be enough. After all, this is your first slip."

(b)

▶ *Kleptomania* is associated with (a) overeating, (b) shoplifting. (b)

(a)

▶ *Dipsomania* is associated with (a) boozing, (b) pocket picking. (a)

Quiz

Write the letter that indicates the **best** definition.

1. (e)
2. (c)
3. (a)
4. (f)
5. (b)
6. (d)

(e) 1. ambivalence	a. fear of small enclosures
(c) 2. aptitude	b. alcoholism
(a) 3. claustrophobia	c. capacity to learn
(f) 4. compensation	d. irresistible stealing
(b) 5. dipsomania	e. conflicting feelings
(d) 6. kleptomania	f. making up for a shortcoming

7. **ego** (ē′gō): the conscious part of the personality, which has to deal with the id, the superego, and external reality, according to Freud. The *ego* does our logical thinking.

8. **id:** the primitive, instinctive, aggressive part of our personality. The pleasure-loving *id,* with which we are born, seeks immediate gratification regardless of consequences, but it is later held in check by the superego and ego, says Freud.

9. **superego:** the moralistic part of the personality which acts as a conscience to control the ego and the id. The *superego* is a product of parental and social training, and it sets up standards of right and wrong.

▶ A baby is like a little animal; it is swayed by the raw, instinctive part of its personality, the ___*id*___.

id

▶ From its environment the child absorbs a sense of what is right and wrong. This developing conscience has been called the s___*uperego*___.

superego

▶ The self-aware, thinking part of the mind is called the e___*go*___.

ego

▶ The unconscious parts of the mind include the primitive drives, or i___*d*___, and the conscience, or s___*uperego*___. The conscious part of the mind, which does our thinking, is the e___*go*___.

id
superego
ego

▶ The uncontrolled impulses of the *id* are likely to be ___*condemned*___ [encouraged / condemned] by society. Such uncontrolled impulses would probably produce (a) rapists, burglars, gluttons, (b) priests, teachers, saints. (___*a*___)

condemned
(a)

▶ Traditional values and ideals of society are represented by the s___*uperego*___. The *superego* strives for (a) pleasure, (b) perfection. (___*b*___)

superego
(b)

▶ The conscious, thinking part of you is called the ___*ego*___. The *ego* operates according to the ___*reality*___ [reality / pleasure] principle.

ego
reality

id superego ego	▸ Personalities can be distorted, says Freud, if either the animalistic ____id____ or the moralistic __superego__ is too strong. One's behavior should be controlled by the conscious aspect of the mind, the __ego__.
(a)	▸ The concept of an *id, ego,* and *superego* was first developed by (a) Sigmund Freud, (b) Charles Darwin. (a)

10. **extrasensory perception** (ESP): ability to gain knowledge without use of the known senses. *ESP* refers to telepathy, clairvoyance, or any other means of perceiving external events or communicating by mental rather than physical means.

(a)	▸ *Extrasensory perception* would be operative if you could send a message by (a) brain waves, (b) Western Union. (a)
extrasensory perception	▸ *ESP* stands for __Extrasensory perception__.
extrasensory perception	▸ You dream that your best friend is calling for help, and the next day he falls down a well. Precognition, as illustrated here, is a type of e__xtrasensory__ p__erception__.
ESP	▸ Most psychologists do not as yet believe in *extrasensory perception* (usually abbreviated __ESP__).
(d)	▸ The term *ESP* does *not* refer to (a) clairvoyance, (b) precognition, (c) telepathy, (d) short-wave radio. (d)

11. **free association:** the free, unhampered, rambling talk by a patient by which his repressions are discovered.

12. **psychoanalysis** (sī′kō-ə-nal′ə-sis): a system of mental therapy, devised by Freud, whereby through free association and dream analysis certain conflictual material is released from the unconscious.

psychoanalysis	▸ Freud's technique of treating mental illness is known as p__sychoanalysis__.

216

free association psychoanalysis	▶ Rambling from one topic to another is called f_ree__association_ a_____. This activity is common during sessions of p_sychoanalysis_.
(a)	▶ The purpose of *psychoanalysis* is to help the patient overcome problems that are basically (a) mental, (b) physical. (a)
psychoanalysis free association	▶ A mental shock that occurred in infancy might be disclosed during a session of p_sychoanalysis_ by means of f_ree_ a_ssociation_.
(b)	▶ Through *free association* one's unconscious wishes find (a) concealment, (b) verbal expression. (b)
psychoanalysis	▶ Psychologists do not accept all of Freud's theories, but he is respected as the father of p_sychoanalysis_.

Quiz

Write the letter that indicates the best definition.

1. (f)	(f) 1. ego	a. Freud's system of treatment
2. (d)	(d) 2. id	b. conscience, or moral control
3. (b)	(b) 3. superego	c. rambling monologue
4. (e)	(e) 4. ESP	d. seat of animalistic impulses
5. (c)	(c) 5. free association	e. thought transference
6. (a)	(a) 6. psychoanalysis	f. thinking part of the mind

13. **hallucination** (hə-loo′sə-nā′shən): the apparent witnessing of sights and sounds that do not exist.

hallucination	▶ "Yesterday upon a stair / I saw a man who wasn't there . . ." —the poet seems to have had a h_allucination_.
(a)	▶ The sights and sounds of a *hallucination* are (a) imaginary, (b) actual. (a)
hallucination	▶ Macbeth imagines that he sees the murdered Banquo sitting in front of him; Macbeth is experiencing a h_allucination_.

(b)

▶ *Hallucinative* drugs make one's sense impressions more (a) dependable, (b) undependable. (b)

---

14. **hypochondria** (hī′pə-kon′drē-ə): excessive worry about one's health; anxiety about minor or imaginary ailments.
15. **psychosomatic** (sī′kō-sō-mat′ik): referring to a physical disorder caused by emotional stress.

hypochondria

▶ Every morning Wilhelm gets up worried, looks at his tongue, and swallows thirty pills; his problem is h*ypochondria*.

(a)

▶ A *hypochondriac* usually believes that his health is (a) failing, (b) perfect. (a)

psychosomatic

▶ Gus has ulcers when he works in an office but not when he works on a farm; his ulcers are probably p*sychosomatic*.

psychosomatic
(a)

▶ Disorders such as asthma, dermatitis, and high blood pressure are sometimes p*sychosomatic*, that is, caused by (a) emotional stress, (b) bacterial infection. (a)

hypochondria
hypochondria

▶ Julius with his imaginary illnesses is an example of h*ypochondria*; he caught his last disease from the *Reader's Digest*. His wife Lydia, overfearful of germs, boils dishes three times before using them—she also suffers from h*ypochondria*.

psychosomatic

▶ Soldiers have sometimes developed a paralysis from fear of combat; such paralysis is p*sychosomatic*.

---

16. **narcissism** (när′si-siz′əm): abnormal self-love; erotic pleasure obtained from admiration of one's own body or mind.
17. **Oedipus complex** (ed′ə-pəs): sexual attraction to the parent of the opposite sex and hostility for the parent of the same sex.

narcissism

▶ *Narcissus* admired his own physical features; thus, Freud refers to such self-love as n*arcissism*.

(b)

▶ *Narcissism* involves a lack of concern for other people and extreme concern for (a) narcotics, (b) one's self. (b)

Oedipus complex	▸ *Oedipus* loved his mother and hated his father; thus, Freud refers to a similar stage in child development as the O__edipus__ c__omplex__.
Oedipus complex	▸ Little Jasper is competing with his father for the love of his mother; Jasper's feelings are referred to as the O__edipus__ c__omplex__.
narcissism	▸ The pretty people in TV commercials often say, "I love my hair—so soft and fragrant," "My skin is baby-smooth," "My breath is twenty-four hours sweet and fresh, thanks to Putro"; such conceited lines suggest n__arcissism__.
(b)	▸ The *Oedipus complex* involves rivalry for the love of the parent of (a) the same sex, (b) the opposite sex. (b)
narcissism	▸ A person who is obsessed with his or her own handsome appearance is exhibiting n__arcissism__.

Quiz

Write the letter that indicates the best definition.

1. (e) (e) 1. hallucination   a. of illness caused by emotions
2. (d) (d) 2. hypochondria   b. love-mother, hate-father phase
3. (a) (a) 3. psychosomatic   c. self-love
4. (c) (c) 4. narcissism   d. anxiety about one's health
5. (b) (b) 5. Oedipus complex   e. seeing what is nonexistent

18. **psychosis** (sī-kō′sis) [*insanity*]: a mental disorder such as paranoia or schizophrenia that involves very serious disorganization of the personality; insanity.
19. **paranoia** (par′ə-noi′ə): a mental disorder marked by delusions of persecution or of grandeur.
20. **schizophrenia** (skit′sə-frē′nē-ə): a mental disorder marked by splitting of the personality, a retreat from reality, and emotional deterioration.

(a)
(b)

▸ *Psychotic* people are (a) irrational, (b) rational. (a) They tend to (a) cope with reality, (b) withdraw from reality. (b)

paranoia	▸ The delusion that people are plotting behind your back and are "out to get you" is a symptom of pa_____.
(a)	▸ Another common symptom of *paranoia* is the delusion of (a) grandeur, (b) inferiority. (a)
schizophrenia	▸ Stanley sits silently for hours, possibly in a fixed position. Such withdrawal from reality is usually known as sc_____.
(a)	▸ A *schizophrenic* tends to be (a) withdrawn and mute, (b) the life of the party. (a)
paranoia	▸ Delusions of grandeur ("I am Napoleon," "I am Jesus Christ") are symptoms of pa_____.
(b)	▸ A major mental disorder is (a) a neurosis, (b) a psychosis. (b)
psychosis	▸ Hardening of blood vessels in the brain of an elderly person may result in a serious mental disorder, or ps_____.
schizophrenia paranoia	▸ The *psychotic* who is rigid and unresponsive probably suffers from _____, the *psychotic* who shouts "They conspire against me—I'll kill them—I'll rule the world!" probably suffers from _____.

21. **rationalization** (rash′ən-ə-liz-ā′shən): justifying of unreasonable behavior by presenting false but plausible reasons to oneself or to others.

conceal	▸ To *rationalize* one of our misdeeds is to _____ [reveal / conceal] the real motives behind it.
rationalization	▸ Whenever Buster, who is overweight, orders another double banana split, he says: "I have to keep up my strength." Buster's excuse is an example of r_____.
(b)	▸ Big Country invades rich Little Country, saying, "We will restore better government." Big Country is probably indulging in (a) pure altruism, (b) rationalization. (b)

rationalization (b)

▶ Self-justification, known as r_*rationalization*_, is probably being used when a football coach explains a 79-6 loss: "We lost because (a) we were outplayed"; (b) them umpires was prejudiced." (_b_)

---

22. **regression:** going back to earlier, less mature behavior as an escape from a present conflict.

regression

▶ Six-year-old Wilmer sees his new baby sister get all the attention, so he begins to wet his pants again. He is trying to solve his conflict by r_*egression*_.

less

▶ *Regression* involves a change to _*less*_ [more / less] mature behavior.

regression

▶ A young housewife keeps running back to the security of her mother's home—this, too, is probably r_*egression*_.

child
regression

▶ A man loses his wife or his job and gets drunk. His escape to the irresponsible condition of a _*child*_ [child / adult] is r_*egression*_.

---

23. **sibling:** a brother or sister; one of two or more children born at different times of the same parents.

siblings

▶ The Grunches have three sons and two daughters of different ages, a total of five s_*iblings*_.

siblings

▶ Suppose you have an older sister and a younger brother. This means that you have two s_*iblings*_.

are not

▶ Twins _*are not*_ [are / are not] referred to as *siblings*.

is not

▶ Wally, an only child, _*is not*_ [is / is not] a *sibling*.

sibling

▶ Competition and jealousy between two brothers or two sisters or a brother and a sister are aspects of s_*ibling*_ rivalry.

24. **trauma** (trô′mə): an emotional shock which has a lasting effect.

major

▶ A trauma is a __major__ [minor / major] emotional shock.

(a)

▶ A car accident gives Nellie a series of nightmares. Its effect has been (a) traumatic, (b) salutary. (a)

trauma

▶ Little Agatha sees her stepfather beat her mother like a gong. Agatha's later hostility to marriage may be due to an emotional shock known as a t__rauma__.

trauma
(b)

▶ A psychoanalyst tries to learn about your every emotional shock, or t__rauma__, because he knows that the effects of a trauma are (a) temporary, (b) lasting. (b)

---

25. **voyeur** (vwä-yûr′): a Peeping Tom; one who obtains sexual gratification by looking at sexual objects or acts, especially secretively.

(a)

▶ A *voyeur* peeks into windows hoping to see (a) sexual acts, (b) television programs. (a)

voyeur
(b)

▶ A Peeping Tom, also known as a v__oyeur__, derives particular pleasure from (a) exhibiting his body, (b) peeking in secret at the nakedness of others. (b)

(a)

▶ The word *voyeur* derives logically from (a) the French *voir*, meaning "to see"; (b) the Latin *vox*, meaning "voice." (a)

an immature

▶ Children go through a stage of intense curiosity about sex. Consequently, *voyeurism* is considered to be an immature [a mature / an immature] way of achieving sexual fulfillment.

Quiz

Write the letter that indicates the best definition.

(e) 1. psychosis
(c) 2. paranoia
(h) 3. schizophrenia
(b) 4. rationalization
(g) 5. regression
(d) 6. sibling
(a) 7. trauma
(f) 8. voyeur

a. a lasting emotional shock
b. justifying with false reasons
c. delusions of grandeur and persecution
d. a brother or sister
e. serious mental disorder (general term)
f. a Peeping Tom
g. escape via less mature behavior
h. splitting of personality; apathy

1. (e)
2. (c)
3. (h)
4. (b)
5. (g)
6. (d)
7. (a)
8. (f)

Review Test

Supply the missing word in each sentence. The first letter of each answer is given.

1. Abnormal self-love is n_____.
2. Morbid fear of small, enclosed places is c_____.
3. That part of the unconscious mind that acts as a conscience is the s_____.
4. A brother or sister is a s_____.
5. A splitting of the personality and withdrawal from reality is s_____.
6. Conflicting feelings, like love and hate, for the same person are known as a_____.
7. A son's desire for his mother and rivalry with his father is the O_____ c_____.
8. Physical illness caused by emotional stress is p_____.
9. Reverting to less mature behavior as an escape is r_____.
10. Excessive desire for alcohol is d_____.
11. Abnormal anxiety about one's imagined illnesses is h_____.
12. A compulsion to do shoplifting is k_____.
13. A lasting emotional shock is a t_____.
14. One who peeks into windows to see sex acts is a v_____.
15. Uncle Fritz claims he is General Grant and that the neighbors are plotting to poison him—Fritz has symptoms of p_____.

Write *True* or *False*.

False 16. The purpose of an *aptitude* test is to measure achievement.
True 17. The *ego* is the conscious part of the personality.
True 18. *Hallucinations* can be caused by drugs.
True 19. *Free association* is a technique used in psychoanalysis.
False 20. A *psychosis* is a fairly common, minor nervous ailment.

False 21. Unusually keen vision and hearing are referred to as *extrasensory perception (ESP)*.

False 22. The *id*, which is powerful during one's infancy, passes out of existence when one reaches maturity.

True 23. A certain blind girl tries doubly hard to master the piano; her efforts are a form of *compensation*.

False 24. *Rationalization* means logical reasoning, the avoidance of fallacy.

True 25. *Psychoanalysis* is a method of treating mental illness.

Key to Review Test

Check your test answers by the following key. Deduct 4% per error from a possible 100%.

1. narcissism	10. dipsomania	19. True
2. claustrophobia	11. hypochondria	20. False
3. superego	12. kleptomania	21. False
4. sibling	13. trauma	22. False
5. schizophrenia	14. voyeur	23. True
6. ambivalence	15. paranoia	24. False
7. Oedipus complex	16. False	25. True
8. psychosomatic	17. True	
9. regression	18. True	

Score: _____%

Supplementary List

1. **abnormal psychology:** the study of the behavior of the neurotic, the psychotic, the feeble-minded, and other abnormal people.
2. **acrophobia** (ak′rə-fō′bē-ə): a fear of high places.
3. **aggression:** behavior that aims to hurt someone or what he stands for.
4. **amnesia** (am-nē′zhə): partial or total loss of memory; specifically, forgetting one's own identity.
5. **atavism** (at′ə-viz′əm): reversion to an earlier ancestral characteristic.
6. **behaviorism:** the doctrine that man reacts automatically, like a machine, to stimuli.
7. **clairvoyance** (klâr-voi′əns): the alleged ability to see objects or to know things beyond the range of the senses.
8. **compulsion:** an irresistible impulse to perform an irrational act.
9. **conditioned reflex:** a response set off by a second stimulus associated with the primary stimulus; for example, secretion of saliva set off in Pavlov's dog by a dinner bell.
10. **defense mechanism** (mek′ə-niz′əm): an unconscious adjustment to block out unpleasant memories, feelings, or knowledge.
11. **dementia praecox** (di-men′shə prē′koks): a mental disorder involving melancholia, withdrawal, delusions, etc.: schizophrenia.
12. **dissociation** (di-sō′sē-ā′shən): a splitting apart of mental elements, involving loss of control over memory and motor processes.
13. **dualism:** the state of being twofold; the theory that a man consists of two entities—body and mind.
14. **Electra complex:** a daughter's unconscious sexual attachment to her father and hostility to her mother.
15. **empathy:** one's participating in the feelings and spirit of another person or thing.
16. **exhibitionism:** a tendency to behave so as to attract attention; self-exposure.
17. **extrovert** (eks′trō-vûrt): a person actively interested in his environment and other people rather than in himself.
18. **fixation:** an abnormal attachment to some person, object, or idea.
19. **Freudian** (froi′dē-ən): pertaining to Sigmund Freud's methods of psychoanalysis, which emphasize the techniques of free association and transference and try to give the patient an insight into his unconscious conflicts and motives.
20. **gustatory** (gus′tə-tōr′ē): relating to the sense of taste.
21. **hysteria** (hi-stēr′ē-ə): emotional frenzy marked by sensory and motor disturbances.
22. **identification:** the putting of oneself in the place of someone else and unconsciously sharing his admirable qualities.
23. **infantilism** (in-fan′tə-liz′əm): extreme immaturity of mind and body in an adult.
24. **inhibition** (in′i-bish′ən): the blocking of one impulse by another.
25. **intelligence quotient** (I.Q.): the mental age multiplied by 100 and then divided by the actual age.
26. **introspection:** analysis of one's own mental and emotional states.
27. **intuition** (in′too-ish′ən): awareness of something without conscious reasoning.
28. **kinesthetic** (kin′is-thet′ik): pertaining to muscle sense or the sensation of position, movement, and tension in the body.

29. **libido** (li-bī′dō): the drive for sex gratification.
30. **masochism** (maz′ə-kiz′əm): the deriving of sexual pleasure from being hurt or humiliated.
31. **maturation** (mach′oo-rā′shən): completion of growth process in the body and the accompanying behavioral changes.
32. **megalomania** (meg′ə-lō-mā′nē-ə): delusions of wealth, power, and self-importance.
33. **melancholia** (mel′ən-kō′lē-ə): a mental disorder characterized by extreme gloominess and depression of spirits.
34. **neurasthenic** (noor′əs-then′ik): afflicted with fatigue, worry, pains, etc., because of emotional conflicts.
35. **neurosis** (nyoo-rō′sis): an emotional disorder, less severe than a psychosis, characterized by anxieties, obsessions, compulsions, and physical complaints.
36. **obsession:** an idea or desire that haunts the mind.
37. **parapsychology** (par′ə): the study of clairvoyance, telepathy, and other apparently supernatural phenomena.
38. **phobia** (fō′bē-ə): any irrational or morbid fear.
39. **pleasure principle:** automatic adjustment of one's thoughts to secure pleasure and to avoid pain.
40. **projection:** ascribing one's own motives to someone else, thus relieving one's ego of guilt feelings.
41. **psychedelic** (sī′ki-del′ik): of a mental state, usually drug-induced, marked by entrancement and blissful aesthetic perceptiveness.
42. **psychodrama:** the acting out of situations related to one's problem, as a form of cathartic therapy.
43. **Rorschach test** (rōr′shäk): the analysis of personality by means of responses to inkblot designs.
44. **sadism** (sad′iz-əm): the deriving of sexual pleasure from hurting one's partner.
45. **stimulus** (stim′yoo-ləs): anything that excites an organism, organ, or part into activity.
46. **subjective:** reflecting a person's feelings and thinking rather than objective reality.
47. **sublimation:** the channeling of psychic energy into socially acceptable activities.
48. **subliminal** (sub-lim′ə-nəl): below the level of consciousness but perceptible by the subconscious.
49. **synapsis** (si-nap′sis): the point where a nerve impulse passes from one neuron to the next.
50. **xenophobia** (zen′ə-fō′bē-ə): fear or hatred of strangers and foreigners.

14

Business and Law

actuary, 1
affidavit, 2
collateral, 4
felony, 6
franchise, 8
indictment, 9
injunction, 10

larceny, 7
libel, 11
lien, 13
negotiable, 5
notarize, 3
perjury, 15
precedent, 16

prospectus, 17
realty, 14
solvent, 19
speculation, 18
subpoena, 12
voucher, 20

This chapter is recommended to only two groups of students:

1. Those going into business or law
2. Those not going into business or law

All citizens, in short, must wet their feet in commercial law. In the words of the jurist Sir William Blackstone, good citizens "cannot, in any scene of life, discharge properly their duty either to the public or to themselves, without some degree of knowledge in the laws" (1753).

Pick up a newspaper and you read of *indictments, injunctions, libel suits,* and *felonies.* Buy a house and you must talk of *realty, collateral, mortgages,* and *easements.* Open a pizza parlor and you bandy words like *franchise, prospectus, solvent,* and *vouchers.* Inescapably you live in a world of business law.

First, master the twenty programed words, then get acquainted with the fifty terms in the supplementary list. You will meet these words again—possibly during life's crises—and you will be grateful that you recognize them.

Exercises

COVER THIS STRIP

1. **actuary** (ak′choo-er′ē): a person who calculates risks, premiums, etc., for insurance purposes.

actuary

▶ The insurance company mathematician who uses statistical records to figure out what rates to charge is called an *ac_____*.

▶ If you wanted to insure your outdoor music festival against rain, the *actuary* would first consult (a) the probabilities of rain on that date, (b) an astrology book. ( )

(a)

actuary
(b)

▶ The statistical expert of an insurance company, who is known as an _____, must be especially qualified in (a) poetry, (b) mathematics. ( )

(b)

▶ If an insurance company keeps charging too low a premium for the company to make a profit (an unlikely situation), the fault is probably that of (a) the filing clerks, (b) the actuaries. ( )

2. **affidavit** (af-i-dā′vit): a sworn, written statement, witnessed by an authorized person.

3. **notarize** (nō′tə-rīz′): to authenticate or certify a document through a notary public.

notarize

▶ A public official known as a notary public will put his seal and signature on your wedding certificate, that is, he will *n_____* it.

(b)

▶ An *affidavit* is a sworn legal statement (a) spoken in court, (b) written and witnessed. ( )

affidavit
notarize

▶ A hit-and-run motorist has smashed your parked VW. If your star witness is too ill to testify in court for you, his testimony should be submitted in the form of an *af_____*, that is, a sworn statement that a notary public would *n_____*.

229

(b)	▸ It is necessary to *notarize* (a) your English composition, (b) a birth certificate. ( )
affidavit (b)	▸ To avoid having to pay out-of-state tuition, a college student sometimes needs a sworn, written statement, or af_____, testifying that he has been a resident of the state for a full year. This *affidavit* must be by (a) a member of congress, (b) somebody who has known the student for the past year. ( )
notarize affidavit (a)	▸ An important function of a notary public is to certify, or n_____, a sworn statement known as an a_____, which deals as a rule with (a) legal matters, (b) doctors' prescriptions. ( )

4. **collateral** (kə-lat′ər-əl): any security, such as stocks and bonds, that guarantees the payment of a loan.
5. **negotiable** (ni-gō′shē-ə-bəl): legally transferable to a third party: said of checks, promissory notes, and securities.

(a)	▸ *Collateral* is (a) security that guaranteees payment of a debt, (b) a tricky football maneuver. ( )
can	▸ A *negotiable* instrument, such as most personal checks, _____ [can / cannot] be made payable to a third party.
negotiable	▸ If a bill of exchange or a promissory note uses a phrase such as "pay to bearer" or "pay to the order of," that financial instrument is n_____.
collateral	▸ Most people who buy a house must borrow money from a bank and must guarantee repayment of that bank loan with some sort of c_____, usually a mortgage on the house.
negotiable collateral	▸ If transferable, your shares of stock are said to be n_____ and they may be used as c_____ to secure a loan.
collateral	▸ A farmer might use his crop or his farm equipment as security for a loan, in other words, as c_____.

Quiz

Write the letter that indicates the best definition.

1. (c)
2. (a)
3. (e)
4. (d)
5. (b)

( ) 1. actuary   a. a written statement made on oath
( ) 2. affidavit   b. transferable to a third party
( ) 3. notarize   c. an expert on insurance risks
( ) 4. collateral   d. security for a loan
( ) 5. negotiable   e. to certify a document officially

6. **felony** (fel'ə-nē): a major crime such as murder or burglary, usually punished in the United States by more than a year of imprisonment.
7. **larceny** (lar'sə-nē): theft. Stealing property valued above a certain amount, possibly $100 or as fixed by state law, is *grand larceny;* stealing a lesser amount is *petit* (or *petty*) *larceny.*

▶ A *felony* is a major crime such as (a) overtime parking, (b) rape. ( )   (b)

▶ *Larceny* refers to (a) theft, (b) wife-beating. ( )   (a)

▶ The crime of kidnapping is a f_____.   felony

▶ The plant manager who misappropriates (steals) several thousand dollars in company funds is guilty of a f_____, specifically, grand l_____.   felony / larceny

▶ The girl who stole a brassiere worth six dollars from a department store was guilty of petty l_____.   larceny

▶ Which of the following is *not* a *felony*? (a) burglary, (b) forgery, (c) murder, (d) hijacking, (e) failure to get a dog license for Rover. ( )   (e)

8. **franchise** (fran'chīz): the right to vote; also, a special privilege granted by the government or by a corporation: as, a *franchise* to operate a bus line, a *franchise* to operate a McDonald's Restaurant.

▶ To exercise one's *franchise* means (a) to jog, (b) to vote. ( )   (b)

(a)

▸ The root *franc,* from Old French, means "free." Thus, the *franchise* granted by the city council to the telephone company or to the waterworks is (a) a special, exclusive privilege, (b) a heavy tax. ( )

franchise

▸ The competition of two or three gas companies in the same town would result in excessive digging and inefficiency; therefore, one company is usually granted the exclusive right to operate, known as a f_____.

(a)

▸ Since a *franchise* restrains others from entering the same business or trade, it tends to establish (a) a legal monopoly, (b) open competition. ( )

franchise

▸ Suppose you want to be the only distributor of Wingding Waterbeds in Snorkelville; you might apply for the local f_____.

franchise
(b)

▸ In 1920 the Nineteenth Amendment to the Constitution gave women the f_____, also known as suffrage, which means (a) the right to suffer in the kitchen, (b) the right to vote. ( )

---

9. **indictment** (in-dīt′mənt): a formal accusation by a grand jury.
10. **injunction** (in-jungk′shən): a legal order requiring that certain people do, or refrain from doing, certain things.

(b)

▸ Amanda's fickle boy friend is found shot to death. The grand jury prepares an *indictment* against Amanda. This means that she (a) is guilty, (b) must face trial. ( )

indictment

▸ The formal accusation by a grand jury is an in_____.

injunction

▸ To prevent a neighbor from erecting a "spite" fence that would shade your yard, you would file an in_____.

(b)

▸ An *injunction* is (a) a word like *and, but, or, for,* and *nor,* (b) a court order to prevent or to enforce action. ( )

indictment

▸ The grand jury has reason to believe that the city manager accepted "payola" (bribes); therefore, the jury brings him to trial by means of an _____.

232

injunction

▶ The Dingle Duo signed a contract to play exclusively for your night club, yet they intend to play for your competitor next week. You can stop them by means of a court order known as an _____.

injunction
indictment

▶ Each night a certain insecticide factory pours lethal wastes into the air; this unneighborly practice is stopped by a court order known as an _____. Later the manager apparently sets fire to the factory for insurance purposes. To bring him to trial, the grand jury issues an _____.

Quiz

Write the letter that indicates the best definition.

1. (d)
2. (c)
3. (a)
4. (b)
5. (e)

( ) 1. felony   a. a special privilege
( ) 2. larceny   b. accusation by a grand jury
( ) 3. franchise   c. theft
( ) 4. indictment   d. a crime such as murder or forgery
( ) 5. injunction   e. a legal restraining order

11. **libel** (līʹbəl): the writing or printing of something false or damaging about someone.
12. **subpoena** (sə-pēʹnə): a legal order directing a person to appear in court to testify.

(a)

▶ You would be guilty of *libel* if you spread lies about a person (a) in your writing, (b) in your speeches. ( )

libel

▶ Defaming your sheriff by word of mouth would be slander; defaming him in a magazine article would be l_____.

(b)

▶ A *subpoena* is a legal order that requires a person (a) to go back to work, (b) to testify in court. ( )

subpoena

▶ You are accused of a felony, but the witness who could clear you says he is too busy to come to your trial. You may have to s_____ him.

233

libel wrote (b)	▶ You might be sued for l_____ if you _____ [said / wrote] that the new scoutmaster was (a) "a remarkable shaper of boys' character," (b) "a drunken pervert who sells dope to the boys." ( )
libel subpoena	▶ In a so-called letter of recommendation to Mr. Shoat, your boss refers to you as "a paranoiac pickpocket and a stinking swindler." You instigate a l_____ suit against your boss and—since Shoat is somewhat reluctant to testify—you request the court to issue a s_____ for Shoat. If Shoat ignores the *subpoena* he is in *contempt of court*.

13. **lien** (lēn): a claim on a property as security against payment of a debt.
14. **realty** (rē′əl-tē): real estate; land and buildings.

(b)	▶ Real estate is known as (a) reality, (b) realty. ( )
realty (a)	▶ A realtor deals in r_____; that is, he helps you buy or sell (a) house and land, (b) stocks and bonds. ( )
(b)	▶ A *lien* on a property is (a) a building or fence that leans against it, (b) a claim against it. ( )
lien	▶ The right of a creditor to control another person's property in order to satisfy a debt is a l_____.
realty lien	▶ When you buy a home or other r_____, you should be aware of any claim, or l_____, of creditors against that property.
lien	▶ Suppose you build a garage for Mr. Grob and he refuses to pay for your labor. You can protect your claim by taking out a l_____ on Grob's property.

15. **perjury** (pûr′jə-rē): the telling of a lie by a witness under oath; false testimony in court, considered a felony.

(a)	▶ *Perjury* is (a) lying, (b) stealing. ( )

perjury

▶ Sonya testifies falsely in court that Bill was playing checkers with her at her apartment at the time of the bank robbery. She has committed p_____.

(b)

▶ *Perjury* refers to (a) ordinary fibbing, (b) lying about a vital matter in court while under oath to tell the truth. ( )

perjury
(a)

▶ Suppose you see your friend Fleegle speed through a red light and cause a three-car smashup, yet you swear in court that the light was green. You are guilty of p_____, an offense regarded by the court as (a) a felony, (b) fairly trivial. ( )

Quiz

Write the letter that indicates the best definition.

1. (c)
2. (a)
3. (b)
4. (e)
5. (d)

( ) 1. libel   a. legal order to appear in court
( ) 2. subpoena   b. a claim on property
( ) 3. lien   c. written defamation of character
( ) 4. realty   d. the telling of lies at a trial
( ) 5. perjury   e. real estate

16. **precedent** (pres′ə-dənt): a legal decision that may serve as an example for a later one.

(a)

▶ A *precedent* is an earlier law case that is (a) similar to the present one, (b) different from the present one. ( )

precedent

▶ Lawyers like to cite prior legal decisions that can serve as a p_____ for the present case.

precedent

▶ Sometimes the divorced father is given custody of the children—let us consider the case of *Spatz v. Spatz* as a p_____.

(b)

▶ The lawyer said that Ringo's lawsuit was without *precedent*. This means that (a) Ringo would lose the case, (b) no case like it had ever been tried in court. ( )

235

17. **prospectus** (prə-spec′təs): a statement outlining a proposed business undertaking or literary work.
18. **speculation:** making risky business investments in the hope of big profits.

▶ A *prospectus* for a business venture is a review of (a) past achievements, (b) future possibilities. ( )   (b)

▶ Before offering a contract, a publishing company will expect to see at least an outline, or p_____, of your proposed book.   prospectus

▶ *Speculation* refers to a kind of (a) ornamenting of garments, with specks, (b) business gambling. ( )   (b)

▶ Much frantic *speculation* has taken place (a) in Wall Street, (b) in the Grand Canyon. ( )   (a)

▶ Buying and selling for quick profit is known as s_____. *Speculation* very commonly involves dabbling in (a) bathtubs, (b) real estate. ( )   speculation / (b)

▶ The new Low-Cal Pizza Company has painted a rosy picture of its prospects in its initial p_____. Better buy shares of its stock if you are interested in s_____.   prospectus / speculation

---

19. **solvent** (sol′vənt): able to pay all one's debts.
20. **voucher:** a receipt showing payment of a debt.

▶ A business firm is *solvent* (a) if it has some money in the bank, (b) if it can pay all of its bills. ( )   (b)

▶ A firm may go bankrupt when it is no longer s_____.   solvent

▶ A *voucher* is (a) a receipt showing that a debt has been paid, (b) a stinging insect. ( )   (a)

▶ When you take an all-expenses-paid trip, you had better hang on to every v_____.   voucher

236

solvent

▶ The Clumpy Cleaners haven't been able to pay salaries for ten weeks. "We're almost clean out of funds," says Mr. Clumpy. "Our company isn't s_____.

voucher

▶ If the Internal Revenue agent doubts any expense in your income tax statement, show him a v_____.

voucher
solvent

▶ The accountant for our Mucilage Manufacturing Company has gone over every bill, asset, and v_____. She says that our future is sticky but that we are still s_____.

Quiz

Write the letter that indicates the best definition.

1. (d)
2. (b)
3. (e)
4. (c)
5. (a)

( ) 1. precedent   a. evidence of payment
( ) 2. prospectus   b. an outline of a future undertaking
( ) 3. speculation   c. able to meet financial responsibilities
( ) 4. solvent   d. an earlier, similar law case
( ) 5. voucher   e. risky investment for fat profit

Review Test

Supply the missing word in each sentence. The first letters of the answers are given.

1. To tell a lie in court while sworn to tell the truth is p_____.
2. A firm that can pay all its debts is s_____.
3. A receipt showing that a payment has been made is a v_____.
4. A judicial decision that furnishes a model for deciding a later, similar case is a pr_____.
5. A major crime such as armed robbery or embezzlement is a f_____.
6. In most towns an electric company is given an exclusive privilege to operate, known as a f_____.
7. A claim on a property, such as a mortgage or a bill for unpaid taxes, is a l_____.
8. You can make a reluctant witness attend a trial by serving him a court order called a s_____.
9. The insurance expert who calculates risks and premiums is an a_____.
10. The grand jury brings a possible criminal to trial by issuing a formal accusation known as an i_____.

Write *True* or *False*.

_____ 11. An *affidavit* requires the signature of an authorized witness.

_____ 12. *Negotiable* bonds can be cashed only by the original purchaser.

_____ 13. If you make false accusations in a radio speech, defaming another person, you are guilty of *libel*.

_____ 14. To secure a loan a person could use his house as *collateral*.

_____ 15. Buying farmland and buildings in the hope of selling at a profit is a form of *speculation*.

_____ 16. *Larceny* is a sexual offense.

_____ 17. *Realty* means "not imaginary."

_____ 18. A *prospectus* might describe a proposed business venture or a proposed literary production.

_____ 19. A notary public is able to *notarize* an affidavit.

_____ 20. An *injunction* is a highway intersection.

Key to Review Test

Check your answers by the following key. Deduct 5% per error from a possible 100%.

1. perjury	6. franchise	11. True	16. False
2. solvent	7. lien	12. False	17. False
3. voucher	8. subpoena	13. False	18. True
4. precedent	9. actuary	14. True	19. True
5. felony	10. indictment	15. True	20. False

Score: _____%

Supplementary List

1. **ad valorem** (ad və-lōr′əm): in proportion to the value: said of a duty on imports.
2. **amortization** (am′ər-ti-zā′shən): gradual settling of a debt by installment payments.
3. **annuity** (ə-noō′i-tē): a sum of money paid yearly to a person during his lifetime.
4. **beneficiary** (ben′ə-fish′ə-rē): a person who is to receive funds or other property under a trust, will, or insurance policy.
5. **broker:** a person who buys and sells securities for his customers.
6. **cartel** (kär-tel′): an international syndicate that aims at monopoly and price-fixing.
7. **cashier's check:** a check backed by the bank's own funds and signed by the cashier.
8. **caveat emptor** (kā′vē-at emp′tôr): L., let the buyer beware, implying that one buys at his own risk.
9. **codicil** (kod′ə-sil): an addition or supplement to a will.
10. **copyright:** the exclusive right for a limited period to print and dispose of a literary or artistic work.
11. **covenant:** a solemn agreement; a formal, sealed contract.
12. **de facto** (dē fak′tō): L., in fact; actually existing, whether legal or not; distinguished from *de jure* (dē joor′i), according to law.
13. **deflationary:** characterized by a decline in prices caused by a decrease in spending.
14. **easement:** the right or privilege of making a special, limited use of someone else's property: as, a right of way.
15. **eminent domain:** the right of a governmental body to take private property for public use upon giving just compensation to the owner.
16. **encumbrance:** a claim or lien upon a property.
17. **ex post facto** (eks pōst fak′tō): L., having retroactive effect: as an *ex post facto* law.
18. **foreclosure:** public sale by court order of property on which the mortgage has not been paid.
19. **habeas corpus** (hā′bē-əs kôr′pəs): L., a writ that would free a prisoner who is held without legal charges; literally, "Have the body."
20. **intestate** (in-tes′tāt): having made no will before death.
21. **ipso facto** (ip′sō fac′tō): L., by that very fact.
22. **jurisprudence:** a system or philosophy of law.
23. **kangaroo court:** *colloq.* an unauthorized and irregular court which ignores or perverts normal legal procedure.
24. **lame duck:** a lawmaker or officeholder who continues in office for a time after his defeat for reelection.
25. **legal tender:** money which may be lawfully used in payment of debts.
26. **litigation** (lit′ə-gā′shən): legal action; a lawsuit.
27. **misdemeanor** (mis′di-mē′nər): a minor offense; a crime less serious than a felony.
28. **moratorium** (mor′ə-tor′ē-əm): legal authorization to delay the payment of debts, as in an emergency.
29. **mortgage** (mor′gij): the pledging of property as security for payment of a debt.
30. **negligence** (neg′li-jəns): the failure to exercise such care as one would ordinarily expect of a reasonable, prudent person.
31. **plenary** (plē′nə-rē): full; attended by all members: as, a *plenary* session.

32. **pocket veto:** veto of a congressional bill, at the end of a session, for lack of presidential action.
33. **preferred stock:** shares which receive dividends or distributed assets first, before common stock gets any.
34. **probate** (prō′bāt): the process by which a will is proved to be authentic or valid.
35. **proviso** (prə-vī′zō): a stipulation or condition that is attached to a contract or a statute.
36. **quitclaim:** a deed giving up one's claim to some property or right of action.
37. **ratification:** approval; confirmation.
38. **requisition:** a formal written order or request, as for certain equipment.
39. **respondent:** the defendant.
40. **restitution:** reimbursement for loss or damage.
41. **scrip:** a temporary paper to be redeemed later for money or other benefits.
42. **statute** (stach′oot): an established law or rule.
43. **stipend** (stī′pend): a salary, pension, or allowance.
44. **submarginal:** unprofitable; unproductive; not worth cultivating.
45. **syndicate** (sin′də-kit): an association of individuals formed to conduct a business enterprise requiring much capital.
46. **tort:** any injury or damage for which a civil suit can be brought.
47. **usury** (yōō′zhə-rē): lending money at an unlawfully high rate of interest.
48. **venue** (ven′yōō): the locality where a legal case is tried.
49. **waiver:** the voluntary giving up of a right.
50. **working capital:** the excess of current assets over debts and obligations.

15

Fiction

alienation, 30	irony of fate, 16	realism, 27
allegory, 23	local color, 9	satire, 24
anachronism, 7	motivation, 12	science fiction, 21
anti-hero, 14	naturalism, 28	sentimentalism, 26
characterization, 11	novel, 1	setting, 8
coincidence, 4	novelette, 2	social criticism, 25
epistolary novel, 17	picaresque novel, 18	stream of consciousness, 15
existentialism, 29	plot, 3	suspense, 5
flashback, 6	point of view, 10	Victorian novel, 20
Gothic novel, 19	protagonist, 13	whodunit, 22

People read fiction mainly for pleasure. As with music or painting or pizza-making, however, one derives increased pleasure the more he knows about his subject. A college student should be aware of the different types of novels: Gothic, Victorian, epistolary, picaresque, existentialist, and so on. He should recognize such attributes as suspense, local color, stream of consciousness, and motivation. A student can enjoy fiction without knowing a myth from a moth, but he can appreciate fiction better and discuss it more intelligently if he understands some technical terms associated with it.

Study the definitions carefully. Fill in the blanks without looking back to the top of the frame.

Exercises

COVER THIS STRIP

1. **novel:** a long fictitious prose story of some complexity, involving characters, scenes, and action. The first English *novel* is usually said to be Samuel Richardson's *Pamela,* published in 1740; the first American novel is William Hill Brown's *The Power of Sympathy* (1789).
2. **novelette:** a short novel, about fifty to a hundred pages long, for example, Ernest Hemingway's *The Old Man and the Sea* (1952).

▶ A *novel* is a long _____ [factual / fictitious] story which _____ [does / does not] involve characters and action.

fictitious
does

▶ If sixty pages long, a story is usually called a n_____.

novelette

▶ Samuel Richardson's *Pamela,* a lengthy fictitious story, was the first English n_____.

novel

▶ Herman Melville's fictitious story *Benito Cereno* (1856) is about seventy pages long and can be referred to as a _____.

novelette

▶ A *novelette* is _____ [shorter / longer] than a short story and _____ [shorter / longer] than a novel.

longer
shorter

3. **plot:** the central plan of action in a story or play; the author's arrangement of episodes. The story consists of certain events in chronological order, whereas the *plot* is the form into which the author organizes those events.
4. **coincidence** (kō-in'sə-dəns): the remarkable occurrence of certain events at the same time, apparently by chance. For example, Longfellow's Evangeline is separated from her lover Gabriel and, years later, as an old nurse, she finds him by chance just as he is dying in an alms-house.

▶ By the *plot* of a novel we mean (a) its general subject, (b) its arrangement of action. ( )

(b)

243

coincidence ▶ When Huck Finn, by sheerest chance, arrives at a distant farmhouse on the very day when Tom Sawyer is expected there, it is c_____.

less ▶ The overuse of *coincidences* in a story tends to make the *plot* _____ [more / less] believable.

(a) ▶ Aristotle says in his *Poetics* that the most important element of tragedy is *plot,* by which he means (a) the plan of action, (b) the moral tone. ( )

plot
coincidence ▶ O. Henry stresses the plan of action, or __*plot*__, but unfortunately his *plot* usually hinges on some incredible chance meeting, or c_*oincidence*_.

---

5. **suspense:** uncertainty as to the outcome; anxiety caused by a tense situation. *Suspense* is an indispensable ingredient of the mystery thriller and the melodrama.
6. **flashback:** an interruption in a story or play to present action which occurred earlier. *Flashback* breaks up the orderly time sequence but often gains psychological values.

(a) ▶ *Suspense* refers to (a) uncertainty, (b) pleasure. (a)

flashback ▶ In the play *Death of a Salesman,* Willy Loman is shown remembering and reliving a hotel episode of an earlier period—this is a f_*lashback*_.

past ▶ The *flashback,* often very effective in drama, jumps to the __*past*__ [past / future].

suspense ▶ During the fourth act of his five-act plays Shakespeare has the unhappy problem of keeping alive the uncertainty and tension known as s_*uspense*_.

(a) ▶ The maintaining of *suspense* is especially important in the (a) mystery story, (b) essay. (a)

suspense
flashback

▸ The condemned killer is strapped to the electric chair in a scene fraught with __suspense__; then suddenly we see him, years earlier, as a boy scout winning a prize at Sunday school—this time shift is called __flashback__.

---

7. **anachronism** (ə-nak′rə-niz′əm): representing something as happening in the wrong historical period. An *anachronism* occurs in *Julius Caesar* when Cassius says, "The clock has stricken three."

anachronism

▸ Raphael's depiction of the Holy Family in medieval clothing is an __anachronism__.

(b)

▸ An *anachronism* is an error involving (a) bad grammar, (b) the wrong period of time. (__b__)

anachronism
(b)

▸ In a western film, critics noticed a time-flaw, or an __anachronism__: above the Indians could be seen (a) an eagle, (b) a commercial airplane. (__b__)

anachronism
(a)

▸ It would also be a historical error, or an __anachronism__, to show Abraham Lincoln using (a) an electric shaver, (b) a feather pen. (__a__)

Quiz

Write the letter that indicates the best definition.

1. (g)
2. (e)
3. (b)
4. (a)
5. (d)
6. (f)
7. (c)

(g) 1. anachronism
(e) 2. coincidence
(b) 3. flashback
(a) 4. novel
(d) 5. novelette
(f) 6. plot
(c) 7. suspense

a. a full-length fictitious story
b. a shift to earlier events
c. anxiety as to how things will turn out
d. a fictitious story shorter than a novel but longer than fifty pages
e. the simultaneous occurrence of unrelated incidents
f. the pattern of story action
g. an event misplaced in history

---

8. **setting:** the physical and spiritual surroundings or environment in which the story takes place. The *setting* of Sinclair Lewis's *Main Street* (1920) is a midwestern village.

9. **local color:** picturesque details—of customs, dialect, and scenery—that bring out a specific story setting. *Local color* is prominent in Bret Harte's portrayal of mining camps, saloons, riffraff, and mining lingo.

▶ *Setting* refers to the story's _background_ [action / background].

▶ Nathaniel Hawthorne's *The Scarlet Letter* (1850) has a Puritan village as its background, or s_etting_____.

▶ *The Scarlet Letter* reflects *local color* in (a) the pillory, Puritan garments, and pious talk, (b) the vengeance theme. (a)

▶ Jesse Stuart's depiction of the dialect, garb, cabins, and oddities of the Kentucky backwoods people supplies the _local_____ color to this ___setting_____ [setting / anachronism].

▶ The *setting* of Truman Capote's *In Cold Blood* (1965) is (a) a Kansas town, (b) the slaying of a family. (a)

▶ Sarah Orne Jewett was a *local colorist,* since her stories depict customs, dialect, and setting that exist (a) anywhere, (b) only in Maine. (b)

---

10. **point of view:** the writer's way of telling his story, whether as participant or as observer, whether as seen by one character or by many characters, whether with objectivity or with editorial comment. *Tom Sawyer* is told in the third person from an omniscient *point of view,* but *Huckleberry Finn* is told in the first person from Huck's *point of view.*

▶ A writer of fiction decides at the outset through whose eyes the story action will be seen; in other words, he chooses and sticks to a definite (a) point of view, (b) all-knowing attitude. (a)

▶ In Poe's "The Tell-Tale Heart" (1843) the narrator says, "I loved the old man," and we know that the *point of* ___view_____ is ___first_____ [first / third] person.

246

should not

▸ Suppose you write a novelette from the first person point of view. Then the secret thoughts and conversations of various non-present characters probably _should not_ [should / should not] be described.

point
third

▸ Horatio Alger pointed out that his "hero" was "poor but honest"—the _point_ of view is _third_ [first / third] person.

---

11. **characterization** (kar′ik-tər-i-zā′shən): the portrayal of people, their physical and spiritual traits and peculiarities. Good *characterization* is consistent and three-dimensional, developed largely by action and dialogue rather than merely by flat abstract description.
12. **motivation:** that which causes a character to do what he does. What *motivations* cause Macbeth to murder Duncan?

characterization

▸ The way people are portrayed is ch_aracterization_

motivation

▸ The passion, grievance, or need which impels a character to act as he does is his m_otivation_.

motivation

▸ Men will not kill, seek divorces, or chase whales without sufficient _motivation_.

characterization

▸ Thomas Wolfe portrayed people so that you came to know their yearnings, their impulses, and their warts—this was effective _characterization_.

motivation
characterization

▸ The sudden reform of sinners and drunkards at the ends of sentimental stories is usually without sufficient m_otivation_—it suggests faulty ch_aracterization_.

---

13. **protagonist** (prō-tag′ə-nist): the main character of a drama or fictional work. Hamlet, Ivanhoe, Huck Finn, and Brer Rabbit are *protagonists* of literary pieces.
14. **anti-hero:** a protagonist who lacks the noble spirit or admirable life purposes usually found in a heroic figure. Modern fiction depicts many an aimless, sinful *anti-hero*.

protagonist anti-hero	▶ The chief character of a novel or drama is known as its _protagonist_. If this *protagonist* is an ordinary, fault-ridden fellow with low aspirations he is an _anti-hero_.
protagonist anti-hero	▶ Clyde Griffith, as the central character of Theodore Dreiser's *An American Tragedy* (1925), is the novel's pro_tagonist_; and since Clyde is depicted as a stupid, blundering killer he is also an _anti-hero_.
is not	▶ A minor character, like Polonius in *Hamlet*, _is not_ [is / is not] the *protagonist*.
against antagonist	▶ Since *anti* means _against_ [around / against], the Greek play character who opposes the main character is called the _antagonist_ [antagonist / protagonist].
shabby	▶ The *anti-hero* of a modern novel usually has a flock of _shabby_ [inspirational / shabby] traits.

15. **stream of consciousness** (kon-′shəs-nis): thoughts and feelings of a character presented as an unceasing, disjointed sequence. *Stream of consciousness* presents a flow of random, fragmented, semi-articulate thoughts from all levels of consciousness and unconsciousness, often as a kind of unpunctuated *interior monologue*.

consciousness	▶ The interior monologue—the puns and the jumble of impressions—in James Joyce's *Ulysses* (1922) reflects the protagonist's *stream of* _consciousness_.
(b)	▶ The thoughts in *stream of consciousness* are (a) uniform and coherent, (b) disjointed and fragmentary. (b)
stream (a)	▶ Authors like William Faulkner and Virginia Woolf, using _stream_ *of consciousness* techniques, have depicted the flow of human thought as a kind of (a) interior monologue, (b) an unbroken chain of logic. (a)

248

Quiz

Write the letter that indicates the best definition.

1. (f)
2. (e)
3. (g)
4. (d)
5. (b)
6. (a)
7. (c)
8. (h)

(f) 1. setting   a. the main character or hero
(e) 2. local color   b. the cause of a character's action
(g) 3. point of view   c. an unadmirable protagonist
(d) 4. characterization   d. how people are portrayed
(b) 5. motivation   e. picturesque, distinctive details
(a) 6. protagonist   f. background of the action
(c) 7. anti-hero   g. the outlook from which the action is described
(h) 8. stream of consciousness   h. jumbled thoughts and feelings

---

16. **irony of fate** (ī′rə-nē): the way that destiny twists or foils the plans of men. Thomas Hardy's characters get a glimpse of happiness but by some *irony of fate* they fail to achieve it.

fate

▸ The *irony of* ___fate___ has a way of providing (a) the expected reward, (b) the unexpected disaster. (b)

(b)

▸ In Stephen Crane's "The Open Boat" (1898) the unselfish oiler who is possibly the most deserving of life is the only man who drowns—this illustrates (a) the irony of fate, (b) that this is the best of all possible worlds. (a)

(a)

irony

▸ The ___irony___ *of fate* would be illustrated if the fire department building (a) needed painting, (b) burned down. (b)

(b)

---

17. **epistolary novel** (i-pis′tə-ler′ē): a novel written in the form of a series of letters. The eighteenth-century *epistolary novel* told a story through an exchange of letters, or epistles, usually between the adventurous heroine and a female friend.
18. **picaresque novel** (pik′ə-resk′): a novel that has a vagabond hero who goes from one adventure to another. *Picaresque novels* such as Tobias Smollett's *Roderick Random* (1748) were popular during the eighteenth century.

epistolary

▸ Samuel Richardson's *Pamela* (1740) and *Clarissa Harlowe* (1748) consist entirely of fictional letters and are called e___pistolary___ novels.

(b)	▸ An epistle is (a) the wife of an apostle, (b) a letter. (b)
	▸ Mark Twain's *Huckleberry Finn* (1884), with its young rogue, episodic adventures, and satire, resembles the p_*icaresque*_ novel.
picaresque	
picaresque (b)	▸ The vagabond hero of a *picaresque* novel is usually involved in (a) a single episode, (b) a series of adventures. (b)
epistolary	▸ J. P. Marquand's *The Late George Apley* (1936), which is told by means of letters, is a modern *epistolary* novel.
picaresque rogue (b)	▸ The protagonist of a *picaresque* novel is a *rogue* [gentleman / rogue] who usually (a) stays in one place, (b) travels from one adventure to another. (b)

19. **Gothic novel:** a horror tale often involving a haunted castle, secret passages, mysterious noises and crimes. Mary Godwin Shelley's *Frankenstein* (1818) is a *Gothic novel*.
20. **Victorian novel:** an English novel written during the reign of Queen Victoria, 1837–1901, and reflecting—unthinkingly or satirically—the leisurely literary style, "decent" tastes, and empty respectability of that period. Distinguished *Victorian novels* were written by Charles Dickens, Thomas Hardy, William Thackeray, Samuel Butler, George Eliot, and others.

Gothic	▸ Novels involving haunted castles and clanking chains—such as *The Mysteries of Udolpho* (1794), by Anne Radcliffe—are *Gothic* [Gothic / picaresque].
Victorian	▸ Complacency, prudishness, and moral earnestness are common to the bulky V*ictorian* novel of the nineteenth century.
Frankenstein (b)	▸ The *Gothic novel*, such as *Frankenstein* [David Copperfield / Frankenstein], stressed (a) cheerful events, (b) terror. (b)
Gothic (a)	▸ Horace Walpole's bloodcurdling *The Castle of Otranto* (1764) was typically *Gothic* [agnostic / Gothic] in dealing with (a) ghosts and madmen, (b) childhood sweethearts and business success. (a)

Victorian nineteenth	▸ English authors like Dickens and Hardy wrote slow-paced *V_____* novels during the _____ [eighteenth / nineteenth] century.

21. **science fiction:** fantasies about time machines, space travel, and future marvels, made credible by technical detail. Modern *science fiction* began with Jules Verne and H. G. Wells.
22. **whodunit** (hoo-dun'it): a murder story dealing with the detection of the criminal; a detective story. The *whodunit*—from "Who did it?"—began with Edgar Allan Poe and Sir Arthur Conan Doyle and is now an extremely popular type of fiction.

science (b)	▸ A novel about cities under the sea is called *sc_____ fiction* since it deals with (a) actual accomplishments, (b) fantastic incidents not yet realized. ( )
whodunit	▸ A novel by Dashiell Hammett which ends in the capture of a slayer is a *w_____*.
(b)	▸ Edgar Rice Burroughs' story of a battle between earthlings and Martians is classified by the librarian under (a) science, (b) science fiction. ( )
science	▸ Ray Bradbury's novel *Fahrenheit 451* (1953) and Aldous Huxley's novel *Brave New World* (1932) contain sharp social comment but are fantasies of future technology and are classed as _____ *fiction*.
whodunit detective	▸ An Erle Stanley Gardner murder yarn is a _____; in other words, it is a _____ [detective / science] story.

Quiz

Write the letter that indicates the best definition.

(f) 1. irony of fate a. fantasies about space travel
(d) 2. epistolary novel b. a detective story
(g) 3. picaresque novel c. a morally righteous novel of the Dickens-Hardy era
(e) 4. Gothic novel
(c) 5. Victorian novel d. a novel in letter form
(a) 6. science fiction e. a grotesque horror story
(b) 7. whodunit f. unexpected twist of destiny
g. a story of a vagabond's adventures

1. (f)
2. (d)
3. (g)
4. (e)
5. (c)
6. (a)
7. (b)

23. **allegory:** a symbolic story in which the actions and characters have a secondary set of meanings; the simultaneous telling of parallel stories. John Bunyan's *Pilgrim's Progress* (1678) is a very obvious *allegory*.

▶ A story like Swift's *Gulliver's Travels* (1726) with two sets of meanings is (a) an allegory, (b) a coincidence. (a)

(a)

▶ If Herman Melville's *Moby Dick* (1851) is symbolic and tells several distinct parallel stories, as critics claim, then it is an *allegory*.

allegory

▶ *Piers Plowman* (fourteenth century) is called an *allegory* because (a) it deals with country life, (b) its simple action has a secondary, spiritual interpretation. (b)

(b)

▶ A long symbolic story such as Samuel Butler's *Erewhon* (1872) is known as an *allegory* because it has (a) one level of meaning, (b) two or more levels of meaning. (b)

allegory
(b)

24. **satire:** wit, irony, or sarcasm used to ridicule abuses and follies. Outstanding *satire* has been written by Horace, Juvenal, Swift, Byron, Rabelais, Voltaire, Lewis Carroll, and others.
25. **social criticism:** the exposure of faults in various aspects of society. The *social criticism* of Sinclair Lewis hits at small town gossip, middle-class conformity, racial discrimination, and medical quackery.

social

▸ Harriet Beecher Stowe's *Uncle Tom's Cabin* (1852) attacks slavery and therefore represents important so__cial_____ criticism.

satire

▸ Had Mrs. Stowe used sarcasm and wit, her criticism might have taken the form of sa__tire_____.

satirists

▸ James Thurber and Aldous Huxley wittily ridiculed modern follies and may therefore be called ___satirists___ [sadists / satirists].

satire
social

▸ Jonathan Swift's *Tale of a Tub* (1704) directs laughter at the faults of Englishmen and is thus sa__tire_____ as well as ___social___ criticism.

(b)

▸ The intention of *satire* is (a) to honor, (b) to ridicule. (b)

criticism
(a)

▸ Another story involving social __criticism__ is (a) John Steinbeck's *The Grapes of Wrath* (1939), exposing the miserable plight of the Okies, (b) Henry W. Longfellow's *Hiawatha* (1855), depicting an Indian romance. (a)

---

26. **sentimentalism:** excessive emotionalism, with emphasis on tender feelings and tears; called *sensibility* during the eighteenth century. Whereas *sentiment* is an expression of delicate, sensitive feelings, *sentimentalism* suggests a soft-heartedness that is gushy and insincere.
27. **realism:** the presentation of everyday life as it is, in accurate, photographic detail rather than in a romanticized way. *Realism* began as a nineteenth-century literary movement that tried to reflect actual life, using commonplace characters and depicting their ordinary impulses, problems, and surroundings.

sentimentalism

▸ In early American novels such phrases as "the sympathetic tears gushed down her cheeks" suggest literary s__entimentalism__

realism

▸ Sinclair Lewis's description of the dullness and dirtiness of Main Street is one of r__ealism_____.

excessive

▸ *Sentimentalism* refers to soft emotions that are ___excessive___ [quiet and restrained / excessive].

253

▸ *Realism* shows people and their surroundings as they __are__ [are / ought to be].

▸ *Sentimentalism,* whether in love poetry or in commercial greeting cards, is emotionally (a) honest and reasonable, (b) overdone. (__b__)

▸ William Dean Howells' *The Rise of Silas Lapham* (1885) reflects ordinary people and their problems and achieves r__ealism__.

▸ The scene describing the death of Little Nell, a classic tear-jerker by Dickens, illustrates __sentimentalism__.

---

28. **naturalism:** an extension of realism tending to stress sordidness and sexuality and to portray man as a soulless animal shaped by his environment and heredity. *Naturalism* is a leading modern literary movement; it denies supernaturalism and looks at man as a puppet lacking free will.

▸ Literary *naturalism* portrays man as (a) a noble creation of God, (b) an animal molded by his environment. (__b__)

▸ The extension of realism known as n__aturalism__ gives close attention to (a) sordidness and sexuality, (b) beauty and high ideals. (__a__)

▸ The *naturalistic* novels of Theodore Dreiser depict man as __brutish__ [god-like / brutish] and as __molded by__ [molded by / rising superior to] his environment.

---

29. **existentialism** (eg′zis-ten′shə-liz′əm): a view of life which maintains that man is alone in a purposeless universe and that he must exercise his own free will to oppose a hostile environment. This *existentialist* theme of man's total responsibility to himself in the midst of conformist pressures is reflected in the fiction of Jean-Paul Sartre, Albert Camus, Franz Kafka, and others.

30. **alienation** (al′yə-nā′shən): a separation from others and from participation; loss of affection. Man's sense of *alienation* from established society is a recurring theme in today's fiction.

▶ Literary *existentialism* stresses (a) the aloneness of man and the hostility of his environment, (b) the togetherness of mankind and the values of living. (a)

▶ The young anti-hero of Camus' *The Stranger* (1946) lacks religion, love, or human involvements; thus, the novel reflects ex_istentialism_ and illustrates man's essential _alienation_ [brotherhood / alienation].

▶ When man loses his faith and sees himself as a short-lived animal in an uncaring world, his sense of al_ienation_ is usually (a) increased, (b) decreased. (a)

▶ *Existentialism* maintains that man must make his choices in a _purposeless_ [meaningful / purposeless] existence.

▶ *Alienated* man, as depicted in the fiction of ex_istentialism_, tends to see life as (a) noble and spiritual, (b) absurd and pointless. (b)

Quiz

Write the letter that indicates the best definition.

(d) 1. allegory   a. emotionalism in excess
(e) 2. satire   b. separation from others
(g) 3. social criticism   c. portrayal of life as it is
(a) 4. sentimentalism   d. a story with a secondary
(c) 5. realism   interpretation
(h) 6. naturalism   e. a witty, often sophisticated attack
(f) 7. existentialism   on follies
(b) 8. alienation   f. Sartre's doctrine of man's
     responsibility to himself
   g. an exposure of social faults, often
     serious in tone
   h. an extension of realism,
     emphasizing sordidness

Review Test

Supply the missing word in each sentence. The first letter of each answer is given.

1. A long symbolic story in which characters and events have a secondary set of meanings is an a_*allegory*_.
2. The background or environment in which the story action takes place is the s_*setting*_.
3. Telling a story through an exchange of letters is the method of an e_*pistolary*_ novel.
4. Bringing out the personalities and individual traits of people in a story is c_*haracterization*_.
5. An extended horror story dealing, for example, with haunted castles and madmen is a G_*othic*_ novel.
6. Picturesque detail which brings out a particular story setting is local c_*olor*_.
7. The portrayal of an event or object in the wrong historical period is an a_*nachronism*_.
8. Each man is alone and must make his own decisions in a meaningless universe, according to ex_*istentialism*_.
9. A protagonist without noble qualities is an a_*nti-hero*_.
10. A remarkable chance occurrence of events at the same time is a c_*oincidence*_.

Write *True* or *False*.

False 11. *Motivation* is the moving about or traveling which takes place in a story.
False 12. In *stream of consciousness* the thoughts emerge in clear and logical fashion.
True 13. *Sentimentalism* is excessive emotionalism.
False 14. *Naturalism* focuses on the pleasanter and nobler aspects of life.
True 15. The *Victorian novel* was written by such authors as Charles Dickens, Thomas Hardy, and George Eliot.
True 16. *Science fiction* sometimes deals with interplanetary travel.
True 17. A *whodunit* is a detective story.
False 18. The *irony of fate* implies that man usually gets what he expects and deserves.
False 19. A *novelette* is an essay, somewhat longer than a novel.
False 20. *Social criticism* refers to the evaluation of the style, merits, and shortcomings of a book.

Write the letter that indicates the best completion.

(a) 21. The *plot* of a novel is its (a) plan of action, (b) moral, (c) background, (d) social criticism.
(d) 22. The *protagonist* of a *picaresque* novel is usually (a) a maiden, (b) a nobleman, (c) a lover, (d) a scamp.
(c) 23. Man's *alienation* refers to his (a) relatives, (b) foreign extraction, (c) aloneness in society, (d) sinfulness.
(b) 24. A *novel* is a long (a) life story, (b) fictitious story, (c) essay, (d) poem or play.
(d) 25. Most *satire* involves (a) suspense, (b) flashback, (c) sentimentalism, (d) irony and sarcasm.

Key to Review Test

Check your test answers by the following key. Deduct 4% per error from 100%.

1. allegory
2. setting
3. epistolary
4. characterization
5. Gothic
6. color
7. anachronism
8. existentialism
9. anti-hero
10. coincidence
11. False
12. False
13. True
14. False
15. True
16. True
17. True
18. False
19. False
20. False
21. (a)
22. (d)
23. (c)
24. (b)
25. (d)

Score: _____ %

Supplementary List

1. **anthology:** a collection of essays, stories, poems, or plays. An *anthology* is often used in college English classes.
2. **commonplace book:** a collection of miscellaneous thoughts, verses, and quotations jotted down for possible later use. Ben Jonson kept a *commonplace book* entitled *Timber,* which includes references to his friend William Shakespeare.
3. **expatriate** (eks-pā′trē-it): one who has left his native land. After World War I, many American *expatriates,* such as Gertrude Stein and Ernest Hemingway, lived and wrote in Paris.
4. **folklore:** the traditional legends, sayings, beliefs, and customs of the people. American *folklore* includes proverbs, riddles, superstitions, ballads, hunting and fishing yarns, and tales of the mountaineer and the cowboy.
5. **incunabula** (in′kyoo-nab′yoo-lə): books printed before 1500. *Incunabula* such as Sir Thomas Malory's *Le Morte d'Arthur,* printed by William Caxton in 1485, are rare treasures today.
6. **lampoon:** a coarsely humorous attack in prose or verse ridiculing someone. The *lampoon* is a particularly strong or malicious brand of satire.
7. **Lost Generation:** a term used by Gertrude Stein to describe the generation of young men and women who were disillusioned by World War I, and the nature of society, and who had therefore forsaken the traditional cultural values. The *Lost Generation* included writers such as Ernest Hemingway, F. Scott Fitzgerald, and John Dos Passos.
8. **motif** (mō-tēf′): a distinctive unifying feature or theme which recurs throughout a work. Ahab's passion for vengeance is a dominant *motif* in *Moby Dick*.
9. **myth:** an old story about gods or racial heroes which explains such things as the origin of the sun and the seasons or of social upheaval; also refers today to a prevailing concept of human nature such as the *myth* of Yankee ingenuity, the *myth* of progress, and the *myth* of the alienated man; also refers sometimes to the fictitious milieu of a particular literary work, as J. R. R. Tolkien's *myth* of the hobbits. Certain poets, such as Blake, Yeats, and T. S. Eliot, have created *myths* as framework for their poetry.
10. **narrative:** a story or an account of happenings. *Narratives* relate action, either factual or fictional, as in diaries, travel literature, ballads, and stories.
11. **Nobel prize** (nō-bel′): an annual prize (about $40,000) awarded in Stockholm, Sweden, to the outstanding writer of idealistic literature. Past winners include George Bernard Shaw, 1925; Sinclair Lewis, 1930; Eugene O'Neill, 1936; T. S. Eliot, 1948; William Faulkner, 1949; Ernest Hemingway, 1954.
12. **novel of manners:** a novel, often satiric, that reflects the customs and habits of a particular social class of a certain period. Novels of manners have been written by Jane Austen, Edith Wharton, and John P. Marquand.
13. **parable** (par′ə-bəl): a short simple story that illustrates a moral or spiritual truth. The Bible presents the *parable* of the prodigal son.
14. **parody** (par′ə-dē): comical imitation tending to ridicule an author or literary work. For example, Bret Harte's "Mrs. Judge Jenkins" (1871) is a *parody* of John Whittier's too-sentimental "Maud Muller" (1854).
15. **pornography** (pôr-nog′rə-fē): obscene writing designed to arouse sexual desire. By definition of the Supreme Court, *pornography* has no redeeming social value.

16. **primitivism:** the belief that primitive cultures are superior in many ways to our corrupt and complicated civilization and that people close to nature have better qualities than those in cities. Rousseau, Cooper, and Hemingway exhibit *primitivism* in their admiration for uncorrupted nature and for simple, red-blooded, earthy people.
17. **pseudonym** (soo′də-nim): a fictitious name or pen name; for example, George Eliot, *pseudonym* of Mary Ann Evans, who wrote *Silas Marner* (1861); Artemus Ward, *pseudonym* of the American humorist Charles F. Browne.
18. **redaction** (ri-dak′shən): the editing and reduction or revision of literary materials for publication. Magazine editors sometimes *redact* a popular novel and print a streamlined version.
19. **saga** (sä′gə): a story of heroic deeds, especially of medieval Icelandic heroes. The Viking *sagas* influenced Longfellow's poetry.
20. **synopsis** (si-nop′sis): a brief summary of the plot of a novel, drama, or other composition. A *synopsis* provides a quick general view of a subject without critical comment.
21. **tall-tale:** a yarn about incredible happenings, usually involving superhuman feats by a character. The remarkable deeds of Paul Bunyan and Davy Crockett occur in typical, humorous *tall-tales* of the frontier.
22. **tetralogy** (te-tral′ə-jē): a series, by a single author, of four related works. A *tetralogy* of dramas, consisting of three tragedies and a satyr play, were presented in sequence at the festival of Dionysus in Athens.
23. **thesaurus** (thi-sô′rəs): a treasury of words, with synonyms and antonyms classified and arranged to help writers. A dictionary and a *thesaurus* are indispensable to an author—talent helps, too.
24. **tone:** an author's attitude toward his material and his readers, whether reverent, jesting, cynical, impersonal, and so on. A nostalgic *tone* often pervades the lyric prose of Thomas Wolfe.
25. **trilogy** (tril′ə-jē): a series, by a single author, of three related works, as in fiction or drama. Eugene O'Neill's *Mourning Becomes Electra* (1931) is a *trilogy,* a series of three plays, in which the ancient Greek playwright Aeschylus's theme of fate haunts an American household.

16
Drama

catharsis, 10
choreography, 25
climax, 7
comedy, 14
conflict, 2
denouement, 8
deus ex machina, 24
dramatic irony, 12
exposition, 3

expressionism, 19
farce, 15
foreshadowing, 4
hamartia, 11
legitimate theater, 16
melodrama, 20
poetic justice, 21
problem play, 18
rising action, 5

soliloquy, 22
Stanislavski method, 23
theme, 1
tragedy, 9
turning point, 6
unities, 13
vaudeville, 17

References to drama are met in every literature course. You should be familiar with the names of various kinds of plays—tragedy, comedy, closet drama, problem play, the Theater of the Absurd—and with basic terms relating to the drama—foreshadowing, dramatic irony, turning point, expressionism. In analytical papers and class discussions you will find that knowing accurate technical terms saves time and windy explanations.

Note that many of these terms apply to other fields beside drama. When you analyze fiction and poetry, you refer there also to theme, conflict, exposition, poetic justice, and so on. Similarly, many literary terms defined in other chapters apply also to drama.

Incidentally, the spelling in this chapter is tricky. Look out for traps like *soliloquy, Stanislavski,* and *denouement.*

Exercises

COVER THIS STRIP

1. **theme:** the major idea of a literary work, stated in general terms; the message; the moral. The *theme* of *Macbeth* is that greedy ambition leads to disaster; the *plot* involves specific incidents.
2. **conflict:** the opposition of forces, or the struggle, necessary to any drama. *Conflict* may be against oneself, against other men, against nature or fate.

theme
(a)

▶ The major idea of a play, known as its t_*theme*_____, is usually stated (a) as a generalization, (b) with full details of names and actions. (a)

conflict
necessary

▶ The opposition of forces, or struggle, known as c_*onflict*_____, is usually considered to be ___*necessary*___ [necessary / not necessary] to drama.

(b)

▶ Dramatic *conflict* refers to a struggle between a character and (a) other people only, (b) various forces, possibly including himself. (b)

theme

▶ The main idea of Ibsen's *The Doll's House* (1879), that housewives should have a voice in running the family, is the play's __*theme*_____.

(b)

▶ If asked to state the *theme* of a play, the student should give (a) a complete synopsis of events and dialogue, (b) a brief generalized statement of its central idea. (b)

3. **exposition:** presentation of characters and background information, usually done in the first act. Ibsen often introduced *exposition* by having two former friends meet and exchange gossip.
4. **foreshadowing:** a hint of some coming event, possibly tragic. Dramatic *foreshadowing* may be provided by a prediction, a dream, blood on a picture, a stormy night.

exposition
(a)

▶ Presentation of characters and the background situation, known as *ex_position*_____, generally occurs in (a) act one, (b) act four. (a)

(b)

▶ *Foreshadowing* refers to (a) the way the front part of the stage is shaded, (b) a hint of what will happen later. (b)

foreshadowing

▶ The spilling of wine on a wedding dress in the second act of a tragic play might be *foreshadowing*.

exposition

▶ When servants in an opening scene discuss their lovesick master, their conversation is *ex_position_*.

foreshadowing

▶ The earthquakes, storms, and warnings which precede Caesar's assassination in Shakespeare's *Julius Caesar* (1599) are *foreshadowing*.

past
foreshadowing
future

▶ *Exposition* deals mainly with the ___past___ [past / future], whereas *fore_shadowing_* looks to the ___past___ [past / future].

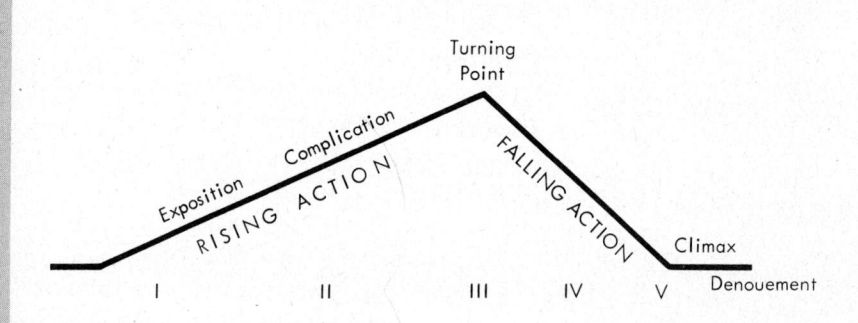

STRUCTURE OF THE TYPICAL FIVE-ACT PLAY
(as analyzed by Gustav Freytag, 1863)

5. **rising action:** the complications of the plot which lead toward the turning point. *Rising action* follows or grows out of exposition and goes on to approximately the middle of a conventional play.
6. **turning point:** that point in a play where the protagonist makes a definite commitment which will lead, by falling action, directly to the climax. The *turning point* often occurs in Act III of a conventional five-act play, as when Iago finally convinces Othello of Desdemona's infidelity.

rising
turning

▶ Plot complications in the opening acts are referred to as the ___rising___ [rising / falling] *action* and lead to the ___turning___ *point.*

262

(b)

▸ In *Romeo and Juliet* a definite part of the *rising action* is (a) Romeo's death, (b) Romeo's decision to go to the Capulet's ball, where he is destined to fall in love with Juliet. (b)

rising
climax
(a)

▸ At the *turning point*, which ends the ___rising___ action and points toward the ___climax___ [explosion / climax], the protagonist makes his (a) definite commitment, (b) bow to the audience. (x)

(b)

▸ In *Macbeth,* the *rising action* includes (a) the final duel between Macbeth and Macduff, (b) the witches' prediction that Macbeth will become king. (b)

---

7. **climax:** the major crisis in which the central conflict is resolved; the point of highest interest. The *climax* of *Hamlet* occurs when Hamlet finally avenges his father's murder by killing King Claudius.
8. **denouement:** (dā-noo-mänh'): the unknotting of complications and resolving of problems following the climax. Sometimes the *denouement* of a play reveals a hidden identity or looks to a future marriage.

climax
(b)

▸ The scene where the main conflict comes to its big crisis, or cl___climax___, is the point of greatest (a) exposition, (b) dramatic interest. (b)

denouement

▸ The *climax* is followed by the unknotting of complications, a process known as the d___enouement___.

climax

▸ Sir Arthur Pinero's *The Second Mrs. Tanqueray* (1893) reaches its point of highest audience interest, or its ___climax___, at Paula's suicide.

climax

▸ In Oscar Wilde's *Lady Windermere's Fan* (1892) Mrs. Erlynne resolves the major conflict by leaving without revealing herself to her daughter—this incident is the ___climax___ [climax / turning point].

denouement

▸ After the *climax* of *King Lear* the futures of the characters are worked out—this is the d___enouement___.

263

climax
denouement

▶ The graph of a conventional dramatic plot would show developments in approximately this order: exposition, rising action, turning point, falling action, c_climax_____, and d_enouement_.

Quiz

Write the letter that indicates the best definition.

(e) 1. climax
(c) 2. conflict
(f) 3. denouement
(b) 4. exposition
(g) 5. foreshadowing
(a) 6. rising action
(h) 7. theme
(d) 8. turning point

a. complications leading to the turning point
b. the presentation of background information
c. the struggle; opposition of forces
d. the point where the protagonist makes a key decision
e. the point of highest dramatic interest
f. the solving of problems, after the climax
g. a hint of coming disaster
h. the play's message or abstract concept

1. (e)
2. (c)
3. (f)
4. (b)
5. (g)
6. (a)
7. (h)
8. (d)

9. **tragedy:** a serious play that ends in disaster or unhappiness for the protagonist because of a moral flaw, fate, or social pressure, but usually with a final awareness by the protagonist of what has really destroyed him, a moral enlargement that paradoxically leaves the audience with some elevation of spirit despite the fall. The hero of early *tragedy* was a person of high rank—for example, King Oedipus, Prince Hamlet, King Lear—but the domestic *tragedy* of more modern times has had a middle-class hero—for example, Willy Loman in Arthur Miller's *Death of a Salesman* (1949).

10. **catharsis** (kə-thär′sis): a purgation of pity and fear, or an emotional cleansing, that we experience vicariously in witnessing a tragic play, according to Aristotle's *Poetics* (circa 330 B.C.). *Catharsis* comes from our pitying the hero and from our fearing a similar misfortune.

serious
(a)

▶ A *tragedy* is a __serious__ [sentimental / serious] play in which the protagonist, possibly because of a moral flaw, finally meets (a) disaster, (b) some new girl friends. (a)

tragedy
catharsis

▶ The emotional cleansing, or purgation, that we experience in seeing *Othello* or a similar tr_agedy_ is called c_atharsis_

catharsis
(a)

▸ *Tragedy,* according to Aristotle, affords the viewer a purgation, or ___catharsis___, of (a) pity and fear, (b) lusts and laughs. (a)

tragedy
enlargement

▸ In spite of his downfall, the hero of a ___tragedy___ usually experiences at the end a spiritual ___enlargement___ [enlargement / warping].

noble
misfortune

▸ The protagonists of Greek and Elizabethan *tragedy* are of ___noble___ [lowly / noble] birth, and the good fortune they enjoy finally turns to ___misfortune___ [complete happiness / misfortune].

tragedy
emotions
(b)

▸ The classic references to an end-in-disaster play, or *tr__agedy__*, and to the resultant *catharsis,* or cleansing of the ___emotions___ [body / emotions], are found in (a) Plato's *Republic,* (b) Aristotle's *Poetics.* (b)

---

11. **hamartia** (hä′mär-tē′ə) : tragic flaw; a weakness in character that leads the protagonist of a tragedy to his downfall. Applying Aristotle's ideas, one might consider Macbeth's *hamartia* to be ambition, King Lear's *hamartia* to be quick temper and love of flattery.

(b)

▸ *Hamartia* refers to (a) ham acting, (b) a tragic flaw. (b)

hamartia
(a)

▸ The hero's character defect, known as ha___martia___, leads him to (a) his downfall, (b) a pile of money. (a)

hamartia
(b)

▸ In Aeschylus's *Agamemnon* (458 B.C.) the king defies the gods by walking on a sacred purple carpet, so his tragic character fault, or ha___martia___, is his excessive (a) humility, (b) pride. ( )

hamartia
flaw

▸ In short, Aristotle's word ha___martia___ refers to a ___flaw___ [virtue / flaw] that brings the leading character to his tragic downfall.

12. **dramatic irony:** awareness by the audience of impending matters of which the characters in the play are not aware; also called *tragic irony*. Dramatic irony occurs when King Oedipus charges that the blind prophet is corrupt, when the audience knows that Oedipus is himself unknowingly corrupt and is, in a sense, blind.
13. **unities:** singleness of time, of place, and of action in a drama, as specified by sixteenth-century French theorists in their misinterpretation of Aristotle's doctrines. The three classical *unities* require that play action should involve a single plot, a single setting, and a single day.

▶ *Dramatic irony* implies that the audience knows vital things about a character that the character (a) also knows, (b) does not know yet. (*b*) — **(b)**

▶ A Nazi falls in love but does not know yet, as the audience does, that his sweetheart is Jewish—this play involves ___*dramatic*___ [Socratic / dramatic] irony. — **dramatic**

▶ The doctrine of the three u___*nities*___, which Shakespeare usually ignored, had to do with time, place, and ___*action*___ [action / characters]. — **unities / action**

▶ The three dramatic u___*nity*___ allowed for one main action occurring in one place and completed in one ___*day*___ [day / year]. — **unities / day**

▶ In Arthur Miller's *Death of a Salesman*, Willy Loman looks forward to job interviews that the audience already realizes will be failures—this is dramatic ___*irony*___. — **irony**

▶ Shakespeare's *The Tempest* (1611) has no subplot and its main action occurs within three hours on a small island; so this play ___*does*___ [does / does not] observe the three classical ___*unities*___. — **does / unities**

---

14. **comedy:** an amusing play with a happy ending. Unlike tragedy, *comedy* does not stress the noble conception of life; instead it pleasantly satirizes human follies and incidents and, according to Aristotle, represents men as worse than in actual life.
15. **farce:** exaggerated comedy marked by ridiculous situations and horseplay. Whereas true comedy has an element of seriousness in it, *farce* aims to produce laughter merely for its own sake.

happily wedding	▸ A *comedy* is an amusing play which ends ~~happily~~ [happily / unhappily], possibly with a ~~wedding~~ [wedding / funeral].
farce	▸ If a play is full of absurd situations and tomfoolery—for example, as in Brandon Thomas's *Charley's Aunt* (1892)—it is called a f~~arce~~.
cheerful (b)	▸ A *comedy* such as Shakespeare's *As You Like It* (1599) not only ends on a _____ [depressing / cheerful] note but the general tone throughout the play is (a) morbid, (b) amusing. ( )
ridiculous	▸ George M. Cohan's *Seven Keys to Baldpate* (1913) is usually called a *farce* because of its slapstick, broad humor, and _____ [believable / ridiculous] action.
farce	▸ Clowning and far-fetched situations are typical of a _____.

16. **legitimate theater**: live stage drama as contrasted with vaudeville, films, and television. *Legitimate theater* does not include subliterary entertainment such as farce, melodrama, and musicals.

17. **vaudeville** (vōd'vil): variety act entertainment. *Vaudeville* was especially popular in the United States during the first quarter of the twentieth century.

legitimate	▸ Live, serious stage dramas like Maxwell Anderson's *Elizabeth the Queen* (1930) belong to the l_____ theater.
do not	▸ Musicals, farce, and television theatricals _____ [do / do not] belong to the *legitimate theater*.
(a)	▸ *Vaudeville* entertains by means of (a) variety acts, (b) one long gripping drama. ( )
vaudeville	▸ Singers, dog acts, and tap dancers were common in early twentieth-century v_____.

(a)

vaudeville
did not
legitimate

1. (i)
2. (f)
3. (a)
4. (h)
5. (e)
6. (g)
7. (b)
8. (c)
9. (d)

(b)

(b)

▶ The great Shakespearean actors Garrick, Booth, and Barrymore were stars of (a) legitimate theater, (b) vaudeville. (   )

▶ A barbershop quartet and a soft-shoe routine might have found a place in old-time v_____, but such acts _____ [did / did not] belong to the professional stage known as the l_____ theater.

Quiz

Write the letter that indicates the best definition.

(   ) 1. tragedy   a. a tragic flaw
(   ) 2. catharsis   b. exaggerated comedy; slapstick
(   ) 3. hamartia   c. live stage drama
(   ) 4. dramatic irony   d. variety act entertainment
(   ) 5. unities   e. singleness of time, place, action
(   ) 6. comedy   f. an emotional purgation
(   ) 7. farce   g. an amusing play with a happy
(   ) 8. legitimate theater   ending
(   ) 9. vaudeville   h. the audience's awareness of the
                              hero's unawareness
                          i. a play depicting the downfall of
                              its chief character

18. **problem play:** a play that comes to grips with a social issue. The *problem play,* also called the *drama of ideas,* has dealt with many social problems, such as husband-wife relationships, racial integration, and the causes of war.
19. **expressionism:** nonrealistic drama which deliberately distorts the stage effects to reflect a character's state of mind or an inherent reality. Eugene O'Neill uses *expressionism* in *The Hairy Ape* (1921) when he depicts a New York street crowd as puppetlike; they are not individuals but an idea.

▶ The *problem play* is a dramatic tug-of-war over (a) some lover, (b) a social issue. (   )

▶ Because Henrik Ibsen's *Ghosts* (1881) explores problems of euthanasia and wifely fidelity it can be classed as (a) expressionism, (b) a problem play. (   )

(a)	▶ In *expressionism* the surface realities are (a) deliberately distorted, (b) accurately depicted. ( )
expressionism	▶ Willy Loman's thoughts are objectified on stage in the _____ism of Arthur Miller's *Death of a Salesman*.
(a)	▶ The *expressionistic* artist in any medium—Vincent Van Gogh, Ernest Toller, T. S. Eliot—distorts the externals in order to reflect (a) an inner reality, (b) his own confusion. ( )
(b)	▶ John Galsworthy's *Strife* (1909) is called a *problem play* because it deals with (a) a fishing trip, (b) labor-management relations. ( )
expressionism (a)	▶ Since it involves scenic distortion, dramatic *exp_____* can best be appreciated (a) at the theater, (b) by a mere reading. ( )

20. **melodrama** (mel′ə-drä′mə): a play crammed with incredible action, suspense, and stereotyped characters, wherein heroism triumphs over villainy. One popular American melodrama is William H. Smith's *The Drunkard: Or, The Fallen Saved* (1844).
21. **poetic justice:** the rewarding of good characters and the punishing of bad characters, according to their deserts. *Poetic justice* is commonly dispensed in melodramas and sentimental novels.

melodrama	▶ A play with suspenseful, incredible action is a *m_____*.
hero poetic	▶ In *melodrama* the final victory is won by the _____ [hero / villain] in accordance with _____ *justice*.
melodrama	▶ Lillian Mortimer's *No Mother to Guide Her* (1905), with its good guys and bad guys and sensational action, is typical of the old-fashioned *m_____*.
justice	▶ The gangsters in film *melodramas* are finally ventilated by bullets, a matter of *poetic* _____.
melodrama poetic	▶ The heroine of a thrilling old *m_____* might be tied to the railroad tracks, but eventually the hero saves her and marries her—that, too, is _____ *justice*.

22. **soliloquy** (sə-lil′ə-kwi): talking to oneself, as if revealing unspoken thoughts. Hamlet's best-known *soliloquy* begins, "To be or not to be."

soliloquy

▸ Talking alone on stage is called *soliloquy*.

(b)

▸ In a *soliloquy* a character speaks as though to himself, and one must assume that he is heard only by (a) his friends on stage, (b) the audience. (b)

soliloquy

▸ In Latin, *solus* means "alone" and *loqui* means "to speak"; thus an actor who speaks as though to himself alone is producing a *soliloquy*.

soliloquy
(b)

▸ The villain Iago, as though thinking aloud, delivers a s_____. We are to assume that Othello, who is also on stage, (a) hears it, (b) doesn't hear it. ( )

(b)

▸ Shakespeare gives Macbeth a dramatic *soliloquy*—life is "a tale told by an idiot . . ."—so that the audience can hear (a) Macbeth's challenge to Macduff, (b) Macbeth's secret thoughts. ( )

23. **Stanislavski method** (stan′i-släv′skē): an acting technique whereby the actor first recalls a parallel emotional situation in which he was once involved and then relives that emotion on stage. The *Stanislavski method* has distinctly influenced American acting.

method
(b)

▸ The *Stanislavski* m_____ requires that in an emotional scene an actor should (a) wave his arms vigorously, (b) relive a similar emotional experience. ( )

Stanislavski

▸ An actor who is to laugh or cry on stage should remember some situation that once made him laugh or cry, according to the S_____ *method*.

method
(b)

▸ The Moscow Art Theater toured this country in 1923 and popularized the *Stanislavski* m_____, an acting technique which depends particularly on (a) stock responses, (b) remembered emotion. ( )

(a)	▸ A "method" actor is one who strives for inner interpretation of a role as taught by the famous stage director (a) Constantin Stanislavski, (b) Ignace Paderewski. ( )
Stanislavski (a)	▸ Because the actor is supposed to recall an emotional experience he once had, the _____ *method* is said to (a) "convert psychology into behavior," (b) "convert sighs into tempests." ( )

24. **deus ex machina** (dē′əs eks mak′ə-nə): any unexpected or artificial trick that resolves the plot conflict. The *deus ex machina* was literally a "god from the machine" who in Aeschylus' *Eumenides* (circa 458 B.C.) was lowered by crane to solve the dramatic crisis below.

25. **choreography** (kōr′ē-og′rə-fē): the art of composing ballets and arranging separate dances. *Choreography* involves grouping, staging, music, and so on.

machina (b)	▸ *Deus ex* _____ means (a) "deuces are wild," (b) "god from the machine." ( )
deus	▸ Any quick, slick solution to a plot—such as an unknown uncle suddenly leaving a million dollars to the bankrupt hero—is a _____ *ex machina*.
(b)	▸ The *deus ex machina* ending is (a) natural and reasonable, (b) unexpected and artificial. ( )
(a)	▸ *Choreography* is the creating of (a) ballets, (b) choruses. ( )
(a)	▸ The dance routines in a musical play such as *West Side Story* are devised by (a) choreographers, (b) a *deus ex machina*. ( )
deus machina	▸ When a Greek god was unexpectedly lowered to the stage to solve a human dilemma, he was literally a _____ *ex* _____.
choreography	▸ The complex and subtle craft of composing ballets is called c_____.

Quiz

Write the letter that indicates the best definition.

( ) 1. problem play
( ) 2. expressionism
( ) 3. melodrama
( ) 4. poetic justice
( ) 5. soliloquy
( ) 6. Stanislavski method
( ) 7. deux ex machina
( ) 8. choreography

a. an artificial, trick ending
b. speaking alone; revealing thoughts
c. creating of dances
d. a drama of ideas or social issues
e. reliving an emotion on stage
f. hero, villain, and incredible action
g. drama with distorted stage effects
h. rewards for the good and punishment for the wicked

1. (d)
2. (g)
3. (f)
4. (h)
5. (b)
6. (e)
7. (a)
8. (c)

Review Test

Supply the missing word in each sentence. The first letter of each answer is given.

1. A serious play which ends in disaster is called a t_____.
2. An exaggerated comedy with horseplay is a f_____.
3. The protagonist's tragic flaw which ruins him is h_____.
4. The major idea of a literary work is its t_____.
5. Speaking when alone on stage is s_____.
6. The unknotting of plot complications is the d_____.
7. A play that grapples with a social issue is a p_____ *play*.
8. The art of devising dances and ballet is c_____.
9. A hint of some coming disaster is dramatic f_____.
10. For the audience to know what the characters themselves do not as yet realize is dramatic i_____.

Write *True* or *False*.

_____ 11. According to *poetic justice,* the good guys are rewarded and the bad guys are punished.
_____ 12. *Expressionism* aims for photographic realism in stage effects.
_____ 13. The *turning point* of a play comes after the *climax*.
_____ 14. *Legitimate theater* includes motion pictures.
_____ 15. *Rising action* includes those plot complications which lead to the *turning point*.
_____ 16. *Catharsis* is the purgation of pity and fear in those who see a tragic drama.
_____ 17. The *melodrama* is notable for presenting characters and actions in unexaggerated, true-to-life fashion.
_____ 18. *Vaudeville* often featured singers, dancers, and comedy skits.
_____ 19. The *conflict* in a drama may be internal—that is, it may involve man against himself.
_____ 20. The *deus ex machina* is considered the logical and most probable solution to the difficulties of the plot.

Write the letter that indicates the best completion.

( ) 21. The three dramatic *unities* do not include the element of (a) place, (b) mood, (c) action, (d) time.

( ) 22. In a five-act play most of the *exposition* is taken care of in (a) act one, (b) act three, (c) act five, (d) the soliloquy.

( ) 23. The *Stanislavski method* depends largely on (a) practiced gestures, (b) constant drill, (c) remembered emotions, (d) tricky makeup.

( ) 24. A *comedy* is a play that (a) teaches a lesson, (b) inspires, (c) shows what people are really like, (d) amuses.

( ) 25. The *climax* of a typical five-act play usually occurs just before the (a) exposition, (b) rising action, (c) turning point, (d) denouement.

Key to Review Test

Check your test answers by the following key. Deduct 4% per error from 100%.

1. tragedy	6. denouement	11. True	16. True	21. (b)
2. farce	7. problem	12. False	17. False	22. (a)
3. hamartia	8. choreography	13. False	18. True	23. (c)
4. theme	9. foreshadowing	14. False	19. True	24. (d)
5. soliloquy	10. irony	15. True	20. False	25. (d)

Score: _____%

Supplementary List

1. **chorus:** a group of characters in Greek drama who comment on the action. The *choruses* of Aeschylus and Sophocles, consisting of twelve or fifteen men and women, dwindled to a one-man *chorus* in the prologue of Shakespeare's *Henry V* (1599).
2. **closet drama:** a play to be read rather than acted. Percy Shelley's *The Cenci* (1819) and *Prometheus Unbound* (1820) are *closet dramas,* poetic but unplayable.
3. **comedy of humors:** comedy in which each character has a dominant trait or "humor," such as stinginess or hypocrisy. Ben Jonson's *Every Man in His Humour* (1598) has in it the braggart Bobadil and the jealous Kitely.
4. **comedy of manners:** witty comedy satirizing human behavior and foibles, especially popular during the Restoration Period, 1660–1700. *Comedies of manners* include William Congreve's *The Way of the World* (1700) and Oscar Wilde's *Lady Windermere's Fan* (1892).
5. **confidant,** masc.; **confidante,** fem. (con'fi-dant'): a trusted friend to whom secrets are confided. The device of the *confidant* keeps the audience aware of the hero's thoughts and plans.
6. **convention:** any unrealistic artistic device that has become accepted by general consent. Audiences have at various times accepted such *conventions* as the soliloquy, the aside, poetic dialogue, and singing dialogue.
7. **dramatis personae** (dram'ə-tis pər-sō'nē): the characters in a play; also, the list of characters. The *dramatis personae* are listed at the beginning of a play script.
8. **dramaturgy** (dram'ə-tûr'jē): the art of writing plays or of presenting them. *Dramaturgy* flourished rather remarkably during the English Renaissance.
9. **histrionics** (his'trē-on'iks): acting; also, overacting or theatricality. *Histrionics* suggests the arm-waving and emotionalism of a second-rate actor.
10. **hubris** (hū'brəs): pride or arrogance, a particular type of *hamartia*. In Greek tragedy the hero with *hubris* is eventually humbled by the gods.
11. **ingénue** (an-zhi-noo'): the role of the innocent, unworldly young woman; also, an actress who plays such a role. The word *ingénue* is related to *ingenuous,* meaning "innocent" or "naive."
12. **masque** (mask): a pageant play with music, dance, and elaborate costumes and settings, originally staged in the Renaissance courts. Ben Jonson wrote several *masques* for which Inigo Jones designed fantastic sets.
13. **morality play:** a medieval allegorical drama that taught some moral sermon. One *morality play* called *Everyman* shows how friends named Beauty, Strength, and Goods desert Everyman when he dies.
14. **mystery play:** a medieval verse play presenting a Biblical scene, originally put on by an English guild or craft. During religious festivals cycles of *mystery plays,* also called *miracle plays,* were shown in the market places of York, Chester, Wakefield, and Coventry.
15. **pastoral** (pas'tər-əl): a play or poem that pleasingly portrays shepherds in a country setting. The *pastoral* play, though artificial and conventionalized, held a charm for Elizabethans.

16. **properties:** any furniture or objects used in a play, excluding costumes and scenery. Tables and sofas are called *set props;* magazines and bottles are *hand props*.
17. **proscenium** (prō-sē′nē-əm): the front part of the stage including the curtain and the decorative arch. The *proscenium* extends from the curtain to the orchestra pit.
18. **raisonneur** (rez-ən-ūr′): a level-headed character who reflects the playwright's own thinking and who comments on the action. The *raisonneur* is the reasonable fellow who vainly warns the hero and others against various follies.
19. **repartee** (rep′ər-tē′): fast, witty retorts, as in high comedy. The *repartee* sparkles in Oscar Wilde's *The Importance of Being Earnest* (1894).
20. **repertory theater** (rep′ər-tōr′ē): a permanent acting company that is prepared to put on any of several plays and that alternates them from time to time. The *repertory theater* has given a rich and varied training to young actors; the tradition continues in summer stock companies.
21. **stock character:** a conventional character who is found in many plays and stories. The dignified butler, the tight-fisted landlord, the flea-brained housewife, and the cruel stepmother are *stock characters*.
22. **stock situation:** a stereotyped plot element. The boaster turns coward, the boy pursues the girl, the talented unknown rises to stardom, women burst into rooms and misinterpret an innocent embrace—these are *stock situations*.
23. **Theater of the Absurd** (ab-sûrd′): plays that picture life as meaningless, incoherent, and futile, and that present wildly irrational or nightmarish scenes which tend to reflect our human isolation in an idiot universe; for example, Eugène Ionesco's *The Bald Soprano* (1950), Samuel Beckett's *Waiting for Godot* (1948), and Arthur Adamov's *Ping-Pong* (1955).
24. **thespian** (thes′pē-ən): an actor or tragedian. The word *thespian* derives from *Thespis,* the "father of drama," and is mildly humorous or pretentious.
25. **tragicomedy** (traj′i-kom′i-dē): a play containing both tragic and comic elements but ending happily. In seventeenth-century *tragicomedy* the villain often repents just before the final curtain.

17

Poetry

anapest, 5
assonance, 17
blank verse, 22
caesura, 7
consonance, 16
dactyl, 6
epic, 18
feminine rhyme, 13
foot, 2

free verse, 23
heroic couplet, 19
hexameter, 10
iamb, 3
imagery, 24
internal rhyme, 14
inversion, 15
masculine rhyme, 12
objective correlative, 25

pentameter, 9
poetic license, 11
quatrain, 20
scansion, 1
sonnet, 21
tetrameter, 8
trochee, 4

It is not enough to say of a verse, "How pretty that is" or "That's a remarkable phrase." To analyze a poem we must be familiar with certain basic technical terms. It is important to know the various figures of speech (see Chapter 11). We must also recognize such aspects of versification as hexameter, anapest, and assonance, and such types of poems as sonnet, epic, and dramatic monologue. Nor should we turn blank at the mention of blank verse, confusing it, perhaps, with free verse.

Analysis cannot hope to explain completely the mysterious nature of poetry, "untwisting all the chains that tie / The hidden soul of harmony"; yet a knowledge of poetic terms can be a real step toward a richer appreciation of poetry.

Exercises

COVER THIS STRIP

1. **scansion** (skan′shən): the analysis of verse to show its meter and rhyme scheme. *Scansion* marks include ˘ for an unaccented syllable, ′ for an accented syllable, and | for a foot division.
2. **foot:** the basic unit of verse meter, consisting usually of two or three syllables of which ordinarily one is stressed. The number of feet to the line determines the meter.

scansion
feet
▸ Metrical analysis, or sc_____, tells you the number and type of _____ [feet / figures of speech] in each line of verse.

scansion
(b)
▸ The process of poetic sc_____ is (a) emotional, (b) analytical. ( )

feet
scansion
▸ The number of metric units, or _____ [bars / feet], in a line of verse is calculated by sc_____.

three
▸ The number of *feet* in Robert Burns' verse "Your locks were like the raven" is _____ [three / seven].

3. **iamb** (ī′amb): an unstressed syllable followed by a stressed syllable; for example, "tŏníght," "děný," "ănd nów," "mў lóve."
4. **trochee** (trō′kē): a stressed syllable followed by an unstressed syllable; for example, "fáster," "dámsěl," "dýǐng," "fling ĭt."

iamb
second
▸ The *iambic* foot, or i_____, consists of two syllables with the stress on the _____ [first / second] syllable.

trochee
first
▸ The *trochaic* foot, or t_____, consists of two syllables with the stress on the _____ [first / second] syllable.

trochee
iamb
iamb
▸ After each example of a metrical foot write *iamb* or *trochee*:
"hanging"—_____
"the sky"—_____
"to dream"—_____

trochee trochee	"drink it"—_____ "Edith"—_____
	▸ After each example of verse write *iambic* or *trochaic*:
iambic trochaic iambic	"To be or not to be . . ."—_____. "Come and trip it as ye go"—_____. "I struck the board and cried . . ."—_____.

5. **anapest** (an′ə-pest′): two unstressed syllables followed by a stressed syllable; for example, "ŏf thĕ mén"; "tŏ rĕjóice"; "ĭntĕrfére."

6. **dactyl** (dak′til): a stressed syllable followed by two unstressed syllables; for example, "síng tŏ thĕ"; "fléeing frŏm"; "rápĭdlў."

anapest third	▸ The *anapestic foot,* or a_____, consists of three syllables with the stress on the _____ [first / third] syllable.
dactyl first	▸ The *dactylic* foot, or d_____, consists of three syllables with the stress on the _____ [first / third] syllable.
	▸ After each sample metrical foot write *anapest* or *dactyl*:
anapest dactyl dactyl anapest anapest	"of the king"—_____ "laughing with"—_____ "fade in the"—_____ "with Elaine"—_____ "in despair"—_____
	▸ After each verse sample write *anapestic* or *dactylic*:
dactylic anapestic	"Maiden most beautiful, mother most bountiful . . ."—_____. "And the sheen of their spears was like stars on the sea"— _____.

7. **caesura** (si-zhoor′ə): a pause within the line of verse, indicated in scansion by two vertical lines, thus ‖. The *caesura* usually coincides with a pause in the thought, as at a major mark of punctuation.

caesura (b)	▸ In scansion the pause known as the c_____ is indicated by (a) a snaky line, (b) two vertical lines. ( )

caesura
(b)

▶ Alexander Pope wrote, "One truth is clear, Whatever is, is right"—here a pause known as a c_____ belongs after (a) "truth, (b) "clear." ( )

caesura
(a)

▶ "Beowulf spake, bairn of Ecgtheow"—here the pause, or _____, belongs after (a) "spake," (b) "bairn." ( )

Quiz

Write the letter that indicates the best definition or example.

1. (e)
2. (f)
3. (b)
4. (a)
5. (c)
6. (g)
7. (d)

( ) 1. anapest   a. the basic unit of verse meter
( ) 2. caesura   b. a foot like "tenderly"
( ) 3. dactyl   c. a foot like "the stars"
( ) 4. foot   d. a foot like "kissing"
( ) 5. iamb   e. a foot like "in her home"
( ) 6. scansion   f. a pause within the verse
( ) 7. trochee   g. metrical analysis

8. **tetrameter** (te-tram′i-tər): a line of poetry containing four feet; example from Lord Tennyson of iambic *tetrameter:* "I come from haunts of coot and hern." Shorter lines are the *trimeter,* three feet; the *dimeter,* two feet; and the *monometer,* one foot.
9. **pentameter** (pen-tam′i-tər): a line of poetry containing five feet; example from John Keats of iambic *pentameter:* "When I have fears that I may cease to be."
10. **hexameter** (hek-sam′i-tər): a line of poetry containing six feet. Longer and less common than the *hexameter* line are the *heptameter,* seven feet, and the *octameter,* eight feet.

tetrameter

▶ A verse containing four metrical feet is a t_____.

pentameter

▶ A verse containing five metrical feet is a p_____.

hexameter

▶ A verse containing six metrical feet is a h_____.

three
two

▶ The *trimeter* line has _____ [three / four] feet, and the *dimeter* has _____ [two / five] feet.

hexameter

▶ The Alexandrine, a line popular in French poetry, is composed of six iambic feet; in other words, it is in *iambic* _____ *meter.*

(b)	▶ A *tetrameter* is to a pentameter as (a) six is to five, (b) four is to five, (c) five is to six. ( )
tetrameter hexameter	▶ A *pentameter* has one more foot than a _____, and it has one less foot than a _____.
four	▶ The final foot of a line is sometimes shortened, or "truncated"; how many feet are there in William Blake's line, "Tiger! Tiger! burning bright"—not counting the feet on the tiger?—_____ [three / four]
(a)	▶ In other words, Blake's line is (a) trochaic tetrameter, (b) iambic trimeter. ( )
	▶ Scan the following verses:
iambic pentam- eter	Thomas Gray's "The curfew tolls the knell of parting day"— i_____ p_____.
trochaic tetram- eter	Thomas Carew's "He that loves a rosy cheek"—_____ _____.
iambic hexam- eter	Edmund Spenser's "God helpe the man so wrapt in Errours endless traine!"—_____ _____.
anapestic pentameter	Robert Browning's "And I paused, held my breath in such silence, and listened apart"—_____ _____.
dactylic hexameter	The Bible's "How art thou fallen from heaven, O Lucifer, son of the morning!"—_____ _____.

11. **poetic license:** a writer's assumption that he may deviate from accepted standards of correctness for artistic effect. *Poetic license* has been cited to excuse violations of grammar, diction, rhythm, rhyme, and historical facts.

(b)	▶ *Poetic license* is sometimes mentioned to excuse (a) lack of productivity, (b) departures from correctness. ( )
poetic (b)	▶ "The owl, for all his feathers, was a-cold"—here Keats has exercised _____ license (a) to alter a fact, (b) to patch his iambic rhythm. ( )

281

▶ Shakespeare's tampering with facts and dates in his historical dramas is usually attributed to (a) poetic license, (b) dishonesty. ( )

(a)

Quiz

Write the letter that indicates the best definition.

1. (b) ( ) 1. tetrameter   a. a verse with five feet
2. (a) ( ) 2. pentameter   b. a verse with four feet
3. (d) ( ) 3. hexameter   c. an author's right to break rules
4. (c) ( ) 4. poetic license d. a verse with six feet

12. **masculine rhyme:** a rhyme limited to the stressed last syllable; single rhyme; for example, "kiss" and "miss," "late" and "fate," "repent" and "consent."
13. **feminine rhyme:** a rhyme of two or three syllables, with the stress on the first syllable; also called double-rhyme or triple-rhyme; for example, "stranger" and "danger," "sleeping" and "creeping," "saddening" and "maddening."

▶ In *masculine rhyme* the similarity of sounds appears in (a) the one stressed last syllable, (b) two or more syllables. ( )

(a)

▶ Two-syllable rhyme, or double rhyme, is called _____ *rhyme*.

feminine

▶ After each pair of rhyming words write *masculine* or *feminine*:

masculine   "hate" and "fate"—_____
masculine   "sheep" and "sleep"—_____
feminine   "flicker" and "sicker"—_____
masculine   "complain" and "refrain"—_____
feminine   "glory" and "story"—_____

14. **internal rhyme:** rhyming within the line; for example, "And nations rush faster toward disaster."
15. **inversion:** a reversal in the natural word order to help out the rhyme or rhythm. *Inversions* are now usually considered undesirable: "And them behold no more shall I."

▶ A rhyme between two words in the same line is called _____ *rhyme*.

internal

282

inversion	▶ A turning about of the normal word order is called _____.
does	▶ "And oh what bliss if her I could kiss"—this verse _____
rhyme	[does / does not] have *internal* _____ and _____
does	[does / does not] contain *inversion*.
	▶ After each line of verse write either *inversion* or *internal* (for *internal rhyme*):
	"We were the first who ever burst"—_____.
internal	"In her attic window the staff she set"—_____.
inversion	"The invited neighbors to the husking come"—_____.
inversion	"For the moon never beams without bringing me dreams"—
internal	_____.

16. **consonance** (kon′sə-nəns): imperfect rhyme in which the words have identical consonant sounds but different vowel sounds; for example, "men" and "mean," "walk" and "weak," "fool" and "fail."
17. **assonance** (as′ə-nəns): imperfect rhyme in which the words have identical vowel sounds but different consonant sounds before and after; for example, "flame" and "rain," "night" and "pine," "blow" and "groan."

(b)	▶ *Consonance* means imperfect rhyme with an identicality of (a) vowels, (b) consonants. ( )
(a)	▶ *Assonance* means imperfect rhyme with an identicality of (a) vowels, (b) consonants. ( )
	▶ After each imperfect rhyme write *consonance* or *assonance:*
consonance	"cling" and "clang"—_____
assonance	"shame" and "raid"—_____
consonance	"note" and "night"—_____
assonance	"creep" and "flee"—_____
(b)	▶ *Consonance* appears in (a) "they hate their fate," (b) "my love doth live." ( )
(b)	▶ *Assonance* appears in (a) "her fears and tears," (b) "to give a kiss." ( )

Quiz

Write the letter that indicates the best example.

1. (f)
2. (e)
3. (b)
4. (c)
5. (d)
6. (a)

( ) 1. assonance
( ) 2. consonance
( ) 3. feminine rhyme
( ) 4. internal rhyme
( ) 5. inversion
( ) 6. masculine rhyme

a. "think" and "drink"
b. "wonder" and "thunder"
c. "Who says the flag is but a rag?"
d. "To me the angry words he spoke"
e. "cord" and "card"
f. "plan" and "map"

---

18. **epic:** a long narrative poem that describes heroic adventures in an exalted style. The *folk* or primitive *epic,* such as *Beowulf* or the *Iliad,* was originally recited by a bard to nobility; the *literary epic,* such as Virgil's *Aeneid* or Milton's *Paradise Lost,* is a more unified and polished work intended for reading.

▸ An *epic* is a lengthy, dignified _____ [essay / poem] which deals with (a) the beauty of flowers, (b) the adventures of heroes. ( )

poem
(b)

▸ A long narrative poem in exalted style is known as an _____; an example of an *epic* is (a) Homer's *Odyssey,* (b) Whittier's "The Barefoot Boy." ( )

epic
(a)

▸ An *epic* such as Milton's *Paradise Lost* has a length of several hundred (a) words, (b) pages. ( )

(b)

▸ The tone of an *epic* poem by Homer or Milton is (a) lofty and dignified, (b) vulgar and uninspiring. ( )

(a)

▸ A long, dignified narrative poem, called an _____, deals with (a) humorous family situations, (b) heroic adventures. ( )

epic
(b)

---

19. **heroic couplet:** two rhyming lines in iambic pentameter, usually expressing a complete, epigrammatic thought, a verse form favored by Alexander Pope; for example, "A little learning is a dangerous thing; / Drink deep, or taste not the Pierian spring."

20. **quatrain** (kwo′trān): a four-line stanza, variously rhymed; for example, "I never saw a moor, / I never saw the sea; / Yet know I how the heather looks, / And what a wave must be."

284

two rhyme (a)	▸ The *heroic couplet* consists of _____ [two / four] lines that _____ [rhyme / do not rhyme] and which usually express (a) a complete thought, (b) part of a run-on thought. ( )
quatrain	▸ A four-line stanza of poetry is called a q_____.
(b)	▸ The rhyming pattern of *quatrains* is (a) always *abab*, (b) variable. ( )
quatrain	▸ Folk ballads make common use of the four-line stanza, or _____.
third	▸ The rhyming pattern of the *quatrain* in Edward FitzGerald's *The Rubaiyat* (1859) is *aaba*, which means that its _____ [first / third] line is unrhymed.
couplet Pope complete	▸ The two-line rhyme known as the *heroic* _____ was a favorite of _____ [Pope / T. S. Eliot], and it usually expresses a _____ [complete / incomplete] thought.

21. **sonnet:** a fourteen-line poem in iambic pentameter with a prescribed rhyming and structural pattern. The *English,* or *Shakespearean, sonnet* consists of three quatrains and a couplet, rhyming *abab cdcd efef gg;* the *Italian,* or *Petrarchan, sonnet* consists of an octave (having eight lines) followed by a sestet (having six lines) and rhymes *abba abba cde cde* (the rhyme scheme of the sestet may vary).

fourteen (a)	▸ The *sonnet* is _____ [twelve / fourteen] lines long and is in iambic (a) pentameter, (b) hexameter. ( )
sonnet (a)	▸ If its fourteen lines consist of three quatrains and a couplet, the s_____ is (a) English, (b) Italian. ( )
sonnet (b)	▸ If its fourteen lines consist of an octave and a sestet, the _____ is (a) English, (b) Italian. ( )

22. **blank verse:** unrhymed iambic pentameter. *Blank verse* is used in the dramas of Shakespeare and Marlowe and in other serious English poetry such as Milton's *Paradise Lost.*

23. **free verse:** rhythmical lines of irregular length without fixed metrical pattern and usually without rhyme; also called *vers libre*. *Free verse* has the rhythms and cadences of natural speech.

(b)
▶ The magnificent *blank verse* of *Macbeth* and *Julius Caesar* is (a) rhymed, (b) unrhymed. ( )

(a)
▶ *Blank verse* consists of lines that are unrhymed and (a) in iambic pentameter, (b) of various lengths and stresses. ( )

free
▶ On the other hand, unrhymed lines of irregular length are _____ verse.

free
(b)
▶ A line of *vers libre,* or _____ verse, has (a) five stresses, (b) no fixed metrical pattern. ( )

free
▶ Walt Whitman, Amy Lowell, and Carl Sandburg often use lines of irregular length and rhythm, known as _____ verse.

is
blank
▶ "For who would bear the whips and scorns of time"—this representative line from *Hamlet* _____ [is / is not] in iambic pentameter; and so this unrhymed drama is in _____ verse.

---

24. **imagery** (im'ij-rē): the various appeals to the senses made by a literary passage; any descriptive phrasing and figures of speech which make us feel, see, hear, smell, taste; for example, "fragrant hair," "gentle rain," "a swarm of golden bees," "The hare limped trembling through the frozen grass."

(b)
▶ A poem has *imagery* if its phrases (a) show imagination, (b) describe how things look, smell, taste, sound, or feel. ( )

imagery
(b)
▶ Phrases like "grassy tomb" or "jolly shepherds" are known as i_____ because they appeal to the reader's (a) curiosity, (b) senses. ( )

(a)
▶ *Imagery* is in the phrase (a) "drunk the milk of Paradise," (b) "ultimate theological conclusions." ( )

286

(b)

imagery
(a)

▸ *Imagery* is in the phrase (a) "The sanitary condition of the restaurant was unsatisfactory," (b) "A black fly landed on the cracked rim of the soup bowl and began to rub its hind legs together." ( )

▸ The appeal to the senses known as i_____ is especially common in (a) poetry, (b) algebra. ( )

---

25. **objective correlative** (kə-rel'ə-tiv): the evoking of an emotion in the reader by the artist's use of such objects, events, or situations as will objectify that emotion or serve as a formula for that emotion. For a discussion of the *objective correlative,* see T. S. Eliot's "Hamlet and His Problems" (1919).

(a)

▸ A poet uses the *objective correlative* to arouse an emotion. For example, to make us feel melancholy (gloomy) he may make references to (a) autumn . . . a wailing wind . . . dead leaves, (b) April . . . sweet showers . . . twittering swallows. ( )

objective
correlative

▸ A poet who wishes to convey a sense of frustration might also use the *ob_____ co_____*. Circle the letters of three phrases below that suggest frustration:

a. green fields
b. a caged eagle
c. the hearty embrace
d. rosy-fingered dawn
e. "Strike three!"
f. the sucking quicksand

(b) (e) (f)

correlative

▸ The poet's emotion may be transferred to the reader by means of symbolic description, in a technique called the *objective* _____.

(b)

▸ The *objective correlative* uses symbols and formulae for a specific emotion so that the reader will (a) be bewildered, (b) feel the same emotion. ( )

objective
emotion
(a)

▸ The phrase _____ *correlative,* referring to a method of arousing a particular _____ [idea /emotion] in a reader, was coined in 1919 by (a) T. S. Eliot, (b) Woodrow Wilson. ( )

287

Quiz

Write the letter that indicates the best definition.

1. (g)
2. (f)
3. (e)
4. (c)
5. (b)
6. (d)
7. (a)
8. (h)

( ) 1. epic
( ) 2. heroic couplet
( ) 3. quatrain
( ) 4. sonnet
( ) 5. blank verse
( ) 6. free verse
( ) 7. imagery
( ) 8. objective correlative

a. appeals to the senses
b. unrhymed iambic pentameter
c. a patterned fourteen-line poem
d. unrhymed verses of irregular length
e. a four-line stanza
f. two rhymed lines in iambic pentameter
g. a long poem about heroic achievements
h. the use of various images and references to arouse a specific emotion

Review Test

Supply the missing word in each sentence. The first letter of each answer is given.

1. The basic unit of verse measure is the f_____.
2. The analysis of rhythm and meter is known as s_____.
3. A long narrative poem describing heroic deeds is an e_____.
4. A four-line stanza is a q_____.
5. Rhyming within a line of poetry is i_____ rhyme.
6. A pause within a line of verse is a c_____.
7. A metrical line of four feet is a t_____.
8. A metrical line of six feet is a h_____.
9. A metrical foot consisting of a stressed syllable followed by an unstressed syllable is a t_____.
10. Twisting poetic words into unnatural order is called i_____.

Write *True* or *False*.

_____ 11. The *anapest* consists of two unstressed syllables followed by a stressed syllable.
_____ 12. *Blank verse* uses an irregular number of metrical feet to the line.
_____ 13. An example of *consonance* is "green" and "grain."
_____ 14. The Shakespearean *sonnet* rhyme pattern is *abab cdcd efef gg*.
_____ 15. The *heroic couplet* is unrhymed.
_____ 16. A *poetic license* costs a small fee and entitles a qualified person to write verse.
_____ 17. The *objective correlative* is used to evoke an emotion.
_____ 18. A *pentameter* line consists of seven feet.
_____ 19. Examples of *feminine rhyme* are "writing" and "biting," "fashion" and "passion."
_____ 20. *Imagery* refers to ingenious twists of plot.

Write the letter that indicates the best completion.

( ) 21. An example of a *dactylic* foot is (a) "dancing," (b) "in the town," (c) "the farmer," (d) "tenderly."

( ) 22. An example of an *iambic* foot is (a) "favor," (b) "depend," (c) "of a cloud," (d) "faltering."

( ) 23. An example of *masculine rhyme* is (a) "cringe" and "lunge," (b) "measure" and "treasure," (c) "ships" and "lips," (d) "dine" and "time."

( ) 24. *Free verse* has (a) regular meter, (b) speech rhythms, (c) rhyming restrictions, (d) stanzaic pattern.

( ) 25. An example of *assonance* is (a) "hate" and "lame," (b) "dinner" and "thinner," (c) "sink" and "drink," (d) "steal" and "stall."

Key to Review Test

Check your test answers by the following key. Deduct 4% per error from 100%.

1. foot	6. caesura	11. True	16. False	21. (d)
2. scansion	7. tetrameter	12. False	17. True	22. (b)
3. epic	8. hexameter	13. True	18. False	23. (c)
4. quatrain	9. trochee	14. True	19. True	24. (b)
5. internal	10. inversion	15. False	20. False	25. (a)

Score: _____%

Supplementary List

1. **Alexandrine** (al-ig-zan′drin): a line composed of six iambic feet; an *iambic hexameter*. The Alexandrine is popular in French poetry.
2. **ambiguity** (am′bə-gyōō′i-tē): an expression having two or more possibly contradictory meanings; also refers to multiple suggestiveness which enriches poetry. William Empson's *Seven Types of Ambiguity* (1931) explores the nature of such hinted suggestions.
3. **ars poetica** (ärz pō-et′i-kə): the art of poetry.
4. **carpe diem** (kär′pi dī′em): "seize the day," a Latin phrase implying that one must enjoy the present moment, for tomorrow may be too late. The *carpe diem* theme appeared in *Ecclesiastes'* "Eat, drink, and be merry" and has run through literature like a scarlet thread.
5. **Cavalier poetry:** graceful, sophisticated, witty verses written during the reign of Charles I (1625–1649) by lyric poets Thomas Carew, Sir John Suckling, Richard Lovelace, and others. *Cavalier poetry* deals typically with beloved maidens and constancy and the importance of enjoying the present moment.
6. **dramatic monologue:** a narrative poem in which a single speaker gives his version of a dramatic situation, meanwhile exposing his own personality quirks; for example, Robert Browning's "My Last Duchess" (1842), which tells a story and incidentally reveals the viciousness of the narrator himself.
7. **elegy** (el′i-jē): a formal, melancholy poem, often a lament for the dead. Notable *elegies* include Gray's "Elegy Written in a Country Churchyard" (1750) and Whitman's "When Lilacs Last in the Dooryard Bloom'd" (1866).
8. **enjambment** (en-jam′mənt): the running on of a sentence from one line of verse into the next without a pause at the end of the line. Such a run-on line is in contrast to the more customary end-stopped line.
9. **haiku** (hī′kōō): a delicate Japanese poem of three unrhymed lines consisting of five, seven, and five syllables, respectively. The *haiku* usually alludes in some way to a season.
10. **in medias res** (in mē′di-əs rēz): in the midst of things, that is, in the middle of the narrative. Homer begins an epic *in medias res,* then describes in flashbacks those incidents which led to this crisis.
11. **invocation:** an appeal for inspiration and guidance from a deity or Muse, at the beginning of an epic. Homer's *Iliad* begins with an *invocation* to Calliope, the Muse of epic poetry.
12. **kenning:** a metaphorical compound name for something in Anglo-Saxon poetry. *Kennings* in Beowulf include "whale-road" for "sea" and "foamy floater" for "ship."
13. **laureate** (lôr′ē-it): a poet recognized as the most eminent in a country. Poets *laureate* of England have included Wordsworth, Tennyson, and Masefield.
14. **light verse:** short, light-hearted poems. Witty, sophisticated *light verse* has been written by Dorothy Parker, Ogden Nash, Phyllis McGinley, and others.
15. **metaphysical conceit:** an ingenious, sustained comparison between things apparently highly dissimilar. In "A Valediction: Forbidding Mourning" (1633) John Donne compares the souls of two lovers to the two legs of a compass.

16. **metaphysical poetry:** highly intellectual, philosophical poetry marked by clashing emotions, jarring versification, and startling conceits, as written by John Donne, George Herbert, and other seventeenth-century writers. *Metaphysical poets* were often intensely analytical of human emotions.
17. **New Criticism:** an approach which concentrates on textual explication of a poem rather than on social implications or historical aspects. The new critics such as T. S. Eliot and Robert Penn Warren favor the "close reading" of a poem and judge it by the coherence of its own aesthetic structure.
18. **ottava rima** (ə-tä′və rē′mə): an eight-line stanza in iambic pentameter, rhyming *abababcc*. The *ottava rima* is used in Byron's "Don Juan" (1824) and in Yeats' "Sailing to Byzantium" (1928).
19. **Spenserian stanza:** a nine-line stanza or poem rhyming *ababbcbcC,* consisting of eight iambic pentameter lines followed by an Alexandrine. This stanzaic form is used in Spenser's "The Faerie Queene" (1596) and in Keats' "The Eve of St. Agnes" (1820).
20. **sprung rhythm:** a rhythm in which each foot begins with a stressed syllable followed by a varying number of unstressed syllables. *Sprung rhythm,* a term coined by Gerard Manley Hopkins, is illustrated in his line: "Look at the stars! look, look up at the skies!"

18

General Literature

aestheticism, 26
Age of Reason, 28
archetype, 6
Aristotelian, 8
belles-lettres, 16
bibliography, 19
biography, 13
Calvinism, 27
canon, 20
classicism, 11

didacticism, 25
epigram, 29
epigraph, 30
epilogue, 24
explication, 17
folio, 21
genre, 15
humanism, 5
memoirs, 14
Middle English, 2

Modern English, 3
neoclassicism, 12
Old English, 1
Platonic, 7
prologue, 23
quarto, 22
regionalism, 18
Renaissance, 4
romanticism, 9
transcendentalism, 10

Literature has its fashions and phases. Classicism gives way to romanticism; didacticism gives way to aestheticism; Platonism gives way to Aristotelianism. Historic periods acquire labels too: Old English, Renaissance, Age of Reason, and so on.

Chapter 18 presents a group of these and other common terms that you will meet in literature courses.

Exercises

COVER THIS STRIP

1. **Old English:** the English language as written and spoken during the period 450–1100; also called *Anglo-Saxon*. *Beowulf* is an epic of the *Old English* period.
2. **Middle English:** the English language as written and spoken during the period 1100–1500. Chaucer's *Canterbury Tales* is in *Middle English*.
3. **Modern English:** the English language as written and spoken since about 1500. Shakespeare, born in 1564, wrote in *Modern English*.

▶ *Old English* is also known as _____ [Anglo-Saxon / early American].

Anglo-Saxon

▶ *Old English* was being written (a) when Columbus discovered America, (b) during the years 450–1100. ( )

(b)

▶ The language written during 1100–1500 was _____ English.

Middle

▶ Chaucer wrote *The Book of the Duchesse* in 1369 using the language of that period, _____ English.

Middle

▶ When *Old English* lost many of its changing word-endings around 1100, the language entered a phase known as _____ English.

Middle

▶ The introduction of printing by William Caxton in 1475 helped to stabilize the language and usher in the period of _____ English. *Modern English* has been used since approximately _____ [1500 / 1900].

Modern
1500

▶ The epic *Beowulf* was written by some unknown genius of about the eighth century in language now known as _____ English.

Old

▶ The first English tragedy *Gorboduc*, written by Thomas Sackville and Thomas Norton in 1562, is in _____ English.

Modern

4. **Renaissance** (ren-ə-säns′): a rebirth or revival of activity in literature and the arts, under classic influence, marking the transition in Europe from medieval to modern history. The *Renaissance* occurred during the fourteenth–sixteenth centuries.
5. **humanism:** a cultural movement of the Renaissance which emphasized human dignity and interests rather than medieval fear concerning the hereafter. Leaders of *humanism* included Petrarch, Erasmus, and Thomas More.

(b)

▶ The word *Renaissance* literally means (a) Dark Ages, (b) a rebirth. ( )

humanism
(b)

▶ An important aspect of the *Renaissance* was the cultural movement known as *hu_____*, which favored (a) monastery life and the divine right of kings, (b) education, peace, and human interests. ( )

Renaissance
classical

▶ William Shakespeare, Christopher Marlowe, and Ben Jonson wrote plays during the era of rebirth known as the *R_____*; this period revived _____ [medieval / classical] learning.

humanism
Renaissance

▶ Man's activity in this world, rather than in an afterlife, was stressed by *h_____*, a cultural movement of the *R_____*.

humanism

▶ Terence's line "Nothing that is human is alien to me" was a kind of guideline for _____ [existentialism / humanism].

---

6. **archetype** (ar′kə-tīp): a pattern of experience which has repeated itself throughout literature; a traditional element that echoes human experience such as the death-rebirth theme or the wicked stepmother theme. According to the Swiss psychologist Carl G. Jung, an *archetype* is part of mankind's "collective unconscious" and the product of countless ancestral experiences, so that we are naturally responsive to it in literature.

(b)

▶ An *archetype* is (a) a fresh literary concept, (b) a traditional story element. ( )

archetype

▶ Since the *femme fatale,* or dangerously seductive woman, pops up often in myths and literature, she must be regarded as an *a_____*.

(a)	▶ A typical *archetype* is the theme of (a) love and mating, (b) repairing a typewriter. ( )
archetype (b)	▶ The theme of the savior hero is also an _____ since it occurs in (a) two or three poems, (b) the literature of most nations. ( )

Quiz

Write the letter that indicates the best definition.

1. (c)	( ) 1. archetype a. a man-centered cultural movement
2. (a)	( ) 2. humanism
3. (d)	( ) 3. Middle English b. language of 450–1100
4. (f)	( ) 4. Modern English c. a traditional literary element
5. (b)	( ) 5. Old English d. language of 1100–1500
6. (e)	( ) 6. Renaissance e. an era of rebirth of learning
	f. language of 1500 to the present

7. **Platonic** (plə-ton′ik): tending to be idealistic or metaphysical; maintaining that nothing is truly real except eternal ideas and that these are therefore the proper object of true knowledge. *Platonic* mysticism was a strong influence on Emerson and the American transcendentalists.

8. **Aristotelian** (ar′is-tə-tēl′yən): tending to be scientific and practical in thinking rather than metaphysical and speculative. The *Aristotelian* thinks about particular things rather than about mystical generalities and uses deductive logic rather than intuition.

ideas	▶ *Platonists* believe in the reality of _____ [ideas / things].
things	▶ *Aristotelians* believe in the reality of _____ [ideas / things].
Platonic Aristotelian	▶ The metaphysical approach is P_____; the scientific approach is _____.
(a)	▶ *Platonic* philosophy was largely responsible for American (a) transcendentalism, (b) inventiveness. ( )

(b)	▸ The *Aristotelian* approach did much to advance (a) religion, (b) science. ( )
Aristotelian	▸ The deductive method of the physicist and the mathematician is _____.
Platonic	▸ Thinkers who are idealistic and spiritual are sometimes said to be _____.
Aristotelian (b)	▸ By contrast, the A_____ is (a) visionary and impractical, (b) logical, practical, and hard-headed. ( )
?	▸ Try to decide here whether in outlook and temperament you tend to be a *Platonist* or an *Aristotelian:* _____.

9. **romanticism** (rō-man′ti-siz′əm): a literary style or movement characterized by a strong interest in nature, exalting of the imagination and of personal feelings, and revolt against rules and traditions. The *Romantic* Period is sometimes said to have begun in 1798, with the publication of *Lyrical Ballads* by William Wordsworth and Samuel Coleridge, and to end in the 1830's.

10. **transcendentalism** (tran′sen-den′tə-liz′əm): a nineteenth-century American philosophical movement, an offshoot of romanticism: it emphasized man's divinity, intuitive wisdom, and personal conscience, also the values of self-reliance, spirituality, brotherhood, and living close to nature. *Transcendentalists* such as Ralph Waldo Emerson felt that man could know eternal truths which *transcended,* or went beyond, his external experiences, a concept derived from the German philosopher Immanuel Kant.

(a)	▸ *Romanticism* was an artistic revolt against (a) rules and traditions, (b) nature. ( )
(b)	▸ *Romanticism* encouraged writers to be (a) scientifically objective, (b) personal and emotional. ( )
transcendentalism self-reliance	▸ One American aspect of *romanticism,* called tr_____, stressed the importance of _____ [obedience to leaders / self-reliance].

romanticism	▶ Shelley's gush of poetic feeling for the skylark is typical of r_____.
Emerson (b)	▶ *Transcendentalists* such as _____ [Emerson / Pope] believed in man's (a) inferiority and ignorance, (b) god-like nature. ( )
(a)	▶ Emerson's *transcendentalist* essays urged people to be self-reliant and optimistic because each man had (a) divinity in him and intuitive flashes of eternal truths, (b) good business opportunities. ( )
romanticism (a)	▶ Love of nature was typical of *rom_____*, as was the exalting of (a) the imagination, (b) dignified control. ( )
transcendentalism (a)	▶ Ralph Waldo Emerson was a spokesman for American *tr_____*; he believed that a man could learn truths through (a) intuition, (b) external experiences only. ( )

11. **classicism** (klas′i-siz′əm): the literary style of ancient Greece and Rome, marked by simplicity, clarity, dignity, balance, and controlled emotion. *Classicism*, in its restraint, is in direct contrast to romanticism.

12. **neoclassicism**: a revival of the classical style in literature and art, occurring in England about 1660–1790. Daniel Defoe's *Robinson Crusoe* (1719) illustrates the clear, rational prose of *neoclassicism*.

(b)	▶ *Classicism* in literature had its origin in (a) Oxford University, (b) ancient Greece and Rome. ( )
classicism (b)	▶ The polished style of *cl_____* was marked by (a) emotional frenzy, (b) dignity and control. ( )
neoclassicism	▶ The eighteenth-century revival of ancient Greek literary *classicism* is known as *n_____*.
classicism later	▶ *Neoclassicism* imitated the spirit of _____ but came along about 1700 years _____ [earlier / later].

observe
neoclassicism

▸ *Classicism* tended to _____ [observe / violate] traditional rules; and the same tendency to conform was a feature of _____ [romanticism / neoclassicism].

Quiz

Write the letter that indicates the best completion.

( ) 1. Aristotelianism
( ) 2. classicism
( ) 3. neoclassicism
( ) 4. Platonism
( ) 5. romanticism
( ) 6. transcendentalism

a. tried to revive literary classicism
b. stressed an idealistic or metaphysical approach
c. favored a practical, scientific approach
d. stressed intuition, personal divinity, self-reliance, and is associated with certain New England writers
e. aimed for dignity and control in ancient Greek literature
f. exalted nature, emotionalism, spirit of revolt, as in *Lyrical Ballads*

1. (c)
2. (e)
3. (a)
4. (b)
5. (f)
6. (d)

13. **biography:** a person's life story, written by another person (if written by himself it is called autobiography). Modern *biography* began with James Boswell's *Life of Samuel Johnson* (1791), with its honest details about an eccentric, talented man.
14. **memoirs** (mem'wärs): a personal record of historical events and people that the author has been associated with. *Memoirs* are a form of autobiography but tend to focus on personalities and events rather than on the inner life of the author.
15. **genre** (zhän'rə): a particular type of literature, such as novel, tragedy, epic, short story, and biography. The old rules which sharply defined the form of each *genre* have begun to dissolve.

biography
(a)

▸ Carl Sandburg's account of Lincoln's life is a b_____ because it is a product of (a) facts, (b) fiction. ( )

biography
genre

▸ The life story of an actual person, called a b_____, has become a popular literary type, or g_____.

memoirs
genre

▸ Winston Churchill's books about the war years are called m_____, another popular g_____.

299

actual	▶ Both *biography* and *memoirs* deal with _____ [actual / imaginary] people and events.
memoirs	▶ Many American presidents, including Grant, Truman, and Eisenhower, have written historical reminiscences known as *m*_____.
is not	▶ *The History of Tom Jones* (1749) is the product of Henry Fielding's fertile imagination, so it _____ [is / is not] a *biography*.
genre	▶ Fielding's *Tom Jones* is a novel and a lively example of that *g*_____.
(a)	▶ A *genre* is (a) a literary type, (b) the head of a French army. ( )

---

16. **belles-lettres** (bel-let′rə): the imaginative and artistic forms of literature, as distinguished from practical and technical writing. *Belles-lettres* include drama, fiction, and poetry.
17. **explication** (eks′pli-kā′shən): close analysis and interpretation of a poem or passage, stressing images, suggestiveness, irony, interrelationships of words, and aesthetic coherence. The art of *explication* has been highly developed by the New Critics.

belles-lettres (a)	▶ An example of *belles-*_____ is (a) Edmund Spenser's *The Faerie Queene* (1590), (b) K. Imhoff's *Sewage Treatment* (1956). ( )
explication detailed	▶ Poetic analysis known as *exp*_____ involves a _____ [general / detailed] interpretation of the text.
artistic (b)	▶ *Belles-lettres* refers to _____ [practical / artistic] writing such as that by (a) the Jet Propulsion Laboratory researchists, (b) Euripides, Shelley, and Dylan Thomas. ( )
are not belles-lettres	▶ Your history and economic textbooks _____ [are / are not] _____-*lettres*.

explication
(a)

▸ Detailed interpretation, or _____, of a poem deals primarily with (a) imagery, irony, ambiguities, etc., (b) social values. ( )

---

18. **regionalism:** the practice of using and developing a special section of the country as background with emphasis on how the customs and surroundings affect the characters. *Regionalism* differs from *local color* in that it reflects the life of a region rather than of a limited locality.

regionalism

▸ Novels and poetry with a New England setting are a type of r_____.

(b)

▸ Literary *regionalism* is illustrated in fiction about (a) the Bronx, (b) the deep South. ( )

regionalism
does

▸ Mark Twain's description of life along the Mississippi also illustrates _____ism, because Twain _____ [does / does not] show the impact of folklore, customs, and river life upon his characters.

Quiz

Write the letter that indicates the best definition.

1. (c)
2. (f)
3. (a)
4. (b)
5. (d)
6. (e)

( ) 1. belles-lettres   a. textual analysis
( ) 2. biography   b. any recognized literary category
( ) 3. explication   c. artistic writing
( ) 4. genre   d. a personal record of historic events
( ) 5. memoirs   e. use of a region as a setting
( ) 6. regionalism   f. a person's life described by someone else

---

19. **bibliography:** a list of books and other writings which deal with a particular subject. Building a *bibliography* is an early step in writing a research paper.

20. **canon** (kan'ən): all the authenticated works by an author. The Shakespeare *canon*, for example, includes 37 plays; it excludes doubtful works.

bibliography

▸ A scholarly writer lists his research sources in a b_____.

(b)	▶ The *canon* of an author is (a) his pistol, (b) a list of his authenticated works. ( )
(a)	▶ The Biblical *canon* excludes (a) chapters considered spurious or not inspired, (b) the Ten Commandments. ( )
is not canon	▶ A so-called Shakespearean play, *Vortigern,* which proved to be a forgery, _____ [is / is not] included in the Shakespeare c_____.
bibliography	▶ A list of one's research sources is called a _____ [biography / bibliography].

21. **folio** (fō′lē-ō′): the largest of books, made from printer's sheets that have been folded into two leaves, or four pages. Original *folio* copies of Shakespeare's plays are rare today.
22. **quarto:** a book about nine by twelve inches, made from printer's sheets that have been folded into four leaves, or eight pages. Smaller volumes than the *quarto,* abbreviated *4to,* are the *octavo, 8vo,* and the *duodecimo, 12mo.*

once (a)	▶ To produce the *folio* the printer's sheets are folded only _____ [once / three times]; consequently, the *folio* (a) is the largest of books, (b) can be tucked into your hip pocket. ( )
quarto	▶ The *folio* is larger than the q_____.
quarto four	▶ To make a q_____ volume, the printer folds a sheet twice, making _____ [four / eight] leaves.
(b)	▶ Because the *quarto* is the product of only two foldings, it measures about (a) four by six inches, (b) nine by twelve inches. ( )
Folio	▶ Shakespeare's collected plays were first published in the largest available format, in 1623, and that volume is called the First _____ [Quarto / Folio].

23. **prologue** (prō′lôg): an introduction to a play or poem. Shakespeare's *Pericles* (1607) begins with a *prologue* delivered by one of the actors.
24. **epilogue** (ep′ə-lôg′): a final comment added to a play, poem, or novel; for example, Shakespeare's *The Tempest* (1611) ends with an *epilogue*.

▸ The *prologue* to a play or to an act comes at the _____ [beginning / end].

    beginning

▸ Ben Jonson's *Bartholomew Fair* (1614) begins with a *prologue*; but its *ep*_____ follows (a) Act I, (b) Act V. ( )

    epilogue
    (b)

▸ Elizabethan and Restoration dramas often ended with a speech to win the good will of the spectators; this was the _____.

    epilogue

▸ The *epilogue* of a play is a speech delivered as (a) an introduction, (b) a farewell. ( )

    (b)

▸ Preliminary remarks are delivered as _____.

    prologue

Quiz

Write the letter that indicates the best definition.

( ) 1. bibliography   a. introduction to a play
( ) 2. canon   b. largest of books
( ) 3. epilogue   c. list of research sources
( ) 4. folio   d. farewell speech in a play
( ) 5. prologue   e. authenticated works
( ) 6. quarto   f. a nine-by-twelve-inch book, smaller than a folio

1. (c)
2. (e)
3. (d)
4. (b)
5. (a)
6. (f)

25. **didacticism** (dī-dak′tə-siz′əm): using literature to teach a lesson or to moralize. Henry Wadsworth Longfellow's *didactic* verses, for example, urge us to "make our lives sublime" and leave "footprints on the sands of time."
26. **aestheticism** (es-thet′ə-siz′əm): the pursuit of art for art's sake; a literary movement of the late nineteenth century that emphasized beauty and style and ignored practical or moral values. The *aestheticism* of Walter Pater and Oscar Wilde failed to win strong support in Victorian England.

(b)	▶ *Aestheticism* involves the pursuit of art (a) to improve society, (b) for the sake of art. ( )
(b)	▶ *Didacticism* is the attempt (a) to entertain, (b) to teach a lesson. ( )
didacticism	▶ John Whittier's tendency to preach against slavery in his poetry is called _____.
(b)	▶ *Aestheticism* stressed the achievement of (a) practical goals, (b) style and beauty. ( )
aestheticism didacticism	▶ Edgar Allan Poe maintained that a poem is the "rhythmical creation of beauty" and must not try to teach or preach; his position is that of _____; like most of today's poetry critics, Poe was opposed to d_____.

27. **Calvinism:** the religious system of John Calvin, emphasizing that man is naturally evil and predestined to eternal hell except for the few saved solely by God's grace. *Calvinism* is reflected in the works of Cotton Mather, Jonathan Edwards, Edward Taylor, and other Puritan writers.

(a)	▶ *Calvinism* held that because Adam disobeyed and ate the forbidden fruit, all men are born (a) naturally wicked, (b) innocent. ( )
Calvinism hell	▶ Therefore, most people, according to C_____, are going to _____ [heaven / hell].
(a)	▶ *Calvinist* Jonathan Edwards preached that we are all "Sinners in the Hands of an Angry God" and can be saved from everlasting flames only (a) through God's grace, (b) by our good deeds. ( )
Calvinism	▶ Michael Wigglesworth's *The Day of Doom* (1662) refers in didactic verse to hellfire, natural depravity, predestination, and God's grace, all in accordance with _____ism.

28. **Age of Reason:** an eighteenth-century period when philosophical men hoped to solve social, political, and other problems by scientific and rational methods. The *Age of Reason,* also known as the *Enlightenment,* saw rising opposition to monarchies, superstitions, and religious doctrines.

▸ The *Age of Reason* encouraged (a) mysticism, (b) rational thinking. ( )

(b)

▸ The attack on traditions during the *Age of Reason* helped to bring on (a) the Revolutionary War, (b) World War I. ( )

(a)

▸ The _____ *of Reason* was _____ [an eighteenth- / a nineteenth-] century phenomenon and is also known as (a) Calvinism, (b) the Enlightenment. ( )

Age
an eighteenth-
(b)

▸ During the *Age of Reason* men like Thomas Paine were confident that political and religious questions could be solved by an appeal to (a) logical thinking, (b) past customs. ( )

(a)

▸ Benjamin Franklin and Thomas Jefferson also were representatives of the *Age of* _____ and consequently turned _____ [to / from] science, democracy, and deism.

Reason
to

29. **epigram:** a brief, clever, quotable saying, sometimes in verse. Example from Oscar Wilde: "I can resist everything except temptation."
30. **epigraph:** a pertinent quotation or motto at the beginning of a book, chapter, or poem. T. S. Eliot's "The Love Song of J. Alfred Prufrock" (1917) begins with an *epigraph* from Dante.

▸ A witty sophisticated observation is sometimes called an *ep_____*.

epigram

▸ A quotation that precedes a literary work is called an *ep_____*.

epigraph

▸ In introducing a poem or story, the *epigraph* usually strikes (a) an off-note, (b) a keynote. ( )

(b)

(b)

epigram

(a)

epigram

▶ An *epigram* is (a) long and dull, (b) short, pithy, and quotable. ( )

▶ When a Shakespearean character says, "Brevity is the soul of wit," he shows appreciation for the _____.

▶ An *epigraph* sheds light on the theme of a literary composition and is placed at the (a) beginning, (b) end. ( )

▶ Shaw's comment, "Youth is a wonderful thing; what a crime to waste it on children," is an _____.

Quiz

Write the letter that indicates the best definition.

1. (c)
2. (d)
3. (f)
4. (b)
5. (e)
6. (a)

( ) 1. aestheticism
( ) 2. Age of Reason
( ) 3. Calvinism
( ) 4. didacticism
( ) 5. epigram
( ) 6. epigraph

a. an introductory quotation
b. teaching and moralizing
c. the attitude of art for art's sake
d. the Enlightenment
e. a short, witty saying
f. a religion stressing original sin, hellfire, and God's grace

Review Test

Supply the missing word in each sentence. The first letter of each answer is given.

1. The rebirth of learning in Europe was called the R_____.
2. A literary type, such as epic or novel, is a g_____.
3. The language of England during 1100–1500 was M_____ E_____.
4. A short final speech to the play audience is an e_____.
5. The pursuit of art for art's sake is a_____.
6. The eighteenth-century revival of classicism is n_____.
7. Teaching or moralizing in poetry is d_____.
8. A list of sources of information is a b_____.
9. A traditional, recurring theme or story element is an a_____.
10. The largest book printed is the f_____.

Write *True* or *False*.

_____ 11. *Explication* is the critical analysis of literary passages.

_____ 12. *Biographies* are usually classed as fiction.

_____ 13. *Beowulf*, an eighth-century epic, was written in *Old English*.

_____ 14. An *epigram* is a night letter which goes at special rates.

_____ 15. The *epigraph* is placed at the end of a novel or poem.

_____ 16. Emotionalism, imaginativeness, and love of nature are common aspects of *romanticism*.

_____ 17. *Platonic* thinking tends to be idealistic and mystical.

_____ 18. *Regionalism* in literature reflects the life of a region.

_____ 19. *Calvinism* maintained that if you did good deeds you would go to heaven.

_____ 20. According to *transcendentalism,* man has divinity within himself and therefore intuitive wisdom.

Write the letter that indicates the best completion.

( ) 21. *Modern English* has been used since about (a) 900, (b) 1100, (c) 1500, (d) 1890.
( ) 22. The *quarto* is smaller than the (a) average book today, (b) duodecimo, (c) octavo, (d) folio.
( ) 23. The *Aristotelian* approach is (a) metaphysical, (b) speculative, (c) practical, (d) idealistic.
( ) 24. *Humanism* emphasized (a) mythology, (b) human activities, (c) religious speculation, (d) medieval learning.
( ) 25. Greek *classicism* is notable for (a) restraint, (b) emotionalism, (c) novelty, (d) distortion.

Write the letter that indicates the best definition.

( ) 26. Age of Reason   a. creative, imaginative literature
( ) 27. belles-lettres   b. the entire authenticated works of an author
( ) 28. canon   c. an introduction to a literary work
( ) 29. memoirs   d. the Enlightenment
( ) 30. prologue   e. a record of personal observations

Key to Review Test

Check your test answers by the following key. Deduct 3% per error from 100%.

1. Renaissance	7. didacticism	13. True	19. False	25. (a)
2. genre	8. bibliography	14. False	20. True	26. (d)
3. Middle English	9. archetype	15. False	21. (c)	27. (a)
4. epilogue	10. folio	16. True	22. (d)	28. (b)
5. aestheticism	11. True	17. True	23. (c)	29. (e)
6. neoclassicism	12. False	18. True	24. (b)	30. (c)

Score: _____ %

19

Academic Terms

Fine Arts

1. **a cappella** (ä′kə-pel′ə): sung without instrumental accompaniment.
2. **aesthetics** (es-thet′iks): the study of beauty, especially as found in the fine arts.
3. **allegro** (ə-lā′grō): lively; faster than *allegretto* but not so fast as *presto*.
4. **andante** (an-dan′tē): a moderately slow movement in music.
5. **aria** (ä′ri-ə): a melody for solo voices, as in an opera or oratorio, usually with instrumental accompaniment.
6. **atonality** (ā′tō-nal′i-tē): *music.* a lack of key or tonal center; a condition wherein no one tone holds a primary position.
7. **avant-garde** (ə-vänt′gärd′): F., the vanguard; especially, in art, those regarded as advanced, daring, and experimental.
8. **baroque** (bə-rōk′): involving fantastic ornamentation and theatrical effects, as in seventeenth-century art, architecture, and music.
9. **bas-relief** (bä′ri-lēf′): sculpture in which the figures project only slightly from the background.
10. **cadenza** (kə-den′zə): a showy musical passage, often improvised, by an unaccompanied instrument in a concerto.
11. **cantata** (kən-tä′tə): a composition involving arias, choruses, and recitatives, to be sung but not acted.
12. **ceramics** (sə-ram′iks): the art of making pottery, earthenware, tile, etc.
13. **chamber music:** music suitable for a small hall, as by an instrumental trio or quartet.
14. **coloratura** (kul′ə-rə-tyoor′ə): brilliant runs, trills, etc., to show off a singer's talents.
15. **connoisseur** (kon′ə-sūr′): an expert in some field, especially fine arts, or in matters of taste.
16. **crescendo** (krə-shen′dō): a gradual increase in loudness.
17. **cubism** (kū′biz-əm): art which uses cubes, cones, and other abstract geometric forms instead of representing nature realistically.
18. **decadent** (-di-kād′nt): deteriorating, as in morals, art, and literature; a writer of a late nineteenth-century group which leaned toward artificial style and abnormal subjects.

19. **dilettante** (dil′ə-tan′ti): one who cultivates an art or science superficially as a pastime.
20. **dynamics:** *music.* the various degrees of softness and loudness in performance.
21. **etude** (ā′tōōd): a technical study for solo instrument.
22. **finesse** (fi-nes′): refined skill; adroitness in handling a delicate situation.
23. **forte** (fôr′tā): *music.* loud.
24. **fresco:** the art of painting on wet plaster.
25. **Hellenic** (he-len′ik): Grecian; pertaining to the ancient Greeks.
26. **impresario** (im-pri-sär′ē-ō): the organizer or manager of an opera company or of concert artists.
27. **intaglio** (in-tal′yō): a design carved below the surface, as on a gem: opposed to *cameo,* a design that stands out in relief.
28. **lapidary** (lap′i-der′ē): pertaining to cutting and engraving precious stones.
29. **little theater:** amateur or community theater; experimental or avant-garde drama playing to a limited audience.
30. **lyric** (lir′ik): a songlike outpouring of emotions and sentiment, as in sonnets, odes, elegies, and hymns.
31. **mimesis** (mi-mē′sis): *drama.* the imitation of human speech and behavior.
32. **mural** (myoor′əl): a painting done on a wall.
33. **nocturne** (nok′tûrn): a dreamy, romantic musical composition appropriate to night.
34. **ode:** a dignified lyric poem of some length which does honor in lofty style to some person or thing.
35. **oratorio** (or′ə-tōr′ē-ō′): an extended composition for voice and orchestra, usually on a religious theme, without acting or scenery.
36. **overture** (ō′vər-chər): the orchestral introduction to an opera or other large work.
37. **percussion instrument** (pər-kush′ən): an instrument which produces its tone when a part is struck; for example, drums, triangles, piano.
38. **perspective:** the drawing of objects as they appear to the eye, exhibiting distance and depth.
39. **pointillism** (pwan′tə-liz′əm): a method of painting by placing small points of pure color on a canvas to produce a blended, luminous effect.
40. **sonata** (sə-nä′tə): a composition in three or four movements for a small instrumental group.
41. **statuary** (stach′ōō-er′ē): a collection of statues.
42. **Stradivarius** (strad′ə-var′ē-əs): a violin or other stringed instrument made by the Stradivari family.
43. **string quartet:** a music group usually playing first and second violin, viola, and cello; a composition for such a group.
44. **surrealism:** the depiction of irrational, incongruous workings of the subconscious mind, especially as manifested in dreams.
45. **symmetry** (sim′ə-trē): harmony of form resulting from a balanced arrangement of parts.
46. **syncopation:** the beginning of a tone on the last half of a beat and holding it through the first part of the next beat.
47. **tapestry** (tap′is-trē): a wall-hanging textile with a decorative design.
48. **tempo:** the rate of speed of a musical passage.

49. **vignette** (vin-yet'): a short literary piece, subtle and delicate; a decorative design or a shaded drawing.
50. **virtuoso** (vûr′choo-ō′sō): one who is eminently skilled in an art such as music.

Natural Science

1. **absolute zero:** the lowest possible temperature, theoretically —273.18 degrees C., at which molecular motion ceases.
2. **acceleration:** the rate of change in velocity.
3. **acoustics** (ə-koōs′tiks): the laws of sound; the sound-transmitting qualities of a room or hall.
4. **adaptation** (ad′əp-tā′shən): a change in structure or function by which an organism adjusts better to its environment.
5. **aerodynamics** (âr′ō-dī-nam′iks): the branch of physics that studies gases in motion, including their mechanical effects and other properties.
6. **alchemy** (al′kə-mē): medieval chemistry which sought mainly to change lead into gold and to find the elixir of perpetual youth.
7. **ampere** (am′pēr): the standard unit of electric current, equal to the current sent by one volt through a resistance of one ohm.
8. **aneroid barometer** (an′ə-roid′): an instrument which measures atmospheric pressure by its effect on the flexible top of a metal box containing a partial vacuum.
9. **anticyclone:** a high pressure area in which the spiral currents flow clockwise in the northern hemisphere.
10. **asexual** (ā-sek′shoō-əl): without sex; reproducing itself without sexual union.
11. **ballistics** (bə-lis′tiks): the science dealing with the flight behavior and impact of projectiles.
12. **Bessemer process** (bes′ə-mər): making steel by forcing a blast of air through molten pig iron to remove impurities.
13. **Bohr theory** (bōr): the theory of Niels Bohr that electrons absorb or radiate energy when changing orbits.
14. **Brownian movement:** the zigzag movement of microscopic particles suspended in fluids, caused by collisions with molecules.
15. **cardiac** (kär′dē-ak′): pertaining to the heart.
16. **catalyst** (kat′ə-list): a substance which speeds up a chemical reaction but itself undergoes practically no change.
17. **centrifugal force** (sen-trif′yə-gəl): the force impelling a thing outward from the center of rotation.
18. **centripetal force** (sen-trip′ə-təl): the force tending to draw a thing inward toward the center of rotation.
19. **congenital** (kən-jen′ə-təl): existing from birth.
20. **cretinism** (krē′tən-iz′əm): idiocy and deformity resulting from a congenital thyroid deficiency.
21. **cybernetics** (sī-bər-net′iks): a comparative study of computers and the human nervous system to help explain brain processes.
22. **cyclotron** (sī′klə-tron′): an apparatus that gives high velocity and energy to protons and deuterons so they can smash nuclear targets.
23. **decibel** (des′ə-bel′): a measure of the volume of a sound; one tenth of a bel.
24. **dominant:** *genetics.* designating a hereditary character which prevails over and masks a *recessive* character.

25. **electrolysis** (i-lek′trol′ə-sis): the decomposition of a chemical solution by means of an electric current.
26. **electrostatics:** a branch of physics that deals with electricity at rest known as static electricity.
27. **fission** (fish′ən): the splitting of an atom, with release of energy.
28. **foot-pound:** a unit of work, enough to raise a one-pound mass a distance of one foot.
29. **fulcrum** (ful′krəm): the support on which a lever turns.
30. **galvanic** (gal-van′ik): of electricity from a battery; convulsive; startling.
31. **gene** (jēn): an element in the chromosomes that transmits hereditary characters.
32. **generic** (jə-ner′ik): pertaining to a genus or class; having a broad general application.
33. **geocentric** (jē′ō-sen′trik): regarding the earth as center of the universe.
34. **geophysics** (jē′ō-fiz′iks): the physics of the earth, dealing with tides, winds, earthquakes, magnetic fields, etc.
35. **gynecology** (gī′nə-kol′ə-jē): the branch of medicine dealing with women's diseases.
36. **gyroscope** (jī′rə-skōp′): a rotating device, used to stabilize ships and planes.
37. **hermetic** (hûr-met′ik): airtight; completely sealed to keep air and liquids from getting in or out.
38. **histology** (hi-stol′ə-jē): the microscopic study of tissue structure.
39. **horticulture:** the cultivation of garden plants.
40. **humus** (hū′məs): organic matter in soils, produced by decay of vegetable and animal stuff.
41. **hybrid** (hī-brid): the offspring of two plants or animals of different varieties.
42. **hydraulic:** using water or other liquid: as, a *hydraulic* brake.
43. **hygrometer** (hī-grom′ə-tər): an instrument for measuring humidity.
44. **immunology:** the branch of medicine which deals with immunity to disease.
45. **inertia** (in-ûr′shə): that tendency of matter to retain its state of rest or of uniform rectilinear motion unless acted upon by an external force.
46. **isobar** (ī′sə-bär′): a line on a weather map connecting points having the same barometric pressure.
47. **isotope** (ī′sə-tōp′): any of two or more forms of a chemical element, each with its individual mass number and radioactive behavior.
48. **kinetic energy** (ki-net′ik): energy resulting from the motion of a body: opposed to *potential* energy.
49. **Lamarckism** (lə-mär′kiz-əm): Lamarck's evolutionary theory that acquired characteristics can be inherited.
50. **malleable** (mal′e-ə-bəl): pliable; capable of being hammered and shaped without breaking: said of metals.
51. **materia medica** (mə-tēr′ē-ə med′ə-kə): drugs and other remedial substances.
52. **maturation** (mach′oo-rā′shən): attainment of maturity; completion of growth.
53. **megaton** (meg′ə-tun′): the explosive power of one million tons of TNT.
54. **Mendelism** (men′də-liz′əm): Gregor Mendel's principles of heredity, which predict characteristics of the offspring in cross-breeding.
55. **metabolism** (mə-tab′ə-liz′əm): the sum of physical and chemical processes which supply energy to the body.

56. **metallurgy** (met′ə-lûr′jē): the science of separating metals from ores and refining them for use.
57. **mutation** (myo͞o-tā′shən): a sudden, transmissible variation from the parent type.
58. **natural selection:** the adaptation of a species to its environment through survival of the fittest.
59. **oscillation** (os′ə-lā′shən): the fluctuation between maximum and minimum values, as of an alternating current.
60. **osmosis** (oz-mō′sis): the passing of a fluid through a membrane to equalize pressures.
61. **periodic table:** an arrangement of chemical elements by atomic number to exhibit groups and families.
62. **pituitary** (pi-to͞o′ə-ter′ē): a gland at the base of the brain that secretes hormones affecting growth and metabolism.
63. **qualitative analysis:** the determining of the ingredients in a substance.
64. **quantum theory** (kwon′təm): the theory that radiant energy is not smooth flowing but discontinuous, and emitted in definite units called *quanta.*
65. **rectifier:** any device, such as a vacuum tube, which converts alternating current into direct current.
66. **resonance** (rez′ə-nəns): reinforced vibration due to the vibration, at the same frequency, of another body.
67. **seismic** (sīz′mik): pertaining to earthquakes.
68. **serology** (si-rol′ə-jē): the science of serums.
69. **sextant** (seks′tənt): a navigational instrument used in determining latitude at sea.
70. **simian** (sim′ē-ən): pertaining to monkeys or anthropoid apes.
71. **solar** (sō′lər): pertaining to the sun.
72. **solstice** (sol′stis): the time when the sun is furthest from the equator, at about June 21 and December 22.
73. **spectrum:** a band of colors observed when a beam of white light passes through a prism.
74. **speleology** (spē′lē-ol′ə-jē): the science of exploring caves; spelunking.
75. **spirochete** (spī′rə-kēt′): any of a genus of spiral-shaped bacteria some of which cause syphilis, trench mouth, and yaws.
76. **spontaneous generation:** the discredited theory that living organisms can originate in nonliving matter.
77. **stalactite** (stə-lak′tīt): an icicle-shaped rocky deposit hanging from the roof of a cave: distinguished from a *stalagmite,* which projects upward from the floor of a cave.
78. **supersonic:** greater than the speed of sound; faster than 738 miles per hour.
79. **taxidermy** (tak′sə-dûr′mē): the art of stuffing animals.
80. **tetanus** (tet′ə-nəs): an infectious, often fatal disease, marked by muscle spasms and lockjaw.
81. **therapy** (ther′ə-pē): the treatment of disease.
82. **thrombosis** (throm-bō′sis): a clotting of blood, forming an obstruction to circulation.
83. **topography** (tə-pog′rə-fē): mapping the surface features of a region.
84. **torque** (tôrk): a force tending to produce rotation.
85. **toxemia** (tok-sē′mē-ə): blood poisoning.
86. **toxicology** (tok′sə-kol′ə-jē): the science of poisons.

87. **trajectory** (trə-jek′tə-rē): the path described by something hurtling through space, especially the path of a projectile.
88. **troposphere** (trop′ə-sfēr′): the atmosphere that contains clouds and winds, below the stratosphere.
89. **Ursa Major** (ur′sə mā′jər): the constellation of the seven stars that form the Big Dipper; literally, the *Great Bear*.
90. **valence** (vā′ləns): the combining capacity of an atom or radical compared with that of a hydrogen atom.
91. **vector** (vek′tər): a quantity, such as force or velocity, that has both magnitude and direction.
92. **ventral** (ven′trəl): pertaining to the belly; abdominal: opposed to *dorsal,* pertaining to the back.
93. **ventricle** (ven′tri-kəl): one of the two lower chambers of the heart.
94. **vernier** (vûr′nē-ər): an auxiliary device which makes possible a more precise setting of a measuring instrument or a tool.
95. **viable** (vī′ə-bəl): physically fitted to live: said of a fetus or of a seed.
96. **viscera** (vis′ər-ə): the internal organs such as the lungs and intestines.
97. **vivisection** (viv′i-sek′shən): cutting into a living animal body in the interests of experimental research.
98. **watershed:** a ridge of high land separating two river drainage basins.
99. **woofer:** a large loudspeaker used to reproduce low-frequency sound waves: distinguished from *tweeter,* used to reproduce high-frequency sound waves.
100. **zenith** (zē′nith): the point in the sky directly above an observer: opposed to *nadir* (nā′dēr), the lowest possible point.

Philosophy

1. **agnosticism** (ag-nos′ti-siz′əm): the doctrine that one cannot know about God or the hereafter, or of anything but material phenomena.
2. **amoral** (ā-môr′əl): neither moral nor immoral; having no connection with morality.
3. **animism** (an′ə-miz′əm): the belief that inanimate objects and natural phenomena, such as stones, sun, and rain, are alive and have souls.
4. **apologetics** (ə-pol′ə-jet′iks): the branch of theology which deals with the defense and proofs of Christianity.
5. **a posteriori** (ā′ pos-têr′i-ō′rī): reasoning from particular instances to principles or from effect to cause; inductive; empirical: opposed to *a priori*.
6. **a priori** (ā′ prī-ō′rī): reasoning from general principle to particular instances or from cause to effect; deductive; based on theory rather than experiment.
7. **Berkeleianism** (burk-lē′ən-iz′əm): the philosophy of George Berkeley, maintaining that ideas are real and that material objects do not exist.
8. **categorical imperative** (kat′ə-gôr′i-kəl): the doctrine of Immanuel Kant that one must do only what he would want others to do in the same situation.
9. **deism** (dē′iz-əm): a belief in God based on reason but rejecting biblical revelation.
10. **determinism:** the doctrine that every action is the inevitable result of a sequence of causes.
11. **dialectics** (dī′ə-lek′tiks): the practice of examining ideas logically, usually by the method of question and answer.
12. **eclectic** (i-klek′tik): selecting what is considered best from various sources; not following any one system but choosing from all.
13. **empirical** (em-pir′i-kəl): depending on practical experience alone, not on theoretical reasoning: as, an *empirical* discovery.
14. **epistemology** (i-pis′tə-mol′ə-jē): the branch of philosophy that investigates the nature, limits, and validity of human knowledge.
15. **fatalism** (fā′tə-liz′əm): the belief that all events are predetermined and inevitable.
16. **free will:** the doctrine that people have the power to choose between alternative courses of action: opposed to *determinism*.
17. **hedonism** (hē′də-niz′əm): the doctrine that pleasure or happiness is the main goal of life.
18. **materialism:** the doctrine that physical matter is the only reality; also, a concern for worldly goods rather than spiritual goals.
19. **monism** (mon′iz-əm): the doctrine that there is only one kind of ultimate substance.
20. **nirvana** (nir-van′ə): *Buddhism.* the blessedness achieved by absorption of the soul into the supreme spirit.
21. **ontology** (on-tol′ə-jē): the study of the nature of reality or being.
22. **oversoul:** the universal spiritual element which unites all human souls, according to Emersonian transcendentalism.
23. **positivism:** the system of Auguste Comte based on positive facts of sense experience and rejecting speculation.
24. **pragmatism** (prag′mə-tiz′əm): the doctrine that ideas have value only in terms of their practical results.

25. **relativism:** the theory that truths are relative and that the basis of judgment varies according to persons, events, etc.
26. **subjectivism** (səb-jek'tə-viz'əm): the theory that all knowledge is subjective and relative, a reflection of one's own consciousness.
27. **syllogism** (sil'ə-jiz'əm): a formula for deductive reasoning, consisting of a major premise, a minor premise, and a conclusion.
28. **Thomism** (tō'miz-əm): the dogmatic theology of Saint Thomas Aquinas, which became the basis of thirteenth-century scholasticism.
29. **utilitarianism:** the doctrine that ideas and things ought to be judged strictly by their usefulness rather than by beauty, tradition, etc., and that conduct should promote the greatest happiness for the greatest number.
30. **volition** (vō-lish'ən): the act of willing; a decision of the will.

Social Science

1. **abolitionist:** one who favored wiping out Negro slavery in the United States.
2. **acculturation** (ə-kul′chə-rā′shən): the process of adopting new cultural patterns.
3. **agrarian** (ə-grâr′ē-ən): relating to farmlands and their ownership.
4. **amnesty** (am′ni-stē): a general pardon, as to political offenders, extended by a government.
5. **Anglican** (ang′glə-kən): pertaining to England, particularly the Church of England.
6. **apartheid** (ə-pärt′hīt): discrimination and segregation enforced against non-whites, as practiced in the Republic of South Africa.
7. **authoritarianism:** a system involving unquestioning obedience to authority, rather than individual freedom.
8. **Benthamism** (ben′thəm-iz′əm): the utilitarianism of Jeremy Bentham, who judged the morality of an action by its production of happiness and who measured that happiness by such criteria as intensity, duration, purity, and extent.
9. **blitzkrieg** (blits′krēg′): a lightning-speed military offensive.
10. **bloc** (blok): a coalition of nations or factions for a common cause.
11. **Bourbonism** (boor′bə-niz′əm): extreme conservatism in political and social issues, like that of the Bourbons.
12. **bourgeois** (boor-zhwä′): middle-class; commonplace, conventional, respectable, and smug.
13. **bureaucracy** (byoo-rok′rə-sē): government by numerous bureaus and officials, marked by inflexible routine and red tape.
14. **capitalism:** an economic system in which the means of production and of distribution are privately owned.
15. **cause célèbre** (kōz sā-leb′r): F., a celebrated legal case; notorious incident.
16. **civil disobedience:** passive resistance.
17. **civil rights:** the rights of all to enjoy life, liberty, and property and the equal protection of law.
18. **Communism:** a totalitarian system of government in which the state owns all means of production and which is characterized by suppression of political opposition and individual liberties.
19. **coup d'état** (koō dā-tä′): F., a stroke of state; sudden, forceful act of politics, such as an overthrow of government.
20. **despotism** (des′pə-tiz′əm): tyranny; government by an absolute ruler.
21. **documentary** (dok′yə-men′tə-rē): presenting factual material, such as news events or social conditions, objectively and without fictionalizing.
22. **egalitarian** (i-gal′i-târ′ē-ən): equalitarian; believing that all men should have equal political and social rights.
23. **espionage** (es′pi-ə-nij): spying to secure military and political secrets.
24. **ethics:** a system of moral standards; code of right conduct for a specific profession or group.
25. **ethnocentrism** (eth′nō-sen′triz-əm): the belief that one's own race, country, or culture is superior to all others.

26. **ethos** (ē′thos): the distinctive spirit or character of a people, group, or culture.
27. **free enterprise:** the economic policy of having private ownership of business with little governmental control.
28. **Gandhiism** (gän′dē-iz′əm): passive resistance to achieve reform, as advocated by Mahatma Gandhi.
29. **genocide** (jen′ə-sīd′): the systematic killing of an entire people or nation.
30. **geopolitics** (jē′ō-pol′ə-tiks): the application of politics to geography, and aiming, as in Nazi Germany, at aggressive expansion.
31. **ghetto** (get′ō): a section of the city in which many members of a minority group, such as Jews or Negroes, find it necessary to live.
32. **granary** (gran′ēr-i): a storehouse for grain; grain-growing region.
33. **greenback:** a piece of United States paper money, printed in green on the back.
34. **Gresham's law** (gresh′əmz): the principle that bad money tends to drive good money out of circulation.
35. **gubernatorial** (goō′bər-nə-tôr′ē-əl): pertaining to a governor or his office.
36. **hinterland:** back country, remote from the coast and the cities.
37. **humanitarian:** a philanthropist; one devoted to human welfare.
38. **husbandry:** thrifty management; the business of a farmer.
39. **Jacobean** (jak′ə-bē′ən): pertaining to King James I of England and his period (1603–1625).
40. **Jim Crow:** *colloq.* discrimination against Negroes.
41. **junta** (jun′tə): a group of political schemers; a faction; a cabal.
42. **laissez faire** (les′ā fâr′): letting people do as they please; *econ.* the theory that the state should not interfere with business.
43. **lingua franca** (ling′gwə frang′kə): any mixed language or jargon such as pidgin English that is used in international trade.
44. **lobby:** a special interest group that tries to get legislators to vote for a bill.
45. **Malthusian theory** (mal-thoō′zē-ən): the theory of Thomas R. Malthus (1766–1834) that if population is unchecked it will outrun its means of support and lead to famine, war, and other disasters.
46. **manifesto:** a public declaration of views and intentions.
47. **mediation:** friendly intervention to settle disputes.
48. **mercantilism** (mûr′kən-ti-liz′əm): the national policy of establishing a favorable balance of trade—that is, more exporting than importing—and of accumulating precious metals.
49. **miscegenation** (mis′i-jə-nā′shən): marriage between members of different races.
50. **monetary** (mon′i-ter′ē): pertaining to money or coinage.
51. **Montessori method** (mon′ti-sôr′ē): a system aiming at self-education of a child through guidance rather than enforced discipline.
52. **naturalization:** the process of becoming a citizen.
53. **nepotism** (nep′ə-tiz′əm): favoritism to relatives, especially in public appointments.
54. **nihilism** (nī′ə-liz′əm): rejection of customary beliefs in religion, government, morality, etc.

55. **oligarchy** (ol'ə-gär'kē): government by a few persons.
56. **opportunism** (op'ər-tōō'niz-əm): the policy of backing whatever furthers one's interests, regardless of basic principles.
57. **pacifism** (pas'ə-fiz'əm): opposition to all war.
58. **partisan:** one who supports a person, party, or cause.
59. **power politics:** international diplomacy backed by a threat of military power.
60. **progressive:** a political liberal; one who favors reforms in legislation or religion.
61. **protocol** (prō'tə-kôl'): the proper courtesies to be observed in diplomatic affairs.
62. **revivalism** (ri-vī'və-liz'əm): a movement to revive religious belief, usually marked by fervid preaching, public confessions, and emotionalism.
63. **scapegoat:** any person or thing that bears the blame for others.
64. **schism** (siz'əm): a split in a church or other organized group caused by differences of opinion.
65. **secession** (si-sesh'ən): formal withdrawal, as of a state from the union.
66. **sedition:** stirring up of rebellion against the government.
67. **Siegfried Line** (sēg'frēd): a fortified defense line constructed in west Germany to face the French Maginot Line before World War II.
68. **social register:** a book listing socially prominent people.
69. **soviet** (sō'vē-et'): any of various governing councils in the Soviet Union.
70. **spoils system:** the practice of distributing appointive public offices to party workers, after a political victory.
71. **standing army:** a permanent army ready for action in peacetime as well as in time of war.
72. **stereotype:** a fixed pattern; a conventional character typifying a special group.
73. **technocracy** (tek-nok'rə-sē): a proposed system of government in which technologists would try to control the industrial and social systems with maximum efficiency.
74. **tory** (tôr'ē): an extreme political conservative; reactionary.
75. **totalitarianism** (tō-tal'i-târ'ē-ə-niz'əm): one-party government, characterized by political suppression and cultural and economic regimentation.
76. **tycoon** (tī-kōōn'): *colloq.* a powerful industrialist; financier.
77. **ultimatum** (ul'tə-mā'təm): a final proposal, the rejection of which may lead to hostile action.
78. **Volsteadism** (vol'sted-iz'əm): national prohibition of liquor sales (1919–1933), named after Rep. Andrew J. Volstead.
79. **yellow journalism:** the featuring of cheap, sensational news to increase newspaper sales.
80. **Zionism** (zī'ə-niz'əm): a movement originally to re-establish a Jewish nation, now to aid Israel.

Miscellany

1. **aboriginal** (ab'ə-rij'ə-nəl): existing at the very beginning.
2. **abscissa** (ab-sis'ə): *math.* the horizontal distance from the *y*-axis of a point on a graph, as measured parallel to the *x*-axis: distinguished from *ordinate,* the vertical distance from the *x*-axis.
3. **abstract:** theoretical; not specific; *art.* nonrepresentational.
4. **Achilles' heel** (ə-kil'ēz): a vulnerable point: Achilles was killed by an arrow that struck his heel, his only weak spot.
5. **advocatus diaboli** (ad'və-kā-'təs dī-ab'ə-lī): L., the devil's advocate; one who deliberately pleads the unpopular side of an argument.
6. **aegis** (ē'jis): *mythol.* Zeus's shield; hence, protecting influence; sponsorship; auspices.
7. **analysis:** separation of a whole into its parts to find out their nature, function, relationships, etc.
8. **annus mirabilis** (an'əs mi-rab'ə-lis): L., year of wonders.
9. **anomaly** (ə-nom'ə-lē): an abnormality; a deviation from the general rule.
10. **aphorism** (af'ə-riz'əm): a short sentence expressing a truth; maxim or adage.
11. **apostate** (ə-pos'tāt): one who has deserted his religion, party, or principles.
12. **archaic** (är-kā'ik): ancient; antiquated, such as a Chaucerian phrase no longer in use.
13. **artifact:** a tool, ornament, or other object made by human work.
14. **asyndeton** (ə-sin'də-ton'): *rhet.* the omission of conjunctions between coordinate sentence elements: for example, "They met, danced, fell in love."
15. **axiom** (ak'sē-əm): *math.* a statement so obvious it needs no proof.
16. **Baconian** (bā-kō'nē-ən): one who believes that Francis Bacon wrote Shakespeare's plays.
17. **Briticism** (brit'i-siz'əm): a word or phrase peculiar to British English: for example, "petrol," "lorry," "lift."
18. **brochure** (brō-shoor'): a pamphlet.
19. **Buddhism** (bood'iz-əm): a mystical religious faith of eastern Asia, teaching that nirvana is reached by right living, right thinking, and self-denial.
20. **calculus** (kal'kyə-ləs): *math.* a method of calculation based on the infinitesimal changes of variables.
21. **cant:** insincere conventional talk; hypocritical twaddle.
22. **carte blanche** (kärt' blänsh'): full authority to do what one thinks best.
23. **computer:** an automatic electronic machine that performs mathematical and logical operations at high speeds.
24. **Conelrad** (kon'əl-rad'): a system of controlling radio signals so they cannot be used by enemy aircraft to locate cities.
25. **congruent** (kong'groo-ənt): agreeing; corresponding; *geom.* coinciding exactly point by point.
26. **consensus** (kən-sen'səs): a collective opinion.
27. **corollary** (kôr'ə-ler'ē): a natural consequence; *math.* a proposition that is incidentally proved in proving another.

28. **correlation:** the kind and degree of relationship between variables.
29. **coup de théâtre** (koo də tä-ä′tr): F., a theatrical or sensational trick.
30. **cui bono** (kwē′ bō′nō): L., for whose benefit?
31. **cul-de-sac** (kul′də-sak′): F., a blind alley; predicament with no escape.
32. **culinary** (kyoo′lə-ner′ē): of cookery or the kitchen.
33. **cum laude** (kum lô′di): L., with praise; with academic honors.
34. **definitive** (di-fin′i-tiv): conclusive; final; most accurate: as, the *definitive* edition.
35. **dernier cri** (der′nyā′ krē′): F., the latest fashion; newest thing; literally: the last cry.
36. **diagnosis** (dī′əg-nō′sis): investigation of facts to determine the nature of a thing; *medic.* recognizing diseases by their symptoms.
37. **dichotomy** (dī-kot′ə-mē): division into two parts; *logic.* the division of a class into two mutually exclusive subclasses.
38. **differentia** (dif′ə-ren′shē-ə): *logic.* a specific attribute that distinguishes one species from another of the same genus.
39. **dilemma** (di-lem′ə): a situation requiring a choice between equally disagreeable alternatives.
40. **dissertation** (dis′ər-tā′shən): a scholarly treatise or thesis, as for the Ph.D.
41. **doctrinaire** (dok′tri-nâr′): of those who apply theories regardless of practical problems; impractical; visionary; theoretical.
42. **doggerel** (dog′ər-əl): crude, amateurish verses, usually comic.
43. **dossier** (dos′i-ā′): a collection of papers and information about a person or matter.
44. **ecclesiastical** (i-klē′zē-as′ti-kəl): pertaining to the church or clergy.
45. **ecumenical** (ek′yoo-men′i-kəl): universal; general; pertaining to the entire Christian church.
46. **emeritus** (i-mer′i-təs): retired from active service but retained in an honorary position: as, a professor *emeritus*.
47. **ennui** (än′wē): boredom; weariness from lack of interest.
48. **epicurean** (ep′i-kyoo-rē′ən): given to sensual enjoyment, especially in eating and drinking.
49. **ersatz** (er-zäts′): substitute, usually inferior.
50. **evangelical** (ē′van-jel′i-kəl): emphasizing salvation by faith in the Bible and in the atonement of Jesus.
51. **ex cathedra** (eks kə-thē′drə): L., from the seat of authority; with official authority: as, an *ex cathedra* pronouncement.
52. **exegesis** (ek′sə-jē′sis): critical explanation of literary passages and phrasing, especially of the Bible.
53. **exempli gratia** (eg-zem′plī grä′shi-ə): L., for example: abbreviated *e.g.*
54. **fallacy** (fal′ə-sē): false reasoning; a misleading argument; an error.
55. **faux pas** (fō pä′): a false step; error; social blunder.
56. **fiasco** (fē-as′kō): a complete and ridiculous failure.
57. **foible:** a personal weakness; slight character fault.
58. **forensics** (fə-ren′siks): the field of debate and public speaking.
59. **format** (fôr′mat): the physical make-up of a book or magazine.
60. **furlong:** one-eighth of a mile; 220 yards.

61. **galaxy** (gal'ək-sē): a vast system of stars: as, the Milky Way; an assembly of brilliant people or things.
62. **genealogy** (jē'nē-al'ə-jē): the line of descent of a person from his ancestors.
63. **glossary** (glos'ə-rē): a list of difficult terms with explanations, sometimes included at the end of a textbook.
64. **Gregorian calendar** (gri-gôr'ē-ən): the present-day calendar with its corrected system of leap years, as adopted in Great Britain and the American colonies in 1752.
65. **guerrilla** (gə-ril'ə): one who engages in sniping, sabotage, and such irregular warfare behind the lines on an invading enemy.
66. **guillotine** (gil'ə-tēn'): a machine for beheading, used during the French Revolution.
67. **hegira** (hi-jī'rə): a journey for safety, like that of Mohammed from Mecca in A.D. 622.
68. **heresy** (her'i-sē): any opinions opposed to the established doctrines, particularly of a religion.
69. **hiatus** (hī-ā'təs): a break, with a part missing; blank space.
70. **hic jacet** (hik jā'sit): L., here lies: inscribed on tombstones.
71. **holocaust** (hol'ə-kôst'): widespread destruction.
72. **holograph** (hol'ə-graf'): a letter or document in the author's own handwriting.
73. **honorarium** (on'ə-râr'ē-əm): a payment as reward for professional services on which no fee has been set.
74. **hooliganism:** rowdiness; vandalism.
75. **hors d'oeuvre** (ôr dûrv'): an appetizer, such as olives or anchovies.
76. **hostage** (hos'tij): a person kept as a pledge that certain things be done.
77. **humanities:** cultural subjects such as literature, philosophy, art, music, and usually history, as distinguished from science and vocational subjects.
78. **hypotenuse** (hī-pot'ə-no͞os'): *geom.* the side of a right triangle opposite the right angle.
79. **ibidem** (i-bī'dem): L., in the same place; in the work just mentioned: abbreviated *ibid.*
80. **idiosyncrasy** (id'ē-ə-sing'krə-sē): a personal mannerism or peculiarity.
81. **impasse** (im'pas): blind alley; deadlock; position from which there is no escape.
82. **in absentia** (in ab-sen'shi-ə): L., in absence.
83. **incendiary** (in-sen'dē-er'ē): causing the malicious burning of property; inflammatory.
84. **incognito** (in-kog'nə-tō): under an assumed name.
85. **induction:** reasoning from particular cases to a general conclusion.
86. **infinitesimal** (in'fin-i-tes'ə-məl): infinitely small; *math.* diminishing toward zero as a limit.
87. **innuendo** (in'yo͞o-en'dō): an insinuation; a derogatory hint.
88. **interpolate** (in-tûr'pə-lāt'): to insert new matter between or among other material.
89. **invective** (in-vek'tiv): a violent verbal attack; abusive words.
90. **isthmus** (is'məs): a narrow strip of land which has water on either side and which connects two larger land masses.
91. **jejune** (ji-joon'): dull; barren; uninteresting: as, a *jejune* novel.
92. **Koran** (ko-rän'): the Mohammedan bible.

93. **lacuna** (lə-kū′nə): a space where something is missing, as in a manuscript; gap; hiatus.
94. **latent** (lā′tənt): *biol.* dormant but capable of normal development.
95. **legerdemain** (lej′ər-də-mān′): sleight of hand; trickery; deception.
96. **lexicon** (lek′sə-kon′): a dictionary or wordbook; vocabulary of a special subject.
97. **literati** (lit′ə-rä′tē): literary or scholarly people.
98. **liturgy** (lit′ər-jē): church ritual.
99. **logarithms** (log′ə-rith′əms): *math.* a method of calculation in which each number is reduced to a power of a common base (the log of 1000 to the base 10 is 3).
100. **logistics** (lō-jis′tiks): *milit. science.* the problem of transporting, supplying, and quartering troops.

* * *

101. **marathon:** a footrace of 26 miles, 385 yards, held at the Olympic games and honoring the Greek messenger who ran from Marathon to Athens to tell of victory over the Persians (490 B.C.).
102. **mean:** the average value, obtained by adding a set of numbers, then dividing by the number of terms in the set.
103. **median** (mē′dē-ən): the middle number in a series of ascending numbers.
104. **microfilm:** the photograph on film of a printed page, much reduced in size.
105. **misogamy** (mi-sog′ə-mē): hatred of marriage.
106. **mnemonics** (ni-mon′iks): memory aids.
107. **mode:** the value which occurs oftenest in a series of data; the norm.
108. **morpheme:** *linguistics.* an indivisible meaningful word-unit, such as *big, pre-,* or *-ing.*
109. **nemesis** (nem′ə-sis): just punishment; retribution.
110. **noblesse oblige** (nō-bles′ ō-blēzh′): F., the obligation of high-ranking people to act honorably and generously to others.
111. **nonce word** (nons): a word coined for a single occasion.
112. **nouveau riche** (nōō′vō′ rēsh′): a person who has recently become rich.
113. **numismatics** (nōō′miz-mat′iks): the collection or study of coins and medals.
114. **objective:** treating the actual physical features of an object rather than one's feelings about it.
115. **obscurantism** (ob-skyoor′ən-tiz′əm): opposition to learning and human progress.
116. **obsolete:** discarded; no longer in use.
117. **octogenarian** (ok′tə-jə-nâr′ē-ən): an eighty-year-old.
118. **optimum:** the condition producing the best results.
119. **ordnance:** military weapons and ammunition.
120. **original sin:** *theol.* the sinfulness inherent in mankind as a result of Adam's disobedience.
121. **paradox** (par′ə-doks′): a statement which seems absurd or contradictory but which may be true.
122. **paragon** (par′ə-gon′): a model or pattern of excellence.
123. **parallel:** *literature.* a counterpart; that which bears a close resemblance.

124. **patois** (pat′wä): the blend of provincial dialect with standard language.
125. **peccadillo** (pek′ə-dil′ō): a petty sin; trifling fault.
126. **pedagogue** (ped′ə-gog′): a schoolmaster.
127. **pentathlon** (pen-tath′lən): an athletic contest involving five events.
128. **permutation** (pûr′myə-tā′shən): *math.* any one of the positions or orders possible within a group.
129. **phoneme** (fō′nēm): *linguistics.* an indivisible unit of sound.
130. **photostat:** a photographic copy or facsimile of printed matter.
131. **pica** (pī′kə): a size of type commonly used in typewriters, with ten letters to the inch: larger than *elite,* which has twelve.
132. **piscatorial** (pis′kə-tōr′ē-əl): of fish or fishing.
133. **polemics** (pō-lem′iks): the art of argumentation.
134. **potpourri** (pō′poo-rē′): a mixture; a medley; a miscellany.
135. **predestination:** *theol.* the fating in advance of all events by God, including each man's salvation or damnation.
136. **prolixity** (prō-lik′si-tē): wordiness; long-windedness.
137. **Promethean** (prə-mē′thi-ən): like the Titan Prometheus, life-bringing, boldly original, creative.
138. **proselyte** (pros′ə-līt′): to convert to a faith; to induce an athlete to attend a certain school.
139. **prosody** (pros′ə-di): the technical study of verse writing, including meter, rhyme, stanza form, and diction.
140. **protean** (prō′ti-ən): like Proteus, very changeable; readily taking on different shapes and roles.
141. **pundit** (pun′dit): an extremely learned man.
142. **quadratic equation** (kwo-drat′ik): *math.* an equation involving the square but no higher power of the unknown quantity.
143. **quintessence** (kwin-tes′əns): the pure essence of a thing.
144. **ratiocination** (rash′i-os′ə-nā′shən): logical reasoning.
145. **rationale** (rash′ə-nal′): the fundamental reasons, or logical basis, of something.
146. **reconnaissance** (ri-kon′ə-səns): *milit. science.* the inspection of an enemy position to get information about troops and terrain.
147. **retribution** (re-trə-byoō′shən): *theol.* punishments or rewards in the hereafter for deeds in this life.
148. **rhetorical question** (ri-tôr′i-kəl): a question asked for literary effect, no answer being expected.
149. **ribaldry** (rib′əl-drē): coarse joking or mocking; vulgar talk.
150. **sacerdotal** (sas′ēr-dōt′l): pertaining to priests.
151. **satyr** (sāt′ēr): *mythol.* a woodland deity represented as part man and part goat; a lecherous fellow.
152. **savoir-faire** (sav-wär-fâr′): tact; knowledge of what to do or say in any situation.
153. **scalar** (skā′lər): *math.* a quantity having only magnitude.

154. **scholasticism** (skə-las'ti-siz'əm): a system of teaching that sticks to traditional doctrines and methods; medievalist learning.
155. **scop** (skop): an Old English bard, minstrel, or poet.
156. **sect:** a small religious group; a faction.
157. **sensationalism:** melodramatic style or subject matter; that which is intended to shock, startle, and excite intense interest.
158. **Shavian** (shā'vē-ən): pertaining to George Bernard Shaw; an admirer of Shaw's works or theories.
159. **shibboleth** (shib'ə-leth'): any phrase or custom regarded as distinctive of a special group.
160. **Shinto** (shin'tō): the state religion of Japan until 1945, emphasizing ancestor worship and the divinity of the emperor.
161. **sinecure** (sī'ni-kyoor'): an easy, profitable job.
162. **sine qua non** (sī'nē kwä non'): L., an absolute essential; an indispensable thing.
163. **smorgasbord** (smôr'gəs-bôrd): appetizers served buffet style.
164. **snafu** (sna'foo'): *milit. slang.* chaotic; out of control; "situation normal, all fouled up."
165. **sobriquet** (sō'bri-kā'): a nickname.
166. **somnambulism** (som-nam'byə-liz'əm): sleepwalking.
167. **soothsayer:** one who foretells the future, as in *Julius Caesar*.
168. **soporific** (sop'ə-rif'ik): causing sleep.
169. **spa** (spä): any resort having a mineral spring.
170. **stance:** posture or mode of standing, as in boxing or golf.
171. **status quo** (stā'təs kwō'): L., the existing condition.
172. **stratum** (strā'təm): a horizontal layer of material, as of clouds or rock.
173. **Sturm und Drang** (shtoorm' oont drängk'): G., storm and stress, designating German romanticism of the late eighteenth century.
174. **sub rosa** (sub rō'zə): L., confidentially; in secret.
175. **subversive:** tending to undermine or destroy.
176. **sycophant** (sik'ə-fənt): a flattering toady; a parasite.
177. **syllabus** (sil'ə-bəs): a summary or outline of a course of study.
178. **synod** (sin'əd): a church council.
179. **synthetic:** artificial; produced by chemicals; not genuine.
180. **tachistoscope** (tə-kis'tə-skōp'): an apparatus that throws images on a screen for a fraction of a second, used in testing attention and reading speed.
181. **tautology** (tô-tol'ə-jē): unnecessary repetition; redundancy.
182. **tenet** (ten'it): a doctrine or opinion held to be true.
183. **Teutonic** (too-ton'ik): pertaining to Germans and other northern Europeans.
184. **theorem** (thē'ə-rəm): *math.* a proposition to be proved.
185. **titanic** (tī-tan'ik): of vast size and strength, like the Titans.
186. **travesty** (trav'is-tē): a farcical imitation intended as ridicule.
187. **truism** (troo'iz-əm): an obvious idea; a platitude.

188. **typography** (tī-pog'rə-fē): the style and appearance of printed material.
189. **ukase** (ū'kās): an imperial decree having the force of law.
190. **valedictory** (val'ə-dik'tə-rē): a farewell speech, as given at graduation.
191. **value judgment:** a judgment which reflects a personal set of values, as in words like "good," "depressing," and "beautiful."
192. **variorum** (vâr'ē-ōr'əm): an edition, as of Shakespeare's plays, that presents variant readings and notes by a number of scholars.
193. **vernal:** appearing in the spring; springlike; youthful.
194. **vertex:** *math.* the point of a triangle farthest from the base.
195. **vertigo** (vûr'tə-gō'): *pathol.* dizziness or giddiness.
196. **Wassermann test** (wä'sər-mən): a diagnostic test for syphilis.
197. **well-made:** having a skillfully constructed or contrived plot: as, a conventional *well-made* play.
198. **Weltschmerz** (velt'shmerts'): G., sentimental pessimism over the world's inadequacies; romantic melancholy.
199. **yoga** (yō'gə): a mystic Hindu practice, involving intense concentration and prescribed exercises.
200. **youth hostel** (hos'təl): a supervised lodging house for young people on bicycle tours, hikes, etc.